SINCERELY LOUISE

SINCERELY LOUISE

To Annette –
a steadfast and
loyal friend –
with love – Gloria

GLORIA BOYD

authorHOUSE®

AuthorHouse™
1663 Liberty Drive
Bloomington, IN 47403
www.authorhouse.com
Phone: 1-800-839-8640

First published by AuthorHouse   11/16/2011

ISBN: 978-1-4685-0542-9 (sc)
ISBN: 978-1-4685-0543-6 (hc)
ISBN: 978-1-4685-0541-2 (ebk)

CONTENTS

PROLOGUE

September 1914

When I tried to comfort Mama, she would push me away, then run to me, gather me in her arms, bury her face in my hair and sob, "Oh, my little Louise, what are we going to do?"

She used to water down the milk in Ruthie's bottle, and when the landlord knocked on the door, Mama would whisper, *shush,* and hold us both so tight we could hardly breath. She'd give Ruthie a sugar cube to keep her quiet until the knocking stopped.

Sometimes when the landlord knocked on our door late at night asking for the rent money, Mama would let him in. I'd lay quiet in my bed, smelling cigar smoke and beer. The next morning Mama would bundle us up and take us to the grocery store to buy food. She would give us pennies to buy candy.

Whenever I asked about our Papa, Mama would tear up, or get angry, and tell me he was dead. I was pretty sure she was lying, because sometimes a letter would come with money in it. Mama would cry then and curse, and I knew it must be from our Papa.

When the letters stopped coming, that's when Mama took us to the farm to live with our German Grandma and Grandpa. I was five then, and Ruthie was only two.

Mama promised to come see us, and when she didn't come, Ruthie cried. After a while when she promised and didn't come, Ruthie didn't cry anymore, She just got more ornery every day. Gram just shook her head, taught me how to milk the old cow, Hilde, and signed me up for kindergarten.

CHAPTER 1

A hot July day in Connecticut, 1916

She said she would come. Other times when she said she would come, she never came. We giggled then, pretending we didn't care. Grampa's farm is far from the nearest town, so far that the green bus comes but once each day.

Today the sun hangs high overhead, paling the summer sky. It is near time. We walk toward the road, kicking at stones, drawing lines in the dirt with our toes. Dust cakes our feet turning them powdery brown. Our wash-weary dresses hang straight down and, save for the large bow in my hair, we are like orphans.

The time she did come, we pushed against each other like kittens in a basket. I was seven and Ruthie was only four. She scowled up at me and asked in her sour, scratchy voice, "Is that our Mama?"

She came mincing toward us, her skirt cropped close around her ankles, her hair flat against her head under a stylish hat with a feather. She was pretty then, and she laughed. Out loud.

Later we sat at her feet, our arms wrapped tight around our knees, listening wide-eyed to her stories, stories filled with promises, while Gram sat tightlipped in her rocker knitting. That night I lay in our bed wondering. I lay still so as not to wake Ruthie, fearing she might be wondering, too.

But now, far off beyond the curve in the road, a dusty swirl angles toward the sun. Slowly a green speck, hardly visible at first, rumbles toward us like a rusty toy, sending crows to resettle. The road shimmers as the bus grows to full size. As it ambles toward us, I take Ruthie's hand and face us toward the farm. I do this, not from pride alone, but for fear when the door hinges open and she won't be the there.

August 1916

Dear Mama,

You promised and we waited. Ruthie cried. She turns five next month. It would please her if you would come for her birthday. Me too. Sincerely, Louise

CHAPTER 2

I edge my three-legged stool close to Hilda. Sun filters through the haze of dusty hay. "Come on, girl," I say, easing my head against her, my curls caressing her bulging paunch.

"It's no wonder I smell like you, you old cow," I whisper.

The milk pail is near full. Ruthie comes in and skids to a stop, scattering the chickens.

"Watch this, Weez," she shouts as she draws the frayed length of clothes-hanging rope in close behind her ankles, swings it high over her head, and jumps. "One! Two! Three!"

Hilde turns, showing the whites of her eyes. Her tail switches, rearranging the barn flies eager for a taste of her flesh.

"Get out of here, Ruthie, you're getting her riled."

"Darn cow," she mutters, not even listening to me. "Now I have to start over. One, two, . . ."

"Quit it! How many times do I have to tell you? Stay clear of the barn when I'm milking Hilde. There'll be real trouble if I don't get this pail full."

" . . . Four, five."

"Git, before she tightens up." I wipe damp hair off my forehead with the back of my hand. Sweat tricks down my arm. "Ruthie? Think you could pump me a cup of fresh water without spilling? I got the barn to sweep yet."

She swings the rope and starts counting again. I aim one of Hilda's teats and squirt her full in the face. She screeches, "I'm telling Gram!" Hilda gives out a high-pitched moo, angles one leg out, topples the pail, and milk spills across the barn floor in hay-strewn rivulets.

"Now look what you've done, Ruthie, all my work for nothing. Gram's going to have a conniption."

"She'll know who's fault it is when she sees that rope. Now get out of here so I can clean up this mess."

"Aw, Weez, I just was showin' ya."

Flies find the milk, and Birdie the barn cat slinks in close. "Just go Ruthie, and next time, stay clear of the barn with your jump ropin'." Her fault or not, Gram is sure to blame me anyway. Seems Ruthie can do no wrong in her eyes. It must be something to be loved like that.

She runs toward the house, wailing her innocence to Gram. I brush off my overalls, grab the broom, and sweep the wet straw toward the yard where it can dry off.

Gram comes storming in, bringing the smell of her baking with her. The cat snarls and scatters. She's looking at me, but I know she's thinking, Mama. She stares at the empty pail, the spilt milk, the flies already gathering, then notices Ruthie's jumping rope layin' on the floor. She must know what happened, but she only points to the empty pail, then at me, and stalks off toward the house.

I know why she has such bad feelings toward me, it's because I reminder her of Mama.

Gram ends up blaming us both and sends us to bed without supper. I wouldn't mind for me; I can do just fine without Gram's chicken liver potpie, but Ruthie gets fierce pains when she misses supper.

Later, lying next to her in bed, I hear her stomach grouching, like a mule itching to get loose. When Gram's door closes and the house is quiet, I slip out of bed. "Stay here Ruthie. I'll bring you something from the kitchen."

A full moon shines through the kitchen window turning everything to pale silver. I open the back door and slip outside and I turn silver too, my hair, my hands, even my toes. I stretch my arms out and look up at the stars. Fireflies angle through the air. From a nearby tree an owl hoots its three-legged hoot. Another answers, and far off, a dog howls. A sudden rush of wind brushes my cheek, and as if with a voice, the night sings out, "*Someone will love you, someday.*"

"Mama?" I whisper as the moon disappears behind a cloud, sending a chill down my back, and I step inside.

Brown smells of liver sausage linger in Gram's clean-swept kitchen. The cracked linoleum bites into my feet, and there on the counter, left out in plain sight, is Gram's bread, with her knife handy beside it. I smile at her goodness, slice off a hunk for Ruthie, a piece for myself, and wipe the knife clean. I rewrap the cloth around the stump of the loaf and tuck it away.

"What took you so long?" Ruthie grumbles and grabs the bread out of my hand.

"Hush up, Ruthie, you'll wake Gram." She's so self-minded I doubt she'll even thank me for bringing her something to eat.

"Tar' nation, Weez, you didn't bring no butter."

"*Any* butter, and quit making crumbs. You want to bring ants? And for tar' nation sakes, Ruthie, will you stop calling me, Weez? My name is Louise, remember?"

The bed squeaks as I fit in beside her.

"Never mind, Weez, it's even good with no butter. I was about to starve to my death waiting for you." She inches close. "Do you feel like talking?"

"Just leave me alone. At least one of us has chores tomorrow."

"Gram sure knows how to bake, don't she, Weez?"

"*Doesn't* she."

"Ain't that what I said?" She yawns and slides under our blanket.

"You said . . . oh never mind, just go to sleep, and don't forget to say your prayers. And remember to pray for . . ." but before I can tell her to pray for Mama, her soft sputtering tells me she is already making her sleep noises.

September, 1917

Dear Mama,

Ruthie turned five this month. She cried when you didn't come. I turned nine in February. Maybe you should write these things down Mama. Do you know Ruthie lies? Sincerely, Louise

CHAPTER 3

May Franklin stares at the unopened envelope on her coffee table. Waves of guilt unsettle her as she fingers her near empty glass. She never could handle these letters from her daughter very well.

She wipes hot tears from her eyes and refills her glass. "Stupid manager," she sniffles, "I had a good idea, and just because it wasn't *his* idea, he fires me. Life isn't fair, and whoever is in charge of this world doesn't seem to care a tinker's damn about me."

She takes a sip and grimaces. She doesn't even like the taste of the cheap gin the bottle holds. It had been sitting on a dusty shelf since her husband left, and that was nearly three years ago. Soon she will just have to pound the streets again and look for another job, or another someone . . . some man . . . to rescue her. It wasn't her first choice, but what else could she do?

Her shoulders slump as she faces the task at hand. She reaches for the envelope, carefully opens it, unfolds the letter, and begins to read. *'Dear Mama.'* A tightening forms between her eyes as she continues; each word spelled correctly, each letter so perfectly formed, and the meaning so clear. "She hates me!"

Through tears, she carefully slips the letter into its envelope and slides it under the frayed pink ribbon so it can rest safely in a shoebox with all the others.

She replaces the box on the high shelf in her closet, grabs her coat, and rushes toward the door. "So help me God, I *will* find a job or someone who will take care of me, so I can get my children back before that woman damages them like she tried to damage me."

CHAPTER 4

When Mama first left us on the farm, a couple of years ago, it took a while for Ruthie and me to get used to our grandmother. She talks mostly German to us. I never saw Gram read a book except the big Bible she brought over from Germany. I don't think she can read English. Ruthie's so ornery I doubt she'll ever learn to read in any language. Maybe that's why Gram is partial to Ruthie and not to me. All her smiles are for Ruthie. She saves her scowls for me, even though I'm the one who does most of the chores.

But even if Gram doesn't like me, I know our Grampa does. He's doesn't talk much, but when he's not ailing, he smiles at me. But sometimes he has trouble recalling where he is, or what he had for breakfast, and he gives Gram headaches. That's why she takes that laudanum she got from the doctor. She keeps it hidden it in an old coffee can high on a kitchen shelf, right next to the baking soda can for her egg money. She doesn't think I know about these things, but I do.

Our Gram's house always smells good. Sometimes it's her cooking and baking, and sometimes it's the roses she brings in from her garden. Ferns were the only plants Mama had in her apartment, and they always smelled like dust. I miss Mama, but the less I talk about her in front of Gram, the easier my life is. There is something between those two that I can't understand. It must have been something bad enough to make Mama run away when she wasn't much older than I am right now. She started to tell me once, but it made her so sad she turned away and said she never wanted to talk about it again.

Grampa and Gram came from Germany to America on a boat when Mama was just a baby. Grampa built the farmhouse himself, Gram told us. She calls the main room, the *wohnzimmer*, which means 'sitting room' in German.

"Your Grampa, himself *dat* table made, too," Gram says in her German way, pointing to the long heavy table. "Wood from our trees, he used." The table is long and wide, and by the scratches and hot kettle marks, I can tell it has seen a lot of years. When I tried to teach Ruthie to spell her name, she started scratching a rough 'R' into the table with a fork. She got halfway done before Gram caught her.

"No!" Gram yelled, raising her hand. Ruthie ran and hid under our bed. I had to sneak food to her that night too. The next time we sat at the table, I gave Ruthie a piece of my school paper and a crayon, so she could practice her letters and not miss dinner. Then Grampa gave her a new bar of Ivory soap, a dull knife, and began teaching her how to carve little animals. I didn't mind too much him paying so much attention to her. I busied myself with homework and drawing pictures of the pretty clothes I would wear when Mama took us to live with her again.

The farmhouse is just big enough for the four of us. It has two bedrooms, one for Gram and Grampa, and one for Ruthie and me. Ours is curtained-off from the main room. When our Grampa isn't ailing so, he's going to build us a door. When we first came, Gram patched us quilts from cloth from her trunk, and from clothes Mama wore before she ran off. Sometimes when I'm in bed, I can breathe in the smell of Mama from the pieces of my quilt. It helps me fall asleep.

The floor in our bedroom tilts a little. I propped up two legs of our dresser with pieces of wood so it wouldn't wobble. Our bed wobbles, but I don't mind that, it still sleeps good.

The kitchen is Gram's favorite room. It's where she does all her cooking and baking. There is a big black stove, a pump for water, an added-on pantry where she keeps potatoes, apples, all her put-up jars of food, and kettles too big to hang in the kitchen.

Gramps chair is near the kitchen, so Gram can keep an eye on him. His chair has big smoothed over wooden arms and a flattened down cushion from his sitting so much. He spends most of his time in that chair, staring out the window, staring at old memories, I guess.

Gram's rocker has carved vines across the back. "My chair, he made, too," she nods. "*Mit* own hands, he carved." And right next to Grams rocker is her big old wooden trunk with shiny hinges. She keeps it locked, and we aren't allowed to touch it. But sometimes when her work is finished and it's too cold for us to play outside, we sit on the floor while she unlocks it and opens the lid. Strong whiffs of camphor and lavender float up, taking over the wood-smoke smell of the house.

"In Germany we grew up in fine house," Gram sighs. "In my head I still see."

"You mean you see where you lived in Germany whenever you open that old trunk?" Ruthie asks as Gram gets that far-off gaze in her eyes and smiles away tears.

She shows us handmade Christmas ornaments, faded family pictures, hand-woven shawls, and old-fashioned shoes and dresses. One dress that was Mama's when she was near my age, but it's so wrinkled it makes my eyes tear up. Gram won't let us touch anything for fear of us getting it dirty, or seeing things she doesn't want us to see.

I know one thing she was hiding in her trunk, but I'll never tell Ruthie. It was an old photograph, one Gram never meant for us to see. She seems proud to show us pictures of her and our Grampa when they were young, and the place in Germany where they lived, but when that other picture slipped out and fell to the floor, I got a good look at it before Gram snatched it back. Her face turned pale. Course I pretended I hadn't seen it, for fear she'd smack me good, but I *did* see it. It was cracked and faded, but right away I knew it was Gram and Grampa, standing stiff in their fine clothes, and Mama when she was about Ruthie's age, standing close, right in front of this very farm house. I could tell it was our Mama, because she looked like me. And there was a baby in Gram's arms. A baby smiling up as her with all the love you can think of. I never told Ruthie about that picture. I knew she'd ask to see it, and then Gram would know I'd seen it when it fell to the floor.

Someday I'll have a trunk of my own, where I can keep my things; things I don't want Ruthie or Mama, or even Gram to see.

"Where' did ya' get all this stuff, Gram?" Ruthie asks, reaching in quicker than lightening, and quicker still, Gram smacks her hand and slams the trunk closed.

It's a good thing Gram didn't see the look Ruthie gave her, or that girl would have gotten a lot more than a slap on the hand. As it is, we'll most likely have to wait a long while before Gram opens her trunk again. I wonder if I'll ever have a dress as pretty as the one our Mama used to wear?

"Louise!" Gram mutters. "No time for dreaming. Clean up *da* kitchen. You clean it good."

"Yes, Gram," I say as I run for the dust cloth. Sometimes I wonder if Gram really has any love for me at all.

I start with the shelf over the stove were Gram keeps her blue-speckled coffee pot and her bent-up kettle for soups and stews, and where the spiders live. Darn spiders. I swish the dust cloth around, shaking out three dead flies and a half-alive spider, which I get with the heel of my shoe. Someday I'll get bitten and then she'll be sorry.

Right next to the stove is a nail that holds the big washtub for keeping our clothes clean and for baths. Gram makes us take a bath every Saturday night with brown soap. I didn't mind taking baths when I lived with Mama. She let us use bubble bath and fancy soaps, and we smelled like flowers when we got through. Everything in Mama's house smelled good; even Mama.

I shake out the dust cloth again and start in on the cupboard shelves along the wall. They hold most everything Gram needs for her cooking and baking. At first I never paid much of a mind to Gram's cooking. I just know whatever she makes tastes real good. It's Gram's potpies and baked goods that win most every blue ribbon at the county fairs. She tacks those ribbons on her bedroom wall over her dresser so she can see them every morning before she starts her day.

She must never have taught our Mama to cook before she ran off. Once Mama made us what she called, I-talian spaghetti, by loading it with garlic and pouring catsup over it. She called it 'Genuine I-talian sauce.' I knew even then, it didn't taste the way it was supposed to. Ruthie was too little to know the difference, and we ate it anyway. It didn't taste bad; it just didn't taste very good, either.

Gram does some secret things to her cakes and pastries. I saw her put sauerkraut in Ruthie's chocolate birthday cake, but I didn't tell Ruthie If she knew, she'd have a conniption.

The neighbor ladies are jealous because Gram wins all the ribbons at the fairs. Whenever they stop by for Gram's strong coffee, they fill the house with their *oh's* and *ah's*, but as they drive off in their buggies, I hear them clucking like a bunch of chickens, "Can't imagine where she learned to bake like that." "She's not about to share her recipes either." "And that strudel! My oh my!"

It is remarks like those that start me thinking. What if I wrote down everything she does when she's in the kitchen; the measurements, how she put things together, how long she cooked or baked things? If I could do that, maybe I could put it all together and someday . . .

"What are you mumbling about, Weez? You sick or somethin'?"

"No," I tell her, as my face heats up. "I was just listening to what those women were saying about Gram, and . . . being proud of her." I cross my fingers behind my back for the lie, because I wasn't thinking that at all.

I can still remember when we lived in Mama's apartment. It wasn't grand but it had electric lights, a telephone, and a *Victrola* that you had to crank to make music. I like to remember those days, but remembering makes me miss Mama 'til it hurts. When Ruthie was napping, she used to read to me, stories like, 'The Secret Garden' and 'Helen's Babies'. She'd sing too; not nursery songs, but real songs, like 'Peg O' My Heart' and 'Teddy Bear's Picnic,' and she would dance me around the floor. But singing "After You've Gone" always made her sad.

While Ruthie napped, I'd stand on Mama's feet, and we would thump around the floor, and the music would get so loud, old Mr. Musser from downstairs would bang on his ceiling. Mama would laugh her high, squeaky, laugh. I'd giggle, and we'd pretend we didn't hear the banging.

Mama would swirl me around fast, always ending with a kiss, but sometimes when she hugged me, her cheeks were damp with tears. My daddy bought the *Victrola* for her before he left.

Mama used to say I had the voice of a nightingale, and she promised I would have singing lessons some day. Ellsworth says I sound like a duck, but I pay him no mind. I like what Mama used to say better.

Sometimes when I'm in bed at night and can't sleep, I wait 'til Ruthie starts her bubbly noises so I know she's asleep, then I make believe we have Mama's *Victrola* here on the farm, and her dance records too, and I'm teaching Ruthie all the steps, while Gram watches to see how good of a teacher I am. I pretend all Mamas promises come true, and she says things like, 'You're the best daughter in the whole world.' She must know some new dance steps by now, and that's when I close my eyes and fall asleep.

But lately those good thoughts have been turning into troublesome nightmares. Gram says you have nightmares when you're my age. She calls them 'schlechte Traume'. Sometimes just as I'm about to sleep a tiny, slimy, green monster slips in beside me and pushes my good dreams all out of shape. He screeches and laughs at me. "She'll never take you back," he squeals. "So what if you are smart and do all the chores. She doesn't give an old shoe for you. Ha-Ha-Ha! It's your long curls she loves, not you. She loves Ruthie best. College? You can forget that. Eighth grade is all you're going to get, and you can't sing worth a cow's tail."

By morning, except for the emptiness that aches around my heart, the nightmare is gone, and that's when I snap at Ruthie, call her a stupid little twerp, even before she deserves it.

November 1918

Dear Mama,

Did you have bad dreams when you were my age? I'll be ten in a few months, and Gram says they're normal. When are you ever going to come and visit? Sincerely, Louise

CHAPTER 5

This Saturday is one of Grampa's better days, and when the sun is right, he's going to take our photograph with his Brownie Box camera. He's making us stand near to Gram's rose bushes in the blazing sun, and I can see we'll have to do a lot of waiting while he remembers how to work the camera.

"Hurry up, Grampa. My feet are burnin' up." Ruthie yells, jumping up and down like a toad in a rainstorm.

"Hush up, Ruthie," I tell her, being too busy arranging my hair to tell her to put shoes on.

"But Weez, the sun's makin' this dress stick on my legs."

"For darn sakes, Ruthie, go stand in the shade 'til he's ready. Can't you do any thinking for yourself?"

I hardly remember ever seeing Ruthie in a dress, except on Sundays. She hates dresses. I get into one every chance I get. If Ellsworth comes by, maybe he'll notice me all dressed up. He whispered to me once, that my hair was the color of the taffy we pulled at school. My face got all hot, and I couldn't think what to say to that, so I stuck out my tongue at him and ran.

Ruthie's hair is truly a sight today. It's short and straight and wild, and stands on end when she runs. She wouldn't let me comb it.

"Wet her down, *Liebchen*," Gram yells when she sees Ruthie. "She's scarin' da hens!" She laughs, holding her hand in front of her mouth, trying to hide her missing tooth, or maybe it's just her German ways.

Gram says our Mama had hair just like mine when she was young. She always gets a scornful look on her face when she mentions our Mama. I haven't found out why yet, but I will. Gram has such hateful thoughts about our mama, but I know enough to steer clear of Gram when her scissors are handy, thinking she might use them on my hair. I put my hand behind my back and cross my fingers, just in case. Ellsworth says doing that helps ward off bad things from happening, and forgives lies.

Way out over the fields clouds begin to build up. Gram comes out of the house with her hair done up neat, and she is hiding something behind her back.

"You look pretty, Gram," I tell her. She doesn't answer, but I can see she's pleased. Gram is funny about hearing nice things about herself, and she isn't much for mirrors either. She made me brush my hair one hundred times this morning, and she starched my hair bow. It's sitting on top of my head, like I might fly away in a good breeze.

"Louise," she says standing close. "Go inside, you put *dis* on." She hands me what she was holding behind her back. It's Mama's dress from her trunk, with all the wrinkles ironed out.

"Oh, Gram!" I shout. "You mean it?"

She nods, and I run into the house to change, thinking as I go, she must have some love in her heart for Mama, or she wouldn't have kept this beautiful dress for so long.

I say a little prayer to myself, to make sure it fits, and it does!

Grampa finally gets the camera in place, shuffles us around a might, and takes my picture just before the sun fades and the raindrops start to fall. Ellsworth missed his chance to be in it. He missed seeing me all dressed up, too.

July 1919

Dear Mama,

Please send me one of my father, so I can remember what he looks like. I hope you are coming for Ruthie's birthday next month. She is getting out of hand. Sincerely, Louise

Gramps takes Louise's picture

CHAPTER 6

"Happy Birthday, Ruthie."

She hardly hears me, for looking down the road for Mama. I could tell her, but she'd have a conniption. Best let her find out for herself. It's a good party anyway, with Gram's chocolate cake with eight candles. Ellsworth comes and brings his cousin, that Homer. Ellsworth gives Ruthie a Baby Ruth candy bar. Ruthie thinks it's named after her. That Homer says he has a present for her and he'll give it to her later. I know he's lying. He just didn't bring her anything.

We make blueberry ice cream and Gram sings German songs to Ruthie. We play games outside and Ruthie follows that Homer around so close she steps on his heels. They disappeared behind the barn for a while, and when they came back Ruthie's face is flushed pink, her clothes are mussed, and she is grinning so hard her face about splits in half. I don't know what went on, but I'm telling Mama when she comes.

Mama never came. She doesn't come for my birthdays, either. When I have children I'll always remember their birthdays, give them presents wrapped in pretty paper, and bake any kind of cake they ask for with pink icing and two kinds of ice cream. And I'll never forget, not ever.

If Mama doesn't come for us soon, I fear Ruthie is going to grow up not remembering her at all. Sometimes I think I'm forgetting her, too.

August 1920

Dear Mama,

Ruthie missed you at her party. She cried. Gram made her a pinafore for dressing up. I doubt she'll ever wear it. She likes overalls the best. I gave her a picture I drew of you. Did you know she is getting tall? You would hardly know her. Unless you come and visit sometime, I guess she will hardly know you either. Sincerely, Louise

CHAPTER 7

There is something special about the farmhouse on crisp fall evenings, like tonight when we all share the light from the hanging kerosene lamp: Gram with her knitting and mending and Gramps dozing in his chair. It times like these I wish we had Mama's *Victrola* and some of her records.

Gramps carved us a checkerboard out of a slab of maple and sliced the pieces from a cedar log. When I try to teach Ruthie how to play, she is more interested in the wood than playing the game. Every time it's her time she scratches at the cedar piece 'til it gives out with a warm smooth smell.

"Teach me to carve, Gramps," Ruthie says, with an almost angelic look on her face. I have to keep telling her, "It's your turn, Ruthie," but she hardly hears. Gramps just smiled and nods, and I know before long he's going to teach her how to hold a knife. Our game goes fine until Ruthie starts cheating.

"Ruthie, you can't move that piece there."

"Yes I can so."

"No you can't. That cheating."

"Who says?"

"I say, now move it back!"

"I will not."

"Keep that up and you'll end up in reform school for sure," I whisper.

That's when she gets all red in the face. Her hair sticks straight out and her eyes slit mean like, and if she didn't look so funny I might be scared of her meanness. My laughing makes her even madder.

With a sharp word, Gram sends us off to bed, but I can see she's hiding a grin. She thinks Ruthie's just fooling around, but I'm worried the world won't tolerate her cheating and lying once she grows up. Sometimes I fear if she doesn't change her ways, she is sure to end up in the reform school. It scares me to think what Mama would do if she knew how mean Ruthie can be. But then, Mama has a temper, too, and Ruthie probably caught it from her.

I lay in bed next to Ruthie. She's making her sleep noises and I can't sleep. At least I won't have to go to school tomorrow because it's Saturday. Since the hens have been layin' real good lately, maybe Gram will take us to town to sell eggs. Some of the egg money goes for her pain medicine. She says the rest is for 'when the hard times come.' She calls her egg money her 'rainy day' money. Every time it clouds over Ruthie stands around waiting for Gram to pass out the pennies. Sometimes I don't know if she's really smart or just plain stupid.

September 1920

Dear Mama,

I think you should know Ruthie lies and cheats, and Gram doesn't even care. Sincerely, Louise

CHAPTER 8

It isn't often that we go neighboring or have company, although it's *Grams* covered dishes that arrive first whenever a neighbor is down with a fever or birthing a baby. Nobody ever says she's boastful or proud, but she doesn't mind people knowing how handy she is in the kitchen. It's her chicken potpies and baked goods that win every blue ribbon at the country fairs. Gram tacks the ribbons on her bedroom wall so she can see them every morning before she starts her day.

Whenever the ladies do stop by for Gram's strong coffee and her famous apple strudel, they fill the house with their "Oh's" and "Ah's," and I hear them say as they drive off in their buggies, "Why you could eat off them floors, they're so clean."

Ruthie can hardly hold her tongue 'til they're beyond hearing distance. "Don't seem right them saying that, when it's us doing the moppin' of the floors."

"When did you ever mop the floor? Besides where would we be if it wasn't for her?"

"Probably in that reform school you keep talkin' about," she mutters.

"Never mind that, Ruthie, just come with me."

She pulls away. "You're not takin' me there now, are you?"

"Just hush up and follow me. I want to show you something."

We climb up the ladder into the hayloft. I let Ruthie go first in case she misses a step. Dust catches the late rays of the sun, lighting our way.

"It's too hot up here. I'm about to faint." Ruthie flops down, fanning herself, copying the ladies in the magazine she stole. She said someone in school gave her the magazine, but I saw her looking at it in the general store last time we went into town. Next thing I knew it was in our bedroom. I told her to keep it under the mattress on *her* side of the bed. Can't think what would happen if Gram knew she stole it.

"What are you gonna' show me, Weez?"

"It's right here." I dig in my pocket and pull out my ribbon. Ruthie gasps.

"Weez. Why are you messing with Gram's ribbon? She'll be hoppin' mad."

"It isn't one of Gram's, it's my ribbon. I won it in our sixth grade spell down."

Ruthie reaches for the ribbon and holds it gentle in her hand. "I could never win something for spelling," she whispers, rubbing out the creases. "How do you know to pick the right letters all the time?"

"Don't know. They just come to me. When I'm thinking the word, I kind of line up letters in my head, like they're hanging on a fence, then knock off the ones that don't belong. Some letters belong, and some don't. I didn't even know what the words mean. The word that won was, *EPIPHANY.* Mrs. Maryweather says I might have one some day, if I'm lucky." I wouldn't know an epiphany if I tripped over one, but I won't tell Ruthie that.

"You see the letters in your head?" she scowls. "I must have been playing hooky when that gift was passed out, 'cause I never seen no letters in my head." She smacks at a fly. "Don't you have to study on it, Weez?"

"Me, study? I don't need to study," I lie. "I'm showing this ribbon to Mama next time she comes."

Ruthie lowers her eyes. "It'll be worn out by then," she mutters as she picks up pieces of straw and lays them, one on top of the other, like she's building a house. "She'll never come again. She hates us."

"Don't say that, Ruthie!"

"Why not? She don't care about us."

"Yes she does. She's just busy that's all. She'll come see us when she can." I don't tell her what I really think.

"I'm sure not gonna' hold my breath," she says, sinking into the hay with a restless sigh. "What did Gram say when she saw your ribbon?"

"I think she was pleased, she even smiled. Said she'd ask Grampa to make me a frame for it when he gets better."

She spins the ribbon by its cord and laughs. "Ha! I'm not holding my breath for either. He ain't never gonna' get better. He gets worse every day."

She's right. Seems like our Grampa gets weaker and thinner every day, too.

Ruthie sits up and scowls at me. "Your boyfriend, Ellsworth, told Homer our Grandpa has the cancer. What does that mean anyway, Weez?"

"Ruth Marie! Ellsworth Wolcott is *not* my boyfriend, and besides, Gramp's sickness is nothing you should be talking about with that Homer. You know, if you talk about something too much it just might come true. He has his good days. If we let him be, maybe he'll get better on his own." I won't tell Ruthie, but I don't believe *that* any more than I believe that a cat has nine lives.

September 1921

Dear Mama,

Gram made me a pinafore for school. It's green. Do you think green is a CONSIDERABLE color for me with my yellow hair? CONSIDERABLE is one of our spelldown words at school. If you ever do come and visit, I will show you the ribbon I won for being the best speller in my eighth grade class. Sincerely, Louise

CHAPTER 9

If kissing makes it so, then Ellsworth Wolcott might well be my boyfriend. It is the tip end of our Indian summer and fall has come in without our knowing it. There's a sharp chill in the air, a hint of winter, I guess.

As Ellsworth and me walk home from school, we stop to pick the last of the apples from Grampa's tree. A breeze stirs the brown and yellow leaves under foot and I shiver. Ellsworth drops my books to the ground and tucks his sweater across my shoulders.

"That better?" he asks, and just out of nowhere, he stretches up and aims a kiss at me. It would have landed square on my mouth, except I turned my head just then, so it hit my cheek. His lips were warm against mine. I don't guess I'll ever forget that feeling on my cheek, warm and soft, like the petals on a rose. "Well, Louise," he says, wiping his mouth with the back of his hand, then rubbing it down the sides of his pants. "How did you like that?"

I touch the spot on my cheek. It is still warm, and I wonder if I should be mad or glad. Just then a blue jay warns in his harsh way, *'Jay, Jay.'* Another answers from a nearby field. "Well, guess I didn't mind much," I tell him, "but you better not try that again."

Didn't ever occur to me before, but Ellsworth is half a foot shorter than me. If I stand up straight I can see over his head. Right off I know I'm never going to marry Ellsworth Wolcott. Ruthie's magazine says when you hear music while someone is kissing you it means true love. All I heard during that kiss were the cicadas left over from summer, the blue jays, and the bees sipping at the apples rotting on the ground. No music, just farm sounds. I did notice Ellsworth's mother put onions in his noon sandwich, but I'm still letting him carry my books home.

Ellsworth and Louise

CHAPTER 10

I know why Grampa favors Ruthie. They share a special gift. When he's not ailing, they sit for hours at the table, carving, even when she could be helping me gather wood for the wood box. She has a whole set of animals she has carved, a horse, a pig, a dog, each one looking a little better than the one before. Bet I could carve like that, if Grampa would teach me, but I can see he's content just teaching Ruthie.

Well, I don't care. I'd probably carve better than she does anyway, and she sure wouldn't like that. Besides, I've got something I'm doing that no one else knows, not even Ruthie. It's my very own secret. I am going to write a book. My teacher, Mrs. Maryweather, says anyone can do it if they have something good enough to say, and I *do*. I've been writing down all Grams recipes on pages in my lesson book, and when I finish, I'm going to turn them into a cookbook. Gram is a great cook, but she holds all her recipes in her head.

I caught her adding a good amount of Gramp's homemade beer to her sauerkraut. Since I've been writing these things down, I watch carefully, to see every little thing she does. I change her handfuls and scoops into measurements in cups and teaspoons, and then write down all her special adding's.

I never had a secret of my own before. It kind of weighs heavy on me. Sometimes in the middle of the night I wake up wondering, is a secret really a secret if no one else knows? What if you have to share it to make it a real one?

I can't tell Gram. She might not take kindly to my turning her freehand cooking and baking into written down recipes without asking. If Ruthie knew, she would just pooh-pooh it, and Mama? I doubt Mama would even care. If God knows about my book, he won't mind, he knows how much I need something in my life of my very own, something to be proud of.

When I put all those recipes into a book, I'll be famous, and won't Mama be surprised at that? I might even give her a free copy.

My notes and recipes are safe in a box under my bed, hidden from Ruthie. At least I thought they were safe, until today when I heard her scuffling around under our bed.

"Ruthie? What are you doing under there? The fumbling noises stop.

"I ain't doing nothin' wrong, Weez."

I look under the bed on her side, and sure enough, she's got the box open, and my notes and recipes scattered all over the floor.

"You little sneak! You shouldn't be getting into my private things!"

If she tells Gram, she'll wreck everything for me. It's not a great secret, but it's the only secret I've got.

"I'm just looking," she says in her innocent voice.

"You had no *right*, Ruthie!"

"What *is* all this stuff, anyway, Weez, and why are you hiding it under the bed?"

"It's none of your business, Ruthie, but if you promise not to tell, not anyone, and when I say promise I mean, if you do tell, I'll write to that reform school myself and have them pick you up so fast your teeth will rattle. You've got to *promise,* and hope to die if you tell. Promise you won't tell until it gets *finished*. Promise?"

"Until what gets finished?" she asks, as if she didn't hear any of my warnings.

"First promise, then I'll tell you."

"I promise, I promise. Now tell me, what's all this paper stuff, anyway?"

"I'm collecting recipes, and I'm going to make them into a cookbook so people can buy it."

"You can't cook, Weez, nothing' I'd eat, anyway."

"Just hush up Ruthie, and listen." I lean close to her. "I'm copying down all of Gram's recipes, and she doesn't know anything about it." "I'm going to surprise her when it's finished."

She scowls, and I can see her trying to figure it out.

"Gram don't have written-down recipes."

"That's just it, Ruthie, She cooks from what's in her head. She pours stuff so fast you can hardly see the amount. That's why I've been watching her real careful, to see what she's adding, so I can write it all down, the amount of each thing, like cups of this, spoonful's of that. I'll write how to mixes them together, and how long she bakes or cooks them, and then I'll have a cookbook. That's the secret."

"That's not a secret, Weez, that's sneaky."

"It isn't sneaky. My face heats up. "Anyway, when it's done and gets put into a book, I'll be famous."

"Gram's gonna' be mad at you."

"Not if you don't tell her. Don't you see? When I'm famous, she'll be famous, too. It'll be a way of keeping all her good cooking and baking ideas going on forever, because they will all be in my cookbook, for everyone to read, 'till kingdom comes."

"I never thought that much about Gram's cooking before," she frowns, "I only knew whatever she made tasted good."

"I saw her put sauerkraut in her chocolate cake."

"You're lying, Weez." She balls up her fists, but I can see the wheels turning in her head. She's thinking back to her birthday cake. She sticks out her tongue and shivers. "I never knew it had sauerkraut in it!"

"But it tasted good, didn't it? And you can't go telling about it, Ruthie, you promised. If Gram finds out, she might make me move out and then where will you be?" I lean toward her and whisper, "She puts some of Gramp's brandy in her pickled cabbage, too, and a sprinkle of red pepper in her prize-winning lemon ginger cookies."

Ruthie sits quiet, for a full five seconds. I can practically see the wheels turning in her head. "I guess that's why those cookies taste so burn-y on my tongue," she sighs.

Maybe I *can* trust her about not telling. I sure hope she doesn't take after our Mama, about *not* keeping promises. I can only hope she forgets all about it. Sometimes having a secret can be a scary thing.

That night after Ruthie is asleep, I lay next to her in our bed, pretending I'm living with Mama. She is having a party, and all the party food is from my cookbook. 'Isn't Louise wonderful,' Mama says. 'Isn't she the best cook that ever was? She will get rich selling her cookbook, and all the boys in the neighborhood will want to marry her and she will live happily ever-after.'

January 1921

Dear Mama,

I have questions about life. Do you have to go to college to become famous? I hope not. By the looks of it, I'll never get there, but I'm going to be famous, anyway. Did you remember my birthday is next month? I'll be thirteen. It's okay if you forget again. Gram forgets sometimes, too. Sincerely, Louise

CHAPTER 11

We might not have electricity on the farm, but we sure do have a Flexible Flyer. Gram must have used up the whole of last year's egg money for that sled. Guess I should be sorry for that, but I'm not.

The snow's taking its time coming, not like last year. What's fallen so far isn't enough to fill a bucket. We've just about given up hope for a sledding storm. Gram made us put the sled back under the house late in February, just after my birthday.

"I don't think it'll ever snow," Ruthie grumbles as she helps me gather stove wood. "Guess heaven got all snowed out from last year."

"There's still time, Ruthie. Last year the snow came late."

"Yeah, but it's already February, and then comes spring."

We stumble into the house with our arms full of wood, and there it is, leaning against the table, the Flexible Flyer, all covered with dust from under the house, and cobwebs sticking to the runners. Ruthie drops her logs. They go thundering across the floor and she pays them no mind. I dump mine in the wood box. Gram makes me pick Ruthie's up and put them away, too.

"Gram?" Ruthie shouts. Does this mean a storm comin'? Do you think it'll be a big one, Gram, really big enough for sledding? You're not just making it up, are you Gram?"

I know what Ruthie's thinking. She's wondering if Gram is lying just to make us feel good, like Mama used to. I want to shake her, tell her Gram wouldn't do that. Gram wouldn't lie, especially about something so dear to Ruthie as sledding.

"Gram knows when the weather's going to change, Ruthie, she's never wrong."

I think Gram is downright spooky when it comes to knowing about things. It's no use me lying to her, either. She'd know right off if I did. She doesn't know when Ruthie lies, because Ruthie is so good at it.

"Okay, Gram," Ruthie shouts. "I believe you! There's a storm coming, just like you said."

Gram points to her nose and nods. "Big storm."

Ruthie squeals and drags the sled to the middle of the room. I help her wipe the cobwebs off and, before she can see it, I stomp on a spider that made it into the house. Ruthie would have a screaming' fit if she'd seen it.

Together we rub the runners with candle wax until they just about sing. Then we wait, and the sled waits too, leaning against the wall, showing off its readiness. The skies cloud over, and just to keep busy, Ruthie and me bring in more wood. We set up the checkerboard, but we don't ever get around to playing.

At about noon, it starts. Slow at first and quiet, forming a soft, whiteness, covering our world. Gram sends us out to hunker down the animals and latch the barn door. We tie a rope from the house to the barn, so if the snow gets deep, we can get to the barn to feed the chickens and milk Hilda.

By bedtime the real storm blows in, lurking around the edges at first, then running straight at us. Like howling wolves it swirls around the house, snuffles under the door, gnaws at the shingles. It whistles through wall cracks and gets the lantern to swinging on its hook.

Ruthie snuggles so close in our bed and I don't know if she's happy or scared. But when her bubbling starts, I know she's asleep. I say a little prayer to keep the animals safe, and add special thanks for Grampa, because he's so good to us. Last summer he made us snow shoes from tree branches. They'll be handy getting back and forth to the barn as the snow piles up.

The snow lasts through the next day. The chickens lay poorly during it all. We lose a few to the cold, but old Hilda comes through just fine with her milk. As long as I don't turn to ice milking her, and hauling the pail from the barn to the house, I guess I'll manage, too.

On the third day of the storm, we eat the last of Gram's strudel. Ruthie near about rips the cupboards apart looking for something sweet to eat. "You must have something good left somewhere," she whines to Gram. "I'd even choke down rhubarb, and you know I get sick over rhubarb. Ain't you got something that'll taste good for a change?"

She can talk mean to Gram at times, but Gram just sits and rocks, shaking her head and speeding up her knitting. But I can tell she's about come to the end of her toleration when it comes to Ruthie.

I help bundle her up when it's time to help me tend to the animals. "Bring an extra bucket," I tell her.

"What for? You're bringing the milk bucket. Why do we we need an extra one?"

"For snow, *Dummkopf,* so Gram can melt it on the stove for fresh water. The pump froze 'cause you forgot to pack it with straw the way Gram asked, remember?" I forgot to remind her, so it's partly my fault.

By the fourth day, the snow eases but still keeps coming down. The road going past the farm turns into part of the fields, and our mailbox disappears. The pump is gone from sight, too, and the door is about jammed shut. But the barn is as pretty as a Christmas card.

Eventually the storm gentles, and falls like a lace curtain, covering the world in silence. When it finally stops, the night sky shows off stars I'd forgotten were there.

The next morning Gram fries up the last of the bacon and fixes a batch of pancakes. She adds the bacon grease to her stew pot simmering at the back of the stove. Ruthie hardly sits still long enough to finish breakfast.

"Guess it's time for this Flexible Flyer," she chirps, sliding her fingers along the shiny runners. I rub frost off the window glass, but I still can't see out for the drifts.

Next thing we know, Ellsworth, and his cousin Homer come plowing through the snow. They must have gotten up when it was still dark. Their shouts are muffled and they throw snowballs at the house. I'll bet that Homer spits on his, making them hard. He better not hit Ruthie with one.

"Hurry up, Louise," Ellsworth yells, "we ain't gonna' wait all day."

I can see he's showing off in front of his cousin. I bundle us into every piece of warmth we own; heavy jackets, mufflers, itchy ski pants, and two pairs of socks each, and help Ruthie stuff rags into her too-big boots so snow can't seep in.

Ducking Homer's snow balls, we wave to Gram and plow through the snow toward the hill beyond the farm, dragging Ellsworth's old sled and our very own shiny new Flexible Flyer. The whole world is white and whisper quiet. Snow-covered branches dip low, and the pale sky holds nary a bird.

When we get to the hill, it takes a half hour of stomping snow down to get the snow the way Ellsworth wants it, slick and hard, so we can fly down as fast as the wind.

Each time we take the hill, we go faster and coast a little further. I can't see beyond our cleared off place, for the drifts. Squealing and yelling we go, two on a sled time after time, down the hill. I let Ellsworth ride on the Flexible Flyer, him on the bottom so he can steer, and me on top. Homer takes Ruthie and she falls off every time. That Homer can't steer worth a nickel compared to Ellsworth.

As the late-day sun flickers through the trees, turning everything blue, it's time to go home. I'm tired and cold and hungry, and Ruthie cheeks are like frosted cherries.

"One more time, Weez," Ruthie whispers through her chattering teeth. "This time I want a chance to go with Ellsworth on our Flexible Flyer. You can go with Homer on his old sled." She wipes a snow-caked wooly mitten across her runny nose.

I don't want to ride down on top of Homer, but Ruthie will have a conniption if she doesn't get her way. Ellsworth grunts when Ruthie flops down on top of him.

"Quit teasing, Ellsworth," Ruthie squeals, "I'm not near as heavy as Weez."

I get on top of Homer and grab hold of him and down we fly, faster than ever. He steers way to the left and then to the right, showing off. I grit my teeth and hang on tight, and before I know it, he swerves, aiming us toward the gate that keeps Hilda from roaming.

Lickety-split we go, bumping across the slick tracks we've already made. I cry out and look up to see if we're going to make it.

The next thing I know, I'm flat out, face down in the snow and Ruthie is standing over me, screaming.

"Oh, Weez! You're all bloody!" She turns to Ellsworth, and through a thick fog I hear her say, "Is she gonna' die?"

"Get out of the way, Ruthie." Ellsworth yells. "She's cut her head, real bad."

Other than the blood seeping warm and sticky down my forehead into my eyes, I feel cold and numb.

"We got to pack it with snow," Ellsworth's voice comes through a thick fog, as if he is far away. He pushes snow under my hat as the low sun's rays form a halo around his head, turning him into 'Angel Ellsworth'.

"Quit doing that to her," I hear Ruthie yell as she slaps the snow out of his hand. "You tryin' to kill her? She's all bloody, even her eye-brows." Her voice comes through to me thick, and full of tears.

Ellsworth pushes her away as I try to sit up. "Stay still, Louise," he says, as he packs more snow under my hat. "This'll stop the bleeding.

Homer! Go back to the farm quick. Tell her Grandma we're bringing her in."

Tears sparkle on Ruthie's cheek. "Please don't die on us, Weez," she says. "At least not until we get you home."

"I'm not dying, Ruthie." I can hear my voice like it's coming from the other side of the fence. "Just help me up. I think I can walk."

"No!" Ellsworth yells. "You're riding back on the sled." His lips pinch tight. "We'll pull you so you won't have to move. Just keep that snow on your head 'til we get you home."

With Ruthie holding me on the sled and Ellsworth pulling it, the sled glides through the snow toward home. I close my eyes. I'm floating on a cloud. For once, I don't have to do the caring for anyone. If only it could always be like this . . . me sliding over the soft quiet snow toward home on our Flexible Flyer, with Ruthie and Ellsworth taking care of me. *"Mama, can you see what they're doing? They're looking out for me."*

The bleeding has all but stopped by the time we get to the farm. Gram looks pale enough to faint as she walks me slowly to the house. Ruthie trails along side, sucking on her soggy mitten.

"I didn't have nothin' to do with it, Gram, honest, hope to die, I didn't".

"Go, Root-tie. Open the bed. Pull down her quilt." She turns to Ellsworth. "You. Go for doctor. Be quick. He'll take her to hospital."

CHAPTER 12

The stuff they give me at the hospital is supposed to put me to sleep. It doesn't work, but I can't feel anything, anyway. The nurse keeps giving me more, and it isn't until after they finish sewing me up that I feel myself spinning, like a swing rope unwinding.

Twelve hours later I wake up, still tired. My ward has four beds. Three are empty. The room has high ceilings, bright lights, and a screen around my narrow iron bed. My head is bandaged, the sheets are scratchy, and the room smells like a just-scrubbed outhouse. A nurse stands over my bed, staring down at me, smiling. She is short and plump with a pile of red curls sticking out from under her white nurses' cap. I always wanted red hair. She must have to tuck it in while she's working. If I had red hair, I wouldn't want to be a nurse and have to keep it hidden.

"Morning, honey," she says, trying to plump softness into my flat pillow. "You got yourself a six-inch cut across the top of your head. How did you manage that? I had to shave a four-inch track of your hair off from one side to the other, so the doctor could sew in those thirteen stitches. Such pretty hair, too," she clucks as she straightens my sheet.

They shaved my hair! "Four inches wide? That's practically my whole head." What will Mama say?

"Don't worry, sugar, it'll grow back." She lets go of my wrist from taking my pulse. "I'll bring you a nice scarf to cover the bandage."

"What did they do with the hair they cut off?"

"It's gone. It was all bloody and tangled," she wrinkles her nose and shakes her head. "Never you mind. Why don't you rest while you can? They'll be bringing breakfast in soon, and don't fuss with the bandage. You don't want to start it bleeding again." She walks toward the door, clicking her tongue. "Can't imagine how you got yourself all cut up like that."

She could have waited for me to tell her, and then she'd know. If I was a nurse, I'd listen to what sick people had to say. I close my eyes and wonder how long 'til my hair grows back.

I must have slept some more, because when I open my eyes, a tray rests on a rolling shelf right over my stomach. The oatmeal has a crust formed, the toast is burnt, and the cocoa is cold. Gram had better bring me something decent to eat, or I'll likely starve.

Gram does come, stomping snow from her big farm galoshes, carrying some of her best cooking in her arms. The hospital has strict orders about children visiting, but Gram pays it no mind. She has Ruthie hidden under her long flowing winter cape.

"They didn't even see me, Weez," Ruthie grins. She likes breaking the rules.

The next day Mama comes. I know it's her even before she gets to my room, by the clicking of her high-heeled shoes. I straighten my sheet, pinch at my cheeks so she won't think I look sickly, and re-arrange the scarf around my head as best I can without a mirror.

She comes in wearing a wide-brimmed, purple hat with enough veils to sail a ship if the wind kicked up. Her pale lavender dress hangs in flowing points just below her knees, her silk stockings match her dress, and a tiny beaded purse dangles from her shoulder on a gold chain. It keeps slipping and she fusses it back in place. Except for her smelling of Evening In Paris, I hardly recognize her.

"Look at *you*," she squeals, flouncing around the room like a haughty hen. "What have you done to yourself, and where did you get that horrid scarf?" She leans over, readjusts the scarf, and aims a kiss at my cheek. I smell beer on her breath. Her cologne makes my eyes water, or is it the 'almost kiss' that brings tears? If I say a word, I know more tears will come, so I only smile. I can hardly remember getting a kiss from Mama.

"This is for you, honey." She tosses a paper sack on my bed.

Two Baby Ruth bars, a captain's hat, a pink flowered dress, I can tell it's not new, and her old red dancing shoes.

"The hat's from a real captain," she says, primping her hair. "It's been around the world twice. The dress is new." I cross my fingers for her lie. "The shoes are for when you grow into the dress. You'll be a knockout when you do. Save it for the day you want to catch a beau."

"Thank you, Mama. It's real nice," I manage to say, but it isn't nice at all, and I don't know why I said it was. My fingers stay crossed. With all this fibbing no use uncrossing them now.

"Are you sure you're all right, honey? You look sort of, . . . peak-ed. In fact you look just awful. What did they do to your hair?"

"It'll grow back, Mama. And I'm fine, just tired is all. The stitches don't even hurt unless I wrinkle my forehead." I show her, and she turns away.

"Well, if you want me to leave, just say so, but I want you to know, it took me two changes of busses to get here and . . ."

A doctor comes in with his clipboard.

Mama turns. As she draws in a breath, her chest rises, setting the silk of her dress to fluttering, and she laughs her perky laugh, as she strolls toward him.

Gram often says things about Mama I don't understand. I watch her now, blinking her eyes, moving her head so her hat veil dances around her face. I remember something in Ruthie's magazines about how modern women use 'charm'. I watch Mama sidle up to the doctor. She stands close, speaks softly to him, and I can tell by her smile she isn't asking about me. She's using 'charm'. Mama isn't a beauty, but she *is* pretty. With her lip rouge and her made-up eyes, She is 'magazine-lady' pretty. And by the way the doctor is looking at her, I can tell he thinks so, too.

She elbows him toward the door. "I'll be right back, honey," she croons looking back at me. "I just want to ask the doctor . . . about your condition."

The captain's hat doesn't fit over my bandage. I wouldn't wear it anyway. It has oily stains around the inside and smells of pipe tobacco. "Coney Island Captain" is printed across the visor. It's perfect for Ruthie. I take two bites of a candy bar and save the rest for her, too.

I lay back against my hard pillow. The sun bathes the room with pale winter light. It might snow again. I try to pat my pillow into place, arrange myself best I can without hurting my head, and wait. A sharp bell declares visiting hours over. A nurse hurries in, clanks the sides of my bed up, and dims the light. I take another bite of candy. She isn't coming back. Tears soften my crisply ironed sheet, and I'm not even crying. I reach for my pad and pencil.

February 1922

Dear Mama,

It is too bad you didn't stay longer. More doctors came in.
I'm sure that would have suited you fine. Sincerely, Louise

I tear the letter into small pieces and aim them toward the waste box. They flutter to the floor like dry leaves, to be swept up and tossed out with the rest of the hospital trash.

CHAPTER 13

The next day Gram comes again, with Ruthie under her coat. Gram holds back a smile, and Ruthie giggles as she pokes her head out.

"Hey, Weez, we brung you some of Gram's apple cake. Are you gonna' give me some?"

"Mama came in to see me yesterday, Ruthie, and she . . . ."

"Noooo!" Her cry echoes up to the ceiling. "Mama came and I didn't even see her?" She breathes hard, her hands working into tight fists. "Why didn't she wait for me?"

"She came during visiting hours. You know they won't let you in then."

"Well, what did she say, Weez?" She bounces up onto the bed. "Did she ask about me?"

"Roo-tee, watch for the head," Gram scolds.

"Did she ask about me?"

"She *did* ask about you, said she misses you very much," I lie. "She said to give you this."

"A present for me?" She grabs the hat, puts it on, and skips around the room. "Oh, Weez, it's beautiful. I'm gonna' wear it forever."

Gram pulls in her lips tight and shakes her head. She knows. I reach toward her and she pats my hand.

They stay for a while until Ruthie gets restless and noisy.

"Come *Liebchen*," Gram says handing Ruthie her coat. "It gets late."

I give Ruthie the rest of the candy." Will you come tomorrow?" I yawn.

"Tomorrow we come," Gram says, helping Ruthie button her coat.

With her mouth all-over chocolate, Ruthie waves goodbye, then runs back to my bed. She leans close and whispers.

"I ain't supposed to tell you, but Grampa made us a door for our room. Act surprised when you get home." She runs back to Gram and they are gone. Just like her to spoil Gramp's surprise.

February 1922

Dear Mama,

> *Thank you for the hat and the candy bars. The dress will be fine when I fix it up with the help from Gram's sewing machine. Pink is an all right color for me. Tomorrow the stitches come out and I go home with Gram. I can hardly wait. Sincerely, Louise*

I miss the farm, but I don't mind being in the hospital. It's quiet, there are no chores, and I've made friends with the nurses. They bring me magazines and let me ride up and down the halls in a wooden wheel chair.

One rosy-faced doctor looked in at me this morning as I sat waiting for my breakfast tray. He was young, and his white coat looked as if it was the first time he'd ever had it on. He peered over his glasses as he checked my chart and shook his finger at me. "Hey, toots," he said in a high scratchy voice, "I see you had a sledding accident. It could have been worse, you know. A few inches higher and you would have sliced the top of your head right off, crushed your skull, and I doubt you'd be sitting here now, waiting for your breakfast."

He pushes his glasses back up his nose and walks away laughing, as if he just told a funny joke. Well, it wasn't funny, and who does he think he is, anyway, calling me, *toots?*

CHAPTER 14

As soon as I walk through the farmhouse door, I see the sign:

WELL—COME HOME WEEZ WE MISS YOU

"Do you get it?" Ruthie squeals. "Do you get the funny way I wrote it? I made you a joke, didn't I, Weez?"

It's not very funny, but I laugh to please her. She's so proud, and she's glad to see me. Gram is glad, too. She made her apple strudel for me, and hot chocolate. It's good to be back with them again. I even think they missed me. Grampa is smiling. I act surprised when I see the door, and say, "Thank you, Grampa." I want to hug him, but I know he wouldn't like it.

It will take a while for my hair to grow back, from their shaving it. It'll probably stick up straight for a while, like Ruthie's. Gram says she'll make me a kerchief to wear. 'So you won't scare da chickens,' she says, making Ruthie screech with laughing. Gram can be so nice sometimes. Makes me think of staying on the farm forever.

I don't want Ellsworth to see me until my hair grows back, but I'm home, and that's all that matters.

Haven't written to tell Mama I'm home. I'll wait 'til my hair grows back before I write, then she can come and see for herself.

CHAPTER 15

Spring comes and my hair has all grown back.

"Good-bye, Weez," Ruthie grins, "Gram and me are going to town and you're staying home."

She is being sassy, because she's going and I'm not. Gram hitches up the wagon. She's wearing her second-best dress and her gray hat that matches, and Ruthie has shoes on.

"Louise," Gram leans down and whispers so Ruthie can't hear. "A chicken for stew we need. While we're gone, do Nealy. Pluck him. Ready him up. I come home, I stew him."

As they pile into the wagon and drive off, Ruthie gives me her ha, ha, ha, smile, but I don't mind. I like being here on the farm without her.

She has never seen me kill a chicken. Since Grampa got too sick to do it, it's been my chore. Gram always has me do it when Ruthie's not around. She thinks seeing it might scar her forever. I guess Gram never thought killing one might scar me, too. Nealy chases Ruthie whenever he can. He only does it because she throws stones at him. I wonder if she'll even notice when he's not around any more.

I watch as the wagon rolls up the hill and disappears. Being on the farm without Ruthie hardly ever happens. Seeing that Grampa is asleep in his room, I decide to wander up through the pasture behind the barn. He won't know I'm gone, and I'll be back before he wakes up.

I wrap the leftover breakfast pancakes in brown paper, and wander up to the pasture behind the barn. There's plenty of time before Gram gets back. Poor Nealy prances across the yard; he doesn't even suspect.

As I walk up the hill, the birds and katydids become quiet. I find a shady spot, and their sounds begin again. A rabbit hops close. I reach toward him and he scurries away. I lay back. What could be better than laying here in the warm grass on a lazy afternoon without Ruthie pestering me, wondering what the rest of the world is doing? A breeze brushes my cheek, the sun flickers through the leaves, and flowers sweeten the air. Bees clumsily dip from one flower to another.

I close my eyes and pretend I'm back in Mama's house. I can almost see her. She will put her arms around me. I'll have on the prettiest dress, and everything will be just the way it used to be. If my father hadn't left, things would be different. Mama would be happy and she wouldn't have taken us to live on the farm. I only wish she would come and visit, or at least answer my letters.

By the time I finally open my eyes it is well into the afternoon. I jump up and for a second everything turns black. I wait till it passes, leave the pancake for the rabbit, and hurry down the hill toward the farm, all the while praying there will be enough time to start the water to boil, catch Nealy, raise the hatchet, and put it to use.

Nealy never asked to be killed, but Gram would skin me alive if I didn't do it. I wait for the blood to stop dripping as he flops around the yard, but I've waited a might too long, and I'll always be sorry for that. With the bloody hatchet in one hand, Nealy's head in the other, I watch as the wagon bumps into the yard.

Ruthie jumps down in time to see the headless rooster flopping around the yard. She turns pale and screams. I hide the hatchet behind me.

She's always hated Nealy, but now, with him flopping around the yard, she's chasing after him, reaching toward him. Blood spatter, tears trail down her cheeks. Ruthie sways back and forth, humming in a low, singsong voice. "Nealy, what have you done with your head?"

Gram steers her into the house, all the while soothing her with German words. As she walks she scowls at me for being late. "Finish up. I give her a warm bath."

Doesn't she see I could use a warm bath, too? But then, I'm not the one having a fit. I'm just the one has to do the killing of the poor bird; pull out his feathers, and get him ready for the stew pot. How does Ruthie think chickens get on our supper table, all juicy and tender with Gram's gravy and all? She never thinks things through. It's some kind of skipping thing her mind does, so she can keep from knowing you have to kill a chicken before you can eat it, and she'll still ask for a drumstick, whenever there's one being served up.

I brush an unwanted tear off my face. I hate this farm. If Mama doesn't take me back soon, I'm going to run away, and who will look after Ruthie then?

April 1922

Dear Mama,

I graduate from the eighth grade this year and that's as far as my school goes. You promised I could live in town so I could go to high school, even think about college. Do you remember? I worry about not finishing school. I worry about Ruthie getting along without me if I ever do leave the farm. Sometimes I worry about you, too, Mama. Sincerely, Louise

CHAPTER 16

Ruthie flops down on our bed and says, "Weez, talk about Mama's house. What was it like when we lived there?"

"I've told you a hundred times, Ruthie."

"Well, tell me again. It's so long ago I can't see them pictures in my mind anymore. I was just a baby, wasn't I?" She squints her eyes almost shut. "Tell about the curtains and the 'lectric lamps and all the mirrors." She sinks back against her pillow and closes her eyes.

I lay down next to her. I can see she's lonesome for talk of Mama. It's a wonder she even remembers her. I sigh and begin the story again.

"Well, there are frilly lace curtains at mama's windows, radiators that give out heat, and mirrors in every room. All her electric lamps have beads hanging on the shades. They tinkle when you walk across the floor and they give out the softest light at night, turning everything pink."

"Tell about the rugs I used to sit on," she sighs.

"You used to crawl around on your hands and knees on Mama's thick, green carpet in the living room, and growl like a bear. You looked like one, too, with your hair all sticking up every-which-way."

"I can't help it if my hair ain't pretty like yours. I hate your hair, Weez."

I pay her no mind and continue. "Well, Mamma gets you ready for your nap and then she reads, *The Little Princess* to you. She reads it twice if you aren't asleep by the first time."

"I remember about the little princess. Do we have that book here?"

"No, it must still at Mama's, if she hasn't thrown it out."

"She better not throw it out. It's my most favorite one."

I shouldn't bad-mouth Mama to Ruthie. She'll know soon enough how Mama is.

"Okay, just be quiet and listen. So after you go to sleep, Mama would brush my hair a hundred times and we would talk. We talked about singing lessons, and when she was going to get a piano. Sometimes we danced to her *Victrola* music. She taught me the two-step and the waltz and . . . You were only two then, still in diapers and too young to dance."

"Never mind about that, Weez. Just tell me about after I wake up, about you asking questions, and about me and the ice cream."

"See, you do remember some of it." I lean back and put my arm around her. "Then I ask our Mama right out, '*When is our father coming back? Are we ever going to see him again?*'"

For a few seconds Ruthie doesn't say a word. Then she looks up at me and asks, "What did our daddy look like?"

I sigh. I hardly remember what our father looked like, so I cross my fingers and lie. "He was handsome. He had dark curly hair and a big smile," I tell her. "He was taller than Mama, and he loved us very much."

Sometimes I *do* remember what he looked like, but it wouldn't do to tell Ruthie. His hair was parted in the middle, he wasn't much taller than Mama, and he had a crocked front tooth.

"I remember seeing him in faded pictures," Ruthie says, staring off into space, "but maybe it wasn't him." She sits up and shrugs. "Maybe you and me never had a father, Weez. Maybe he's just in your made-up stories."

"That's crazy talk, Ruthie. Anyway, after that you started screaming because you wanted your diaper changed. You could be a real pain sometimes. And while Mama changed your smelly diaper, she said, '*How about if we go into town and buy you both some ice cream?*'"

"And I yelled, '*Strawberry*', didn't I, Weez?"

"No you didn't! You could hardly talk then. If you think you know that story so well, you can finish it yourself, and I'll do the listening."

"Okay, I'll tell the rest." She snuggles up close, not noticing how she is bothering me. "And Mama gets me ready, and I get strawberry and it dripped all down my front, and Mama wiped it off so hard she made me cry." She stops, thinking about the part she just told. "She didn't mean to make me cry, did she, Weez?"

"Course not, Ruthie, and, I get a three-scoop cone—chocolate, chocolate, chocolate, with chocolate sprinkles and . . ."

She buts in. "Then I see a kitten and start screaming for one, and Mama gets mad and hollers, 'No more talk about cats!' I guess she thought a kitten would be more trouble than you and me put together, didn't she, Weez?"

"I guess so," I say, wondering myself. "Anyway that's when it happened. After we finished our ice cream, instead of going us back to her house, she takes us to the farm, and that's how we got to live with Gram."

I remember thinking Gram must have known we were coming, because as soon as we arrived she gave us gingersnap cookies still warm from her oven, but all she gave Mama was a mean, hard look.

"That was the last time we ever had ice cream, wasn't it, Weez?"

"And we'll never know any more about our father," I say, holding back the tightness in my throat, "unless Mama decides to tell me."

"Sometimes Mama has a way of saying things without really saying them, don't she, Weez, I mean about kittens and fathers?"

She jumps down from the bed, and I know story time is over, for this time anyway.

CHAPTER 17

"It's tonight, Weez. Do you think we should stay in our clothes or get into our nightshirts?"

"Nightshirts? What *are* you talking about, Ruthie?" I shake my head, wishing she'd just go somewhere and let me be.

"What do you *think* I'm talking about? I'm talking about the new moon, so we can see the stars. Gram said we could. You forgot, didn't you?"

"Of course I didn't forget," I lie, "I just wanted to see if you remembered." I hate it when she catches me up like this and I have to pretend to keep up with her.

"You think you're so smart, Weez? You said when the next new moon happened, you'd take me up the hill, and take our quilts so we could watch stars shoot across the sky, and you forgot, didn't you? Seems like I've got a better remembering thing going in my head than you do in yours."

We haven't talked about the new moon since before spring. How can she remember a thing like that? "Ruthie, how come you know it's tonight?"

"Because it's right here in the all-min-ik."

"The what? You mean, *almanac*?"

"That's what I said! You never listen to me, Weez."

"Where'd you ever see an almanac, Ruthie?"

"At the hardware store." She gives me her sideways look. "I didn't steal it, Weez, Mr. Brewster said I could have it, honest." She points to a page. "See? It's right there, the seventh day of May; nineteen twenty-two, and that's today. There's a picture of an all black moon. All black means it's the new moon."

"You took that almanac when Mr. Brewster wasn't looking, didn't you? Ruthie, you know that's stealing. You've got to take it back."

She scowls, sticks out her bottom lip, and mutters something under her breath. She's got the pages so wrinkled and smudged I doubt it would do any good to take it back now. But she is right about what it says, and if it's a clear night, the stars will be bright enough so we won't need a lantern.

"So what do we wear?" Ruthie asks.

"You can just wear your bare skin, for all I care, and if you ever take something without paying again, Gram is going to hear about it. Then you really will end up in reform school."

Ruthie shakes off my words as if I'd never said them. I doubt she even heard me. She's too much for me to handle; she needs a real mother.

Gram's makes us hot chocolate in case the night cools, and I grab a big stick and a quilt off our bed.

"I'll carry the hot chocolate and the stick," Ruthie says. "You can carry the rest."

I end up carrying the quilt, extra sweaters, and the lantern. We start walking.

With every stirring of the wind, every sound of a twig breaking, I am grateful for the lantern. She may be right about the animals, but I'm not saying a word. Slowly we make our way up behind the barn toward the empty field.

"Don't walk so fast, Weez. I can't keep up. Ouch," she whimpers. "Darn, stupid old rock."

"Hold my hand, Ruthie, and be careful." Her hand is clammy cold, even with the warmth of the night.

"Do you think the Big Dipper's still there, Weez?" she whispers as we reach a clearing.

"Of course it's still there. It'll always be there. Look here. This is a flat spot. Let's stop here."

I set the lantern down. "Grab the corner of the quilt Ruthie, so we can spread it out. Be careful you don't knock over the cocoa. Good thing Gram thought of it; the wind's kicking up."

Ruthie giggles. "Never knew the wind could kick, and besides I forgot the cocoa."

"You forgot the cocoa while I carried *everything?*"

"I brought the stick, didn't I?"

I might have known. Well, just lay down next to me and be still."

I dim the lantern till it hardly burns. Ruthie moves closer and we lay still, staring at the star-speckled sky tucked in all around us. Some twinkle, one streaks off in a silent path across the sky.

"Oh . . . Ruthie pinches my arm and whispers, "Did you see that, Weez?"

I nod and whisper back. "A shooting star. Most of the others are locked so firm in place, millions of years can't pry them loose."

An owl screeches. "Maybe he saw it, too." She pinches my arm again. "Look, Weez. I see it," she squeals. "The Big Dipper. There it is, just like in the picture!"

"Hush, Ruthie. You're supposed to whisper when you look at stars."

"Weez? If the stars making the handle of that dipper ever shoot across the sky, we won't be able to call it a dipper anymore, will we? Because a dipper needs a handle."

"You don't have to worry about that, Ruthie, the dipper will always be there, for ever and ever. I learned that in school. You see that group of stars? That's the Seven Sisters."

"Who would ever want seven sisters," she grumbles.

"Nobody, if they're as ornery as you are."

She gives my shoulder a nudge and snuggles close. We lay still, staring up at the dark sky, letting it wrap around us, like Mama's arms used to.

"There's one," I whisper, and three seconds later, "and another." We sigh and watch as another streaks silently across the sky then disappears.

"Wish on it. Ruthie," I whisper, wondering if star-wishing may be the same as praying. Just in case, I think a wish to myself about Ruthie and her lying, and her cheating at checkers. Can't hurt I guess, especially if I give something in return, like maybe letting her win our next game.

"I wish people could be like that dipper," she says, breaking the silence.

"Most of them are." I say, not quite believing it.

"But not all, huh Weez?"

Letting my thoughts settle, I wait before answering. "No, not all, I guess."

Ruthie sighs, sending a shiver through her to me, drawing us closer. "I know one who ain't, Weez."

I know full well who she has in her mind. Suddenly the wind kicks up and it turns cold. "Wish we had that hot chocolate right now," I say, "sure would taste good."

"Gosh, Weez," Ruthie mumbles, "I didn't mean to forget it."

I've hurt her feelings, and I know she didn't mean to forget. "Never mind, Ruthie. We'll have it with Gram when we get home. We'd better start back now. I gather up the quilt and turn up the lantern.

"Hold my hand, Weez?"

"Sure, but we'd better be quick, before those wild animals get us."

We giggle and shout warnings to all the wild creatures that might be hiding behind every tree, as we light our way through fields of deep, damp grass, toward Gram, her hot chocolate, and the safety of the farm.

CHAPTER 18

Getting ready for Christmas starts the week after Thanksgiving. Each morning Gram gets to her baking right after chores and doesn't finish 'til near dark.

Clouds of flour circle up from her baking board as she rolls out cookie dough. Whiffs of cinnamon and clove and cardamom find their way into every corner of the house. Soon we start humming *Oh Tannenbaum* and *Silent Night,* and Gram lets us decorate cookies with raisins and colored sugar and black walnuts. But there is no sampling until Christmas Eve day. Ruthie manages to sneak a few, but I stick to Gram's rules. I hope Gram notices that.

Grampa mostly sits in his chair, breathing in the goodness of it all. As the big day gets closer, the house is filled with smells of red cabbage, cranberry sauce, and savory dressing for the goose. It's a wonder we can sleep for the waiting.

One afternoon before Christmas I find Ruthie in the barn muttering half aloud. "Now-I-lay-me-down to sleep," she crosses herself, "I pray-the-lord-my-soul-to-keep." She crosses herself again, twice.

"Ruthie, how come you're praying this time of day and in the barn? That's a nighttime prayer, and we just finished breakfast. Besides, we never cross ourselves. Where did you learn that?"

"From Mary Margaret in school. She says praying don't work unless you cross yourself. She ought to know; she's Catholic. She's going into a convent some day."

"I don't think Gram would like you crossing yourself. What are you praying for, anyway?"

"I'm making sure I get a kitten for Christmas."

I roll my eyes and don't say a thing. No use spoiling it for her, but that night at dinner, I say a silent prayer myself. *Please God, when Birdie has her kittens, could Gram let Ruthie keep just one? I'll even do extra chores, if you'll see that Ruthie gets a kitten.*

Turning so Gram can't see, I cross myself, just in case. Can't do much harm.

But then I think maybe she doesn't deserve a kitten. She's got to get over her meanness first. She'd probably pull its ears and drop it from the barn loft to see if it bounces. I take back my prayer and the crossing of myself. Let her do her own chores. She's no more able to care for a kitten than I am to fly.

Two days before Christmas a delivery truck delivered a giant box to the farm. Nothing like this has ever happened since we've been here. As soon as Gram signed a paper saying she had received it, the two deliverymen hoisted the box into the house.

"Over *dare*, put it," Gram tells them as she points to her bedroom. Ruthie is so curious she inches close and pokes at the box. Gram gives Ruthie her tight-lipped look and shakes her head.

"What do you suppose it is, Weez?" Ruthie whispers behind her fist. Do you think it's something for me?"

"How should I know? It's big enough to be a new stove. Gram sure could use one."

A stove! That's no Christmas present, and why would she want it in her bedroom?"

"Well, what ever it is, we'll just have to wait."

"Do we have to go to church on Christmas Eve, Gram?" Ruth asks, "and why do we have to eat supper before we light the tree candles?"

Gram scowls and doesn't answer.

If Ruthie's not careful, she'll push Gram too far with her questions. "Don't fret," I tell her. "We'll get to open our presents and eat some of Gram's cookies when it's time."

Miss Maryweather gives out old books for Christmas presents. Last year each person in my grade got to take home one volume in the *Book of Knowledge.* I got the number eleven volume and I've read it through, cover to cover, about a fourteen times. I just wish I hadn't gotten the one that told all about spiders. Ruthie had the notion she wanted to hear every word about those spiders, over and over again. She asked a million questions. 'Why do they need so many legs? Why do some have claws and fangs? How can they grow to be ten inches long? How come some are poison and can shoot eight feet through the air if they have a mind to? Can their poison kill you?" That's why I read it over so many times, so she would remember and quite asking.

Hearing about those spiders gave her nightmares. She would wake up screaming and I had to shake out our quilts four times to make sure there weren't any of them in our bed. I should have read her the part about butterflies instead of spiders.

This year, Mama sent our packages in the mail. I knew when they came she wasn't coming herself. My package is the size of a shoebox, all wrapped in store-bought paper. This year my feet took such a notion to grow, so if it's shoes, I doubt they'll fit.

"I know there's a kitten in my box," Ruthie grins, shaking it, and trying to hear it purr.

"Don't be dumb, Ruthie. Mama can't box up a kitten and send it through the mail. You should know that."

She scowls and I can see she's trying to figure a way that could happen.

"Maybe she told it to hold its breath." She puts her ear to the box. "Listen, Weez," she whispers, "I think it's crying. Maybe we should open it, to give it some air."

"Whatever it is, you'll have wait until Christmas morning, and it's not a kitten. What do you want a kitten for, anyway? You'll just forget to feed it or squeeze it so hard it would choke."

"Quit sayin' that, Weez. I want one so it can grow up and have more kittens. Then I can play with them all."

Whatever is in her box, I hope she likes it. Would be just like her to spoil Christmas for the rest of us.

CHAPTER 19

We wake on the morning of Christmas Eve to a two-inch falling of wet snow. After breakfast, Ruthie and me take Grampa into the woods to cut down a tree. I do the chopping, while Grampa props against another tree and motions me how to hold the axe. He's mostly given up talking, but we still understand what he means.

Ruthie pepper me with snowballs. She's got good aim, but she doesn't know how to pack the snow tight, so hers don't hurt at all.

When I'm finish chopping, I drag the tree home, while Grampa leans on Ruthie.

We shake off the snow and set the tree up in the parlor, and the freshness of it fills the room. It towers so high the top curls against the ceiling.

"How come it looked so small out in the woods," Ruthie asks, and in here it looks to be the tallest tree in the whole world?"

I could recite the lesson we learned in school on optical illusions, but I doubt she could sit still long enough to listen, much less understand.

"It isn't the tallest in the world, but it's probably the tallest in Connecticut," I tell her but . . . I can tell by her slant-y-eyed look she knows I'm teasing. For once she lets it go and we begin the decorating.

Gram opens her trunk. With gentle hands, she lifts out her ancient ornaments. An angel, a silver bell, a bunch of grapes, each grape wrapped in cellophane paper, and a sailing ship made of painted glass. There is a cloth elf with Mama's name on it. She must have made when she was a girl. I hold it gently in my hand, and it brings tears. Ruthie makes a grab for it, but Gram snatches it away and puts it high in the tree out of reach. We hang acorns tied with colored yarn, and striped candy canes Gram bought from town.

"Let's make a paper chain to drape on the tree," Ruthie says, bringing out her magazine. I get Gram's scissors and start mixing up some flour paste. Then Gram sees the magazine.

"Where you got that from?" she asks, and before I can think up something halfway near the truth, Ruthie pipes up.

"From school, Gram. Mrs. Maryweather gave it to me, so we could use it for decorations." She makes wide innocent eyes for Gram and beams a smile at me. Lies come so easy to her. As Gram scowls her doubts, Ruthie piles it on thicker still.

"Mrs. Maryweather *ex-cribes* to lots of magazines," she lies. "Gives 'em to us kids means she won't have to throw 'em away. We're just doing her a favor by taking 'em, Gram."

A hollow-eyed smile widens across her face. I bite my lip, like I might be going to tell on her. She balls up her fists and gives me her squinty-eyed look.

"Be careful with the scissors," is all I say. Someday her lying is going to get her into more trouble than she can handle.

When we finish decorating the tree with Gram's decorations and the paper chains, Gram sets out a plate of decorated cookies and cups of hot chocolate. Then she pushes out the big box that has been in her bedroom.

"Early present for us," she says with a big grin. "Useful present."

We help her cut and pull away the cardboard box, and there, standing big and proud and brand new, is a shiny new sewing machine, with the name *Singer* stamped in the metal.

"What's that, Gram?" Ruthie asks, wrinkling her nose. She probably thought it was going to be something for her, like a piano or a go-cart.

"For making clothes," Gram said, "for you two *unt* me." But now we get ready to go to church. You two push, I pull."

We manage to get the machine back into her bedroom and the three of us set off in the wagon for the carol sing at the church.

Grampa stays home in bed. I saw Gram give him one of her pills and I guess that will make him sleep until we get home.

The church is aglow with tall candles, and Gram's eyes tear up through the singing. Ruthie gets into a real tizzy wanting to get home, and Gram gets fretful, worrying about Grampa. We don't even stay for punch and cookies. No one asked me what I wanted to do.

Ruthie fidgets all the way home in the wagon. "Let's not eat supper 'til after presents, please, Gram?" Ruthie whines. Gram doesn't bother to answer, just coaxes the horse to keep moving.

We hurry into the house, and there is Grampa sitting wide-eyed and frail, in his chair with one of Gram's quilt tucked clumsily around his knees, and under the tree is an assortment of presents that had been hidden in their bedroom. Grampa's pale face looks pale and sad. He probably though Gram had forgotten about him.

Merry Christmas Eve, Grampa," I say to him. His eyes cloud over. He probably thought Gram had forgot him.

Ruthie pokes at the presents while Gram fixes our Christmas Eve supper. Hard-boiled eggs in cream sauce, poured over her homemade biscuits. She says it was that way in Germany the night before Christmas. She won't let me help, but I watch for her special adding's, so I can write them down later. She adds dry mustard, which turns the sauce yellow and spicy. If Ruthie knew there was hot mustard in the sauce, she wouldn't eat it. She'll never guess that the mustard is what makes it taste so good, not until she reads it my cookbook.

I wonder if Gram will be proud when my cookbook is finished, or if she'll think I'm sneaky, like Ruthie said. Guess I'll put a message in in the front of book thanking her for helping me become almost as good a cook and baker as she is. Gram will like that.

When the supper dishes are dried and put away, we light the candles on the tree. What a wonderful sight it is; everything is perfect, as perfect as it can be without Mama.

I help Grampa up as we all stand around the tree, holding hands, and hum along with Gram as she sings the old German Christmas song, 'O Tannenbaum.' Grampa has tears in his eyes watching Gram, and I'm thinking, he's singing along with her in his head.

When we're through singing, Gram sits Grampa in his chair, and makes us take turns opening our presents, one at a time. It about drives Ruthie to crying, she is so full of eagerness.

"Open the one from me, Weez. Hurry up." She jiggles up and down, and chews on a hank of her hair. "It's a plant," she shouts, taking all the surprise from it. "I grew it myself. You like it don't you, Weez?"

I hold up a cleaned-out coffee can full of dirt with it's sprig of greenness drooping over the side. "It's just what I wanted, Ruthie. Thank you for it."

Ruthie beams. "I knew you'd like it. It'll be a flower soon. You just have to keep it watered."

"I was wanting a plant just like this," I say, reaching to hug her, but she pulls away. I cover my disappointment and quickly say, "Now open the one I'm giving you, Ruthie."

She grabs it and tears off the paper, not even noticing my hand-drawn Christmas designs on the paper.

"Oh, it's a scarf," she says as she winds it twice around her neck, and races around the room pretending she is a steam engine, with the fringed ends flowing out behind her like smoke. "Toot, toot," she says, "aren't I grand?"

Grampa smiles, while Gram holds her hands in front of her mouth and laughs out loud.

"I knitted it myself," I tell her, but she's too much into her showing off to hear me. She doesn't even think to say thank you.

Gram gives us green and white-checkered pinafores she made. They're trimmed with lace from her trunk.

I give Gram a book of empty pages I strung together with yarn, with hand drawn pictures of roses on the cover.

"It's an album, Gram, so you can put all your pictures in. I made it myself."

"Good," she says, patting it gently. Her eyes smile, and I can see she is pleased.

Ruthie gives Gram the baby robin she carved from red cedar.

"It's for you, Gram," she says.

Gram's hug to Ruthie gets my fists to tighten. Why did she have to give it to Gram? Ruthie told me she was going to give it to me.

Grampa hands Ruthie a little wooden horse carved from white pine. She pretends to be thrilled, but I can see her interest is already pointing toward the box from Mama.

He gives me a carved frame he made for my spelling ribbons. I lean over to stroke his hand, and he smiles.

"I'm next for Mama's present," Ruthie squeals as she wrestles off the store-bought wrapping without a notion to saving it.

Ruthie opens the box. It *is* a cat, but it's a toy stuffed cat, with glass eyes, and it meows when you squeeze its stomach. Gram's lips pinch tight at the sound. What is it about cats that rile her so? She tolerates Birdie because she has to, otherwise the barn would be overrun with mice, but whenever Birdie has kittens, Gram does away with them before they even have a chance to open their eyes.

Ruthie would have ripped the tail off the stuffed cat from Mama, if we weren't watching. Gram gives Ruthie a warning look, and she settles, saying in a voice as sweet as apple butter, "Just what I wanted. Now I have two cats, one from Grampa and one from . . ." she grits her teeth, "from . . . her."

I open my box from Mama and pull out a genuine boar bristles hairbrush, and it *is* just what I wanted. I must have gotten the idea of fussing with my hair from Mama. I certainly didn't get it from Gram. Never once have I seen her hair done in any other way than her loose slipping-down bun on the top of her head.

Grampa's glazed-over eyes watch as the three of us sing *Silent Night* one last time.

When we finish singing she lets us snuff out the candles. "Save da good ones for tomorrow," Gram says. My throat tightens thinking of Mama not being here.

Ruthie takes the lantern to our room. I want to hug Gram and wish her a Merry Christmas, but she is too busy tending to Grampa to notice.

When I slip into our bed and I don't hear Ruthie's regular bubbling noises. She may be crying about Mama's present, but she's so quiet I'm far from knowing for sure. I wonder if Mama is thinking about us tonight? Before I go to sleep I write Mama another letter.

December 1922

Dear Mama,

Sorry you didn't make it here for Christmas this year. You should see how good our house smells from Gram's baking. Thank you for the hairbrush. It was just what I wanted. Ruthie is pleased with the stuffed cat. She says it's not as good as a real one, but she thanks you anyway. Oh, yes, I almost forgot. Merry Christmas and A Happy New Year too. Sincerely, Louise

Five days after Christmas a litter of kittens is born in the barn, but Gram manages to take them before Ruthie finds out, leaving Birdie to suffer with unused milk.

CHAPTER 20

March 1923

Dear Mother.

My birthday came and went again. Don't you care at all???

Signed,—your just turned fifteen year old daughter who will graduate from the eighth grade this year and there aren't any grades here beyond the eighth. What am I supposed to do if you don't take me out of here? Louise.

P.S. I don't much care anyway.

There are times when I don't do what Gram says; after all, I'll be fourteen on my next birthday. She can't make me curtsy when I meet a neighbor either, and when I go wading in the stream I don't wear all my clothes. When Ruthie hits me, sometimes I smack her back. I'm old enough to have a mind of my own.

Whenever Gram thinks I've done something wrong, she says, 'You're just like your mama.' She spits the words out as if that's the worst thing I can be. She never says that to Ruthie, although Ruthie is a lot more like Mama than I am, except for her dark every-which-way hair.

Gram keeps Ruth's hair short and she is forever threatening to cut *my* hair too. I don't think she really would cut it; it's just her way of getting back at me for reminding her of Mama.

It's Ruthie I worry about. Ever since Mama gave me a hairbrush for Christmas, Ruthie has been even more envious of my curls. Every night before we go to bed, I undo the long braid that hangs clear down to my waist, and brush out the farm dust and tangles with my new brush. Ruthie watches, all the while pulling more stuffing out of her Christmas cat.

I give my hair one hundred strokes every night, and it would be helpful if Ruthie would braid me up again so I can sleep in comfort, but she won't. Says she's too tired, but I know it's because she's jealous. Her short, ragged hair looks just like her stuffed cat. Poor cat. It already is missing one leg and it's head is hanging' loose. Ruthie named it Milky Mouse.

April 1923

Dear Mama,

Pay no mind to my last letter if it made you sad or angry. I may have been coming down with something. Sincerely, Louise

CHAPTER 21

Winter finally gives way to spring, sending me and Ruthie deep into the woods to hunt wild flowers, pure white Indian pipe, lady's slippers, and if we're lucky, Dutchman's breeches and Jack-in-the-pulpit. Gram says, "don't pick." She says wild flowers are just for looking at. She doesn't mind if we pick the violets because they grow everywhere. We bring back enough to fill three glass canning jars; one in Grampa's room, one for the table, and one for the dresser in our room.

Grampa is getting worse. He stays in his room most of the time now. Gram talks to him in a soft voice and keeps him cleaned up and fed. On his better days she walks him to the outhouse. On his bad days he uses the chamber pot. Gram keeps his room dark, and, except for the violets, it has a sickly sweet smell, like mice droppings, so Gram mostly keeps his door closed. When it's cold, she puts heated stones in his bed to keep his feet warm and piles on the quilts, even though it's coming near summer.

Sometimes when I take him his supper tray, Grampa stares at me as if he doesn't know me. His words are muddled, and all I want to do is back out of his room and close the door. Sometimes he reaches out with his bony fingers, like he wants me to stay, but when I come close, he shakes his head and waves me away. That's when I know it's probably Ruthie he wants.

"Hope you feel better, Grampa," I tell to him, "I pray for you every night."

But that's a lie, because mostly I forget. To make up for it I write another letter to Mama.

April 1923

Dear Mama,

*Grampa is ailing. He doesn't say it, but I think it would
please him if you came for a visit. Just don't tell Gram you are
coming. Sincerely, Louise.*

We sit at the table with Gram for an early supper. Ruthie dips
homemade bread into her bowl of Gram's potato cabbage knackwurst
soup. If she knew Gram slips ginger and a pinch of red pepper in it,
she wouldn't eat it. I have all Grams' secret things written down in the
recipe for my cookbook.

"Weez," Ruthie says between bites, "the almanac says Easter is on
the first day of April this year. That's April Fool's Day, isn't it?"

I scowl, remembering she stole that almanac. "You ought to know,
Ruthie."

"Does that mean we don't have to go to church that day?"

"No, it just means someone might play a trick on you."

"Not if I play one on them first, you wait and . . ."

The door to Grampa's room creaks open. He stares at us with his
watery eyes. His pale skinny legs stick out below his faded nightshirt
like dead sticks as he stumbles toward the front door. Gram's hand
flies to her throat as she runs toward him. They gaze at each other,
each seeming to shrink in size.

My eyes tear up. Ruthie whimpers as she bolts out of her chair, and
runs to our room.

Gram folds her arms around our Grampa. She looks at me and
whispers, "You, finish up. Get her to bed." Then slowly walks our
Grampa through the door.

I clear our plates and hurry to our room. Ruthie is laying face
down on our bed, whimpering. I settle in beside her and gently rub
her back.

Through the window I can see Gram as she slowly walks our grandfather to the old apple tree. She helps him slip to the ground, buries her face in his chest, rocking him back and forth.

My breath catches and I sob, knowing for sure, I will never see our grandfather alive again.

CHAPTER 22

Ruthie takes over feeding the animals while I help Gram build a box for our Grampa. We use the pinewood pieces he had already cut to proper lengths before he got so sick. The pieces fit perfectly. He probably never guessed it would be Gram and me nailing the pieces together. Gram goes at building his box like she does with her knitting when she has something preying on her mind. She hardly takes time to breath until the job is finished.

I've never seen a dead person before, and I don't know what to say to Gram. Can't imagine the farm without our Grampa. I never want to die; I never want to be laid in the ground in a wooden box. If I do, I want a little hole drilled in the top, so my spirit will be able to fly up and over the fields, so I can look down and keep an eye on what's going on below.

I don't know if Mama would care if I died, though I think Gram would. With Grampa gone, maybe she will have more time for me. I cross my fingers behind my back for fear Grampa might hear, and think I wanted him to die.

Neighbors and people I don't even know come to pay their respects to our Grampa. Men come with their hats in their hands, women with cakes and pies, and some of their finest covered dishes. Mrs. Wolcott brings a cooked ham and branches from her early blooming dogwood tree.

Gram dressed Grampa in a crisp black suit from Gram's trunk, and shiny black shoes. Ruthie can't seem to get enough of staring at

Grampa in his box, like she's waiting for him to get up and fix himself a plate of food.

We bury Grampa in the very spot near the old apple tree where he walked to when he laid down and died. I guess that's where he wanted to be. The preacher says the words, and we all bow our heads, except Ruthie, who keeps staring at where his box is buried. Gram stares, too, like she's seeing something else. We all walk back to the house for refreshments, and when the people have said their goodbyes and the wagons are gone, Gram takes our hands, and we walk again to where Grampa is.

"He picked a fine place, Gram," I say. "Right near his favorite tree."

Gram's eyes glisten. She pinches her mouth and nods. She keeps silent as we stand, me on one side of her, Ruthie on the other. She hasn't said a word since Grampa left us, not even to thank the neighbors for coming. I wish she would talk. It's not good that she won't talk.

"It's a real nice resting spot, isn't it Gram?" I say.

She nods again and gathers her arms tight around her starched black grieving dress. "The sweet clover grows thick here, Gram, with plenty of sunshine and rain. We can bring fresh flowers every day 'til they stop blooming. It's nice here, near his apple tree, and there's . . ."

" . . . Room for one more," Gram whispers, as if she's talking right to Grampa.

With a sob, my tears finally come. "Don't fret, *Liebchen*," she whispers as we walk back to the house. But I do fret. Mama didn't even come for the funeral. She should have been here. How will she feel if no one comes when she dies and gets buried in the ground?

Every day Gram goes to water the flowers around Grampa. She speaks low to him with German words, while Ruthie and me stand near. I wonder if Grampa knows we are here, and can hear Gram's words?

The days pass just as always, only now there is no need to carry a tray in for Grampa, and no one to keep Gram warm in her bed at night.

April 1923

Dear Mama,

We buried Grampa and now I don't have a father or a grandfather. Sometimes I wonder if I even have a mother anymore. Sincerely, Louise

CHAPTER 23

We'll be wearing our gingham dresses with the lace collars to church on Easter. It's the only time we get to wear our best dress other than Christmas. I wish Grampa could see us.

Ruthie stands in front of me with her hands on her hips, sassy-like. "Guess what, Weez?" she says in her, I-know-something-you-don't-know voice. "We're having an egg hunt on Easter. You want to come?"

"If this is one of your made-up ideas Gram doesn't know about, Ruthie, I don't want to hear it."

"We don't need you. Me and Ellsworth thought it up together."

My cheeks burn. *Her and Ellsworth?* Why, that little imp! She has no right making plans with Ellsworth. *I'm* the one that should be making plans with Ellsworth. I've been waiting for him to try to kiss me again so I could say no, but I don't want him pairing up with Ruthie, or have her taking up his time with any egg hunt, either. She's not . . . well, she's only a little kid.

"Easter Eggs?" Gram asks, within earshot of what we had said. She is not smiling and I'm wondering if she's thinking of Grampa being fresh in the ground.

"It's a dumb idea, Gram. I told Ruthie you'd say no," I say, hoping she will.

Gram's eyes squint up, her lips pinch tight. "No harm in it," she says, looking over at me. "You help her with Ellsworth, you understand? See she don't make trouble, and you too."

Sometimes I think Gram can see right into my thoughts. I go to hug her but she backs away. "Get on with you," she smiles, and that smile makes me think maybe she cares for me just a little.

Every afternoon before Easter, Ellsworth rides over in his pony cart and the three of us do the planning the Easter egg hunt. I'm glad Ellsworth's cousin that Homer is in bed with a bad cold. Maybe if Ruthie doesn't see him for a couple of days, she'll forget him. Don't know why Mrs. Wolcott lets him stay with them. He's always up to no good. I'd send him packing if he lived with us.

Gram shows us how to color eggs using onionskins, beets, red cabbage, and walnut shells. She says in Germany it's the rabbits that lay the chocolate eggs. Ruthie believes it, but I know Gram is making it up. German rabbits can't be much different than our rabbits, and I never saw them laid even regular eggs, much less chocolate ones. But I don't let on to Gram. She said if we lived in Germany and didn't believe rabbits laid chocolate eggs, our baskets would be empty.

"How many eggs do you think we need to color, Ellsworth?" Ruthie asks. "I think a hundred, don't you?"

Ellsworth shrugs *his I-don't-know shrug*, as if he doesn't want to listen to her. I don't think he ever tried kissing Ruthie. It took all his courage for him to kiss me.

"We'll get as many as they lay," I say, pretending she's talking to me." Our hens never give us more than twenty in a week, but it won't do any good to tell her that.

"I know what, Ellsworth. Let's have a parade," she says, turning her back on me and giving her whole attention to Ellsworth. "We can give rides on Hilda for money . . . and dress up the pigs and teach them to march, and . . . let's think up something for that old goose to do."

"Don't be silly, Ruthie," I say before Ellsworth can come up with an answer. "Hilda won't let anyone ride on her back. And you can't teach pigs to march, neither. If you think you can make that old goose do anything, except chase after you, you've got no sense at all. So let's just finish coloring the eggs."

Ruthie sulks until Ellsworth gives her a piece of *Black Jack* chewing gum. He knows how to calm her down even without saying a thing.

Ellsworth's pony balks when we plait her tail with ribbons, but when we're done, she snorts and paws the ground like she knows she looks fancy.

Ruthie grabs her old straw hat and tries to climb up onto Hilda's back. Hilda shakes her off and she tries again. "Gram," I yell, "she'll get hurt."

"Enough Roo-tee!" Gram hollers from the house. "Leave Hildie be!"

"I told her it wouldn't work," I whisper to Ellsworth.

Ruthie limps toward us and brushes off. I can tell she's going to try again as soon as Gram isn't looking. She edges toward me and whispers, "I'll fix you, Weez. You just wait. You can stay here with that old lady, but I'm leavin'. I'm running away, and they'll blame you for my going."

"I wish Gram could hear you say that, Ruthie. If you don't stop acting up, you'll ruin it for all of us. Just forget about riding Hilda."

She elbows me away, and grabs Ellsworth's hand as if she owns him. "Ellsworth, I thought up a new idea. Let's have races, three-legged ones, like we had in school, and the one where you walk on your hands while . . ."

I cut her off before she can finish. "Ellsworth and I have already decided on races," I tell her. "We made a list."

She stamps her foot and narrows her eyes to slits like I knew she would. "You never asked *me* about no list."

"We got the list already made, see?

1. Carrying an egg in a spoon.

2. Push peanuts across the yard with your nose.

3. We'll have an egg toss."

"Well I'm not doing any of that baby stuff," she pouts.

I can see she's nearing her boiling point. "Ellsworth," I whisper. "If we don't let her do what she wants, she'll have one of her fits. Let her think up the prizes."

Ruthie balls up her fists and comes at me on a run. "Quit talking like I ain't here. This is my idea, mine, and Ellsworth's. I hate you, Weez," she says and starts punching me.

"Get off me, Ruthie. You're spoiling everything."

"You're the one's doing the spoiling, making a list with Ellsworth, leaving me out. I'll show you." She comes at me again. I grab her arm hard. She lands a punch right in my eye. Ellsworth stands there doing nothing.

"*Roo-tee!*" Gram whoops from the doorway. "You come here this minute."

Ruthie jumps off of me, and runs crying to Gram. She moans as if she's in pain. "She hurt me, Gram. *Oh*, I think she broke my arm."

"I hardly touched you, Ruthie! And look at my eye. It's starting to swell already. I can hardly see out of it. Gram?"

But Gram is too busy tending Ruthie to take any notice of my eye.

"Look at that, Gram," Ruthie says, letting her arm hang loose. Gram takes her into the house.

Ellsworth stands from one foot to the other, looking helpless. He could have stuck up for me.

"That girl belongs in reform school," I tell him.

"She didn't mean it, Weez. She was just mad."

"You're sticking up for her, too? Can't you see she's trouble? She started it and now she's blaming me. And don't call me Weez."

Why did I ever want him kissing me again? He doesn't care a hoot about me. Nobody cares. Not Mama, not Gram, not even Ellsworth. It always ends up like this. Tears sting my eye worse. I can't go to church with a black eye. But if I don't go to church, God won't hear me pray for Mama. Maybe Gram has a German remedy for black eyes. Drat that Ruthie anyway. Everyone's going to laugh when they see me at the egg hunt. Maybe if I hide in the barn no one will notice. Maybe nobody will even care.

I can't ever guess what Gram said to Ruthie, but whatever it was, it worked. Ruthie comes skipping toward me, smiling her she-loves-me-better-than-she-loves-you, smile.

"Gram's got the egg coloring ready, Weez," she sings out. "Look at my arm. It got better real quick. Come on. We've got a million of eggs to color. What are you waitin' for, Weez?"

May 1923

Dear Mama,

> *Ruthie is getting worse than ever. I just thought you ought know. We are having an egg hunt on Easter Sunday. If you come, don't notice my eye. It hardly hurts anymore. Sincerely, Louise*

Easter morning comes, and it's raining buckets. It beats down like it'll never stop. I can barely see through my swollen eye. Gram says we can't go to church. She fears the wagon will get stuck. Ruthie sulks and blames me for the rain. But I know whose fault it is. *He* let Ruthie give me a black eye. Now *He*'s sending rain so we can't get to church so *He* won't hear my bargaining and Mama won't ever change. What is the matter with this world?

I was going to give all my Easter basket candy to the poor, in exchange for *His* help with Mama. I would have gone to church—even with my purple eye—and now I can't. I guess what's between me and Mama is meant to be, too, but I don't understand. God is supposed to know best, but this time I sure wish he hadn't sent rain. Now we'll have to eat all the hard-boiled eggs ourselves.

For Easter breakfast Gram fixes bread slices dipped in batter and fried. We lather each piece with butter and jam. I catch her doing her secret adding's. This time it's a hefty sprinkling of cinnamon and a dash of vanilla to the batter. We have hot chocolate and real oranges. Ruthie won't eat a thing except her Easter basket candy. I eat a chocolate egg from my basket, wondering when Gram had a chance to buy them.

"It's your fault it rained Weez," Ruthie says through a mouthful of her chocolate egg. "You never wanted an Easter hunt, anyhow."

I want to tell her who really sent the rain, but Gram doesn't like us talking out loud about God. Except for, 'Now I lay me down to sleep.' She says all talk of God should be done inside our heads or in church.

After breakfast I lay on our bed wondering if praying at home *is* as useful as praying in church. I guess the only way I'll know is if any of Mama's promises come true.

Even in the pouring rain, Ellsworth comes over and brings us chocolate bunnies. I think he likes me, because he gives me the most. I give him a basket full of of our colored eggs. Even after that, we still have so many we'll be eating hard-boiled eggs three times a day for a whole week. Standing next to Ellsworth, I can see he's grown since under that tree. I think I'm beginning to like him a little more, too.

May 1923

Dear Mama,

We didn't have an egg hunt. God sent rain instead. Ellsworth came over. He got soaked but he brought us chocolate bunnies anyway. Ruthie ate hers all at once and got sick. Gram gave her castor oil and sent her to bed. This time Ruthie got what she deserved. I'm not sure, but I think Ellsworth likes me. Sincerely, Louise

CHAPTER 24

"Louise." Ruthie comes running into the chicken house.

"How come you're calling me 'Louise' instead of 'Weez'? You sick or something?"

"It's not me, Weez, it's Gram."

That wide-eyed look on her face only comes when she's expecting her world to turn inside out. Something must be wrong. "Just wait 'till I take these eggs in the house, Ruthie."

"No, don't go in. I have to warn you first," she whispers.

"Warn me about what?" Right away goose bumps appear on my arm. "What is it, Ruthie?"

She pulls on her hair, chewing on the ends, making it stand up in spikes as we walk toward the house. "Gram is talking to our Grampa."

"Don't be a smart-aleck, Ruthie. Grampa isn't here, he's dead."

"But she *is*, Weez." Tears shine in her eyes. "She's sitting in her rocker talking to him like he's right next to her, and I just know she can hear him talking back. Hurry, Weez."

My heart pounds. "Don't lie about Gram, Ruthie," but somehow I know she's not lying.

"Just come! See for yourself."

She pulls me through the door. The room is dark after the brightness outside. Gram is sitting in her rocker. I hold the egg basket close. "Gram? Gram, are you all right?"

She turns toward me, slow like, and puzzled, like she doesn't know who I am. Tears catch in my throat, making it hard to talk.

"It's me, Gram, Louise, don't you know me?"

She shakes her head and stares up at me, trying to get her senses straight, I guess.

"Louise?" She asks, as if she isn't sure.

Ruthie stamps her foot. "Don't be that way, Gram. You hear? You *know* that's Weez. I don't want you being sick this way."

Gram's shiver comes clear up from her swollen legs. "Sick? Who says sick? I just talk with Grampa. He helps me look for my medicine. Get away now. You shouldn't listen."

"You're having a spell, Gram." I reach out to her.

"No spell! Go!" She pulls away. "He's gone now. See? It's fine."

She looks around for a second and shakes her finger at me. "Say *nutin'* to your mama, you hear?" She eases herself up from her chair, straightens her apron, and fingers the bun on the back of her head. "Only *dat* many eggs?"

"I'll go get some more, Gram. You feel okay?"

"Okay, yes. It's good sometimes to talk. You both go now. Get eggs." Ruthie stares at her. Gram softens. "Go, *Liebchen*. See to dem eggs."

We head back to the hen house, knowing there are no more eggs.

"Don't she know he's dead, Weez?" Ruthie whispers. "Don't she remember us burying him down near the apple tree?"

"I think she gets lonely for him, Ruthie. And don't say *don't*. You know you're supposed to say *doesn't*."

"What's the difference? Nobody cares how I talk, not even Grampa." She looks back toward the house. "You don't care do you, Grampa?" she whispers.

"Stop that, Ruthie. Stop that right now."

"Good-bye, Grampa." She waves him a kiss and ducks out of my reach.

I reach under a hen and collect one more egg, still warm. "Someday, Ruthie, if you ever move in with Mama, you'll have to be sensible."

"I ain't moving in with Mama." She puts a piece of straw in her mouth, pretending it's a cigarette. "Do you think she'll make us stay on the farm to see to Gram, now that she's talking to Grampa, like he's still here? Do you think that?"

"I think that straw in your mouth has chicken poop on it."

She sputters, wipes the back of her hand across her mouth, and glares at me.

"I ain't stayin' here alone. If she takes just you, I'm runnin' away for sure." She stamps her foot, and stares toward the apple tree.

"Ruthie, don't you know it takes more than you saying it to make things happen? The world isn't going to change just because you stamp your . . ." But she's gone, off to visit Gramp's grave again.

Gram keeps her visits with Grampa mostly to herself. She said not to tell Mama. Mama couldn't do anything about it, anyway, even if I did tell her.

June 1923

Dear Mama,

> *Everything is fine on the farm. You don't need to come to see for yourself. We manage fine without you. Sincerely, Louise*

CHAPTER 25

May turns out to be dry enough for haying. Ellsworth and his dad come to help Gram and me. They bring their tractor and hired man, and we work for two days, with just short spells for meals. Gram drives, while the rest of us use pitchforks and bale. I watch her. Sometimes I think I can see Grampa sitting next to her, but it's probably just the heat.

I get so tired haying, I'm almost sick. Each day when we finish, I stagger into the house, undo my braid, shake my hair loose, and flop on my bed, too tired to plait it up for the night; too tired to take off my boots; too tired to eat the stew Gram has kept warming on the back of the stove. All I can think of is sleep.

If my being so sound asleep hadn't lasted 'til morning and heard Ruthie squeaking the floorboards near out bed, I might have stopped her from doing what she did. I would have seen her nasty, slit-eyed grin.

She must have crept out of bed early and sneaked into Gram's mending basket. I didn't know until my ear she nicked my ear.

"Ouch," I yell, grabbing my bloody ear. I jump up and see my curls laying on the floor; laying there like dead things.

"No!" I yell, but it's too late. I reach back, and they're gone. All my long curls are gone. "Ruthie," I say, in a slow, beyond-angry voice. "You're going to be sorry for this."

I chase her clear into the yard, with what's left of my hair sticking out in clumps, looking almost like hers. I grab her arm. "You're not going to get away with this. When Mama hears, you know where she'll send you? To that reform school, that's where, and I hope they never let you out."

Ruthie jerks away and laughs her screech-full laugh, and I chase her again. She laughs because she knows she can run faster than me and Ellsworth put together.

"Just wait," I shout through tears. "You just wait!"

Ruthie runs toward the house. "Gram," she yells. "Keep her away from me."

I sink flat out in the dirt, sobbing, sobbing 'til no more tears will come. Mama will never love me now.

A chicken struts toward me and pecks my head. I reach for it's neck, but it flaps its useless wings and skips out of reach.

Gram comes, waving her arms, taking me inside. She won't even let me talk while she tends to my bloody ear. Ruthie comes in and Gram makes us hot cocoa. We sit glaring at each other, each sipping cocoa, each with short spiky hair.

Gram sends Ruthie to bed without supper. I hope she's waiting for me to bring her something, because she can wait 'til kingdom come and breakfast, to get any food from me, and I hope she starves.

August 1923

Dear Mama,

Ellsworth and his dad helped Gram and me with the haying. Don't be mad, everything is fine. Sincerely, Louise

P.S. Did I tell you I now have short hair?

CHAPTER 26

Gram trims my hair as best she can. She says it'll look better in a week or two. I'm thinking it will take longer, but before it matters much, Mama comes storming through the door.

"Mama," Ruthie squeals. "How come you're here? It's not my birthday. You're taking me back? I'll get my clothes."

Mama pushes past her. "Where is she? Where is that old woman?"

For a moment the room is dead quiet, like after thunder, before the rain starts. I peek through the curtain on our bedroom door just enough so that my scissor-cropped hair won't shout out to the whole room. Short strands slip loose from the hair clip and fall across my forehead, it being so thick. She sees me and pulls me through the curtain.

"Oh, Louise," she sighs, as tears streak down her cheeks, running her eye makeup down with them. "Your beautiful hair!"

I don't ever remember her crying before, and she's crying over *me*. My breath catches and I have trouble breathing.

"It's all right, Mama," I say, ready to forgive her everything. "It'll grow back. Besides, it's easier to take care of now."

I wait for her to hug me, but she storms past me, and heads straight for Gram.

Gram is sitting quiet in her rocker, mending one of Gramp's old shirts she still wears around the house.

Mama glares down at her. "You knew I loved her hair," she snaps through tight lips. "How could you do it?"

"Just hair! Why should you care?"

"That's why you did it, isn't it, because you knew I loved it long. You remember, old woman, when you did the same thing to me?" She looks toward me, shakes her head, and then looks back at Gram. "You had no right," she stamps her foot. "Who gave you the right?"

Ruthie slinks behind me, biting her fingers. Gram rises from her chair.

Like two angry cats, Mama and Gram circle each other.

"But Mama," I try to tell her, "it wasn't . . ." Ruthie whimpers like a hurt kitten.

"You shut up." Mama words sting like a slap.

Gram points toward the door. "Go, *Roo-tee*, go now! To the barn."

Mama flares up. "Don't you dare tell my daughter what to do, not when I'm standing right here."

"Here? When are you here?" Gram's eyes flash. She stands tall and ridged.

Ruthie ducks behind me but I push her away. I still haven't forgiven her for what she did. Just wait until Gram tells Mama it was Ruthie who cut my hair, mot Gram.

"You had no right to cut her hair." Mama points at me in a way that makes my heart ache.

"In my own house I have rights, Gram snaps.

I put my hands behind my back and cross my fingers. When is she going to tell her it was Ruthie who did it?

"You call this a house?" Mama yells. Why, it's no better than that barn out back. Look at this place, not even running water."

Gram's back stiffens. She pounds the table. Dishes rattle. "You don't like it? Take '*dem* and go. Take *dem* both, and go." Gram shakes her head from side to side. "*War effort*," she mutters. "Make money. Hell with war effort. Mind your kids, I say." She circles Mama. "Stop fooling around, *Dummkopf*."

Mama backs up, ready to pounce. Her eyes slit narrow, like Ruthie's. "You don't know what you're talking about. You know why I left. Don't I have a right to live my life?"

"You ain't no *Dummkopf,* Mama," Ruthie shouts from the doorway. "Let's go, get us out of here."

Mama's breath catches. "Oh, honey, you know I . . . I . . . I'll come for you, real soon. As soon as I can, I promise."

Mama looks toward me, and then turns away as if I don't matter. I thought she was going to say she cared, even with my hair short, but her concern is all going toward Ruthie. If Gram isn't going to tell on her who cut my hair, I have a good mind to tell on her myself.

Slowly Mama and Gram's anger wears down. Gram pats down Gramp's shirt; Mama fusses her hair into place. Ruthie inches toward Mama as Mama's temper flairs again.

"You didn't have to chop it off clear up to her ears."

I step forward ready to tell what really happened, but Gram's eyes flash at me.

"Yours grew back," she says calmly. "Hers will, too."

She's not going to tell on Ruthie. Her hand reaches in her apron pocket and takes out the thick hank of hair that was mine, and holds it out to Mama. It's all wound around with pink ribbons.

"You want *dis*?" she asks.

I want to tell her, No, Gram, it's mine. Don't give it to her, but the look on Mama's face stops me. I finger the frayed ends of what's left of my hair on my head.

"Spun gold," Mama whispers, holding the ribbon wrapped curls in her hands.

"It's passed now," Gram says. "Louise. Go put dishes on da' table. Get ready for supper."

Mama looks at Gram. "You want me to stay?" Gram shrugs.

"Well, now," Ruthie says, wiping her nose clear up to her elbow. She gives Mama her ear-to-ear smile. "You're staying for supper, ain't you, Mama? You can sit next to me."

Doesn't she remember? She did the cutting. She caused the trouble. That little ninny acts like we're giving a party and it's just for her.

"It's sausage and sauerkraut, Mama," Ruthie chirps, innocent as a babe, "and Gram's apple strudel. You got to clean your plate before you get dessert; Gram says." She smiles up at Mama,

Mama looks at Gram. "*Mutti*?" she asks, using a word that gives Gram a start." Is it all right if I stay?" Gram looks down, closes her eyes, and shrugs.

Mama takes Ruthie's hand. "Why, I haven't had Gram's sausage in a month of Sundays," she croons.

"That's okay, Mama, it's still good," Ruthie throws her arms around her. "I knew you'd stay."

Mama gives her a hug, but I can see she is nervous. She's not used to Ruthie's ways. She has never stayed for supper since we've been here.

"I'll set another place." I say, pushing past Ruthie.

I should be the one Mama hugs. It was *my* hair that got cut. I'm the one should ask her to stay, but I don't care if she stays or not.

I wanted everything to be perfect if she ever did eat supper with us. And now the dishes don't match. Ruthie has broken most of Gram's good ones. I can see by Gram's face she won't be digging out one of her good tablecloths from her trunk.

Using the outhouse as an excuse, I run outside to straighten my hair as best I can and pink up my cheeks. There are just enough roses left in Gram's garden for the table. Won't do to have Mama think we live like country folk.

Back in the house, Gram has changed into her second best dress and her hair bun is tight.

Ruthie didn't even wash her face. She must think she looks good enough, and Mama will take her home just as she is. Well, she's wrong on both counts.

At supper Mama is into her promising again. Ruthie gets so excited she's ready to pack her bag right off.

"Calm down, Ruthie," I say. "Mama isn't going to . . ."

Mama breaks in, "I might not be able to take you just yet, sweetie, but soon, I promise."

Gram lips tighten. She knows.

Ruthie smiles, and I can tell she's thinking she can change Mama's mind. How can Mama make out like she'll be taking her? She no more means to do that than there's an angel at the foot of my bed copying down my prayers.

Just before dessert Mama stares over at me and clicks her tongue. "We'll just have to get you to the beauty parlor for a decent bob, one of these days . . . real soon."

I can't take any more. After clearing the table I slip off to the barn as if the chickens need feeding. Ruthie is about to stop me. She knows the chickens have already been fed. Gram pulls her back. Mama must know, too. She used to live on the farm. She knows at this hour the chickens are settled 'til morning.

I can still hear her talking.

"We'll go to the circus, Ruthie, would you like that? And how about singing lessons?"

Singing lessons? I can't believe what I'm hearing. Doesn't Mama remember? Ruthie can't carry a tune in a milk pail. I want to scream through the window, *I'M THE ONE WHO CAN SING, MAMA!*

We will always live on the farm I just know it. She'll never take us away. We will be here 'til there's no farm left. And the way it's going, with Grampa dead and Gram carrying on the way she is, that won't be very long at all.

I wait outside and watch through the window, and when Mama is showing signs of leaving, I go in to help Gram with what will be one of Ruthie's fits when she realizes she isn't going with Mama.

Gram fixes hot cocoa for us both before we go to bed. She even tucks us in, for the first time ever. I smile up at her and put my arm around Ruthie. As I lay awake and listen to Ruthie's breathing, it comes to me again. Sometimes good things do come out of bad, if you wait long enough.

It's been two weeks, and I'm almost used to having short hair. Mama promised she'd take me to a beauty shop to have it cut proper. Well, I'm not holding my breath on that one; I'll just wait until it grows again.

My teacher, Mrs. Maryweather, told us once that people could change their bad habits, like lying. I want to believe that, for Mama's sake. If she can change, maybe she'll start caring about me again. But Mrs. Maryweather also said, bad habits can get passed on to children. That's why I'll have to keep a good watch over Ruthie.

Louise with short hair

CHAPTER 27

It's been six months since we buried Grampa, and this afternoon, since milking is done, I'm here lazing around under his apple tree, waiting for the smells of supper to call me in.

I think of him often, especially when I'm near his resting place. Running my hands over the soft grass, I watch as butterflies dance through Gramp's flowers. I smile, thinking, maybe he's watching, too. Ruthie comes running up, scattering my thinking and the butterflies.

"Hey, Weez, remember how Grampa used to love blueberry pie?"

"Pie? Yes, I guess." Seems we're both thinking of him. Sit here and close your eyes, Ruthie. Doesn't it seem as if he's thinking of us, too?"

She shakes my arm. "Let's go pick some."

I open my eyes and stare at her. "What?"

"Blueberries, Weez. Maybe Gram will bake us a pie."

"Oh, Ruthie, Blueberries don't come this early in the summer, silly."

She flops down and lays her head on my stomach. "What if I'm dead by then?"

"Don't say things like that."

"Well, I might be. Grampa is. Maybe Mama is, too. Maybe that's why she don't come, 'cause she's already dead."

"*Doesn't* come," I sigh, and she's not dead.

Sometimes being her sister is too hard. I squirm, arranging her bony head so it isn't squashing my stomach. Death makes you wonder no matter what age you are, I guess, but I wish she'd stop talking about it. I'd much rather be picking out pictures in the clouds and thinking about Grampa as he was, than getting into this with her today.

"Do you think she's dead and just don't want us to know?"

"Ruthie. Mama is *not* dead."

How can you be so sure?"

"She isn't even sick. Besides, Gram would tell us."

"I've been thinking," Ruthie says with a long sigh. "If Grampa has dirt piled on top of him under his tree, how can he get up to heaven?"

I can see a burden of her questions heading my way. I don't understand these things anymore than she does.

"Things just happen, Ruthie. It's like his spirit can go up, even when the rest of him is still in the ground." I start fiddling with her spiky hair. She pushes my hand away.

"I won't ever die," she says. "I'm going to live forever. When I leave this farm I'll do everything in the world there is to do."

There she goes again, with her big plans. "Everything dies sometimes, Ruthie, even trees and farm animals and birds."

"I think someone around here does some helping with the animals, especially the chickens." She turns her head and gives me her slant-eyed look. "And kittens, too."

"Well, just remember, eggs hatch out new chickens, and mama cats are always giving out with more kittens."

"That don't account for Grampa. Who's gonna give out with a new Grampa?"

"It doesn't work that way and you know it. Remember when Gram said, 'his time has come'? Well, that doesn't mean he'll come back, or that we have to stop remembering him."

She reaches for a tall weed, flicks it at a passing butterfly, and I can see I'm not telling it right.

"I guess it has something to do with love," I say, wondering where I'll go from here.

"Love? You mean love makes people die?"

"No! Of course not! Not exactly, anyway."

"You don't know nothin', Weez." She says, pushing her head hard into my stomach. "I just hope when I'm your age, I know more about love and dying than you do."

"You picked a darn hard thing to talk about, just before supper."

"But I want to know. Why did Mama leave us if she loves us? If she don't love us, that means maybe we're going to die, too."

"Ruthie, you're getting it all mixed up."

"Well, un-mix me, Weez," she sits up and stares at me, waiting.

"Well, you've heard about the 'Great War'," I say, trying to turn the subject so she can understand.

"No. They talked about it in school, but I don't listen to that stuff."

"Well, you should, Ruthie. Anyway, it started over in Europe."

"What's Europe?"

"For gosh sakes! You should be learning this in school, and don't interrupt."

"I'm only in fourth grade, we're just learning our tables, and don't swear or I'll tell Gram."

"I didn't swear. Anyway, the Great War was started the year after you were born. That's when Mama brought us here, something about the 'war effort'.

"War effort! What's that mean?" She plunks her head back on my stomach.

"It's just what I heard Gram say. I think Mama was a nurse or something during the war. People get wounded in a war, and I guess she thought she could help with bandages and things. All I know is, she said she would come get us when she could afford it."

From the house, Gram starts banging the dishpan, reminding us to come help with supper.

"She should have stayed home to take care of us, and I know something else, too. Your stomach is grumblin' so loud it's botherin' my thinking."

I push her off me and we walk back to the house shooing away bees, and dodging thistles. At least her questions are over. How can I make her understand why Mama left us, when I don't even have it clear in my head either? Maybe next time I visit with Grampa I'll see reasons written in the clouds. I didn't tell Ruthie the war ended a long time ago. I knew she'd right off start stuffing her clothes in a bag, and be running to catch the bus headed for Mama's house.

March, 1924

Dear Mama.

I was wondering if you had a job yet? It's getting harder and harder trying to explain things to Ruthie. I think she could use a mother, if that isn't asking too much. Sincerely, Louise

Ruthie, "that" Homer, Louise, Ellsworth

CHAPTER 28

The weather finally gets far enough along to ripen the wild blueberries out on the hill, and Gram promises us pie if we pick enough. I hurry to finish my chores, round up a bucket for me, and a small pail for Ruthie. She always eats more than she picks, usually so many she gets sick.

Gram says her weak stomach runs in the family. Mama has it, too, but least it didn't pass on to me.

Ruthie comes running into the house.

"They were pleased I asked them to come, Weez."

"Asked who to come where?" I ask, knowing darned well she means Ellsworth and that cousin of his to pick blueberries with us. I'm not keen on having that Homer come along, but there he is, trudging up the road with Ellsworth, weaseling along in his baggy overalls like he's already done something bad.

"I bet Homer picks more than you, Weez, and if you say he can't come, I'm tellin' Gram about you copying her recipes."

"You promised you wouldn't, Ruthie. All right, he can come, but that's the last time I'm telling you any of my secrets."

"Wear hats," Gram hollers after us. That sun, it gets hot."

We have hats, but I know Ruthie will rid herself of hers as soon as we get out of sight. Gram doesn't know half the bad things that girl does.

The four of us, each carrying a pail, hike along the rocky path through the woods to the far side of the hill overlooking the farm.

Ruthie runs ahead. "Look, Weez, millions of 'em!" The bushes shimmer with tightly packed green stubby branches, each heavy with hundreds of dark blueberries.

"Don't think there's been a better year for blueberries in an age," Ellsworth says, in his slow, tight-lipped way.

It's hard to hear what Ellsworth says sometimes, much less know what he's thinking, unless you see his eyes. When he comes to school with bruises on his arms or a limp, his eyes tell his story, and Mrs. Maryweather gives him a special hug and some of her bread-and-butter pickles during lunch. We all know it's that Homer that's doing it.

That Homer's a no-good from the start. He plays hooky most every day, and he's got the nastiest mouth in the county. I know he's teaching Ruthie some of the cuss words she uses. Too many times I've caught him and Ruthie coming out from behind the barn with guilty grins, too. No telling what they've been up to. 'We *ain't been doing nothing, Weez,*' Ruthie says looking slightly woozy, *'not even smoking.'*

"Let's see who can pick the most," Ruthie yells, popping a handful of berries into her mouth.

"Hey kid," Homer, says. "You'll never win if you don't stop shoveling all them in your mouth, piggy face." He gives her a hard shove, knocking her to the ground.

"You leave her alone if you know what's good for you," I snap, wishing Ellsworth would say something, too.

Ruthie winces as I help her up and brush blood and dirt off her arm. "I'm okay, Weez. He didn't mean to hurt me." She blinks back tears and smiles up at Homer.

"How about if we have a prize for the one who picks the most?" Homer says, starting to pick already. He has wild red hair and freckles. His front teeth make him look like a gopher, and he's always hanging around Ruthie. If I don't keep her away from him, she's sure going to end up in real serious trouble.

Ruthie wipes her nose up her arm. "What will the prize be, Homer, something pretty swell?" I can see she's practicing using his city words.

Homer digs his thumbs under his armpits and swaggers toward me. "Let's have it be a kiss from the one the winner picks."

Ruthie's face pinks up as she races to the nearest bush. She thinks she's going to win, and I know who she'll pick to kiss her.

"Come on, Homer, let's pick on the same bush," she says.

Seeing their heads together, I remember seeing them coming from behind the barn . . . smoking . . . kissing maybe, and who knows what all . . . and that red face of hers. Maybe it's time to tell Mama.

We hardly make an impression on the hill, even after an hour. Ellsworth wins with the most berries, although it's close between him and me. Ruthie and Homer didn't even try, but by the color of their lips, I'll bet they'll be sick by the time we get home.

"Who do you want the kiss from, Ellsworth?" Ruthie asks, causing his face to turn red clear back to his ears. "How about me? You want a kiss from me?"

Ellsworth shakes his head and faces me. My legs go weak. He stands real close and looks into my eyes. He's grown at least two inches since the last time we stood this close. His voice is quiet, so quiet I can hardly hear him.

"I guess it's not fair, since you told me that other time I wasn't to try again," he whispers, in his slow, thin-lipped way.

"A prize is a prize, Ellsworth," I whisper back, "unless you don't want to."

Ruthie and Homer stand still as fence posts, waiting.

"Think I'll choose a better time," Ellsworth says, loud enough so they can hear. Ruthie comes running over, stares up at him with her jaw jutting out, just like Homer's.

"You mean you ain't gonna' kiss anybody? You ain't gonna' collect your prize?" Ruthie swings her pail toward me spilling some berries. "Guess he don't love you no more, Weez," she grins.

If ever I wanted to smack her good, it's now. My cheeks sting as I start walking fast toward the farm. Maybe she's right. He probably doesn't like me anymore.

Ruthie throws up on the way home. I have to hold her head and practically carry her the rest of the way. I doubt I'll ever have a craving for Gram's blueberry pie after this.

Ellsworth doesn't say a word until Ruthie is inside, and Homer has hightailed it home. We stand looking at each other, him fidgeting, and me not wanting to go inside. He looks at me, and takes a deep breath. I wonder if he's thinking of kissing me again.

"Louise, you know it's not right, you having such bad feeling about your Mama.

I bite my lip. Why is he talking about Mama? She's no concern of his. I turn toward the door and he reaches out and stops me.

"I just want to say this, Louise. Your Ma, she must have had a really bad time keeping enough food in the house when your Pa left. It must have been hard on her, not having him around. Did you ever think that leaving you and Ruthie with your Gram might have been the best thing she could do for you? Maybe the only thing she could do?"

I felt my face heat up. Mama is none of his business. I don't want to hear anymore. Pushing past him, I run into the house nearly running into Gram.

"Go home now, Ellsworth," she says. "It gets late. Tell Ruthie to come home or she misses dinner."

How did Ellsworth know so much about my father? They must talk about Mama at his house. They have no right to mess around in our business. I don't feel like eating, so I tell Gram I'm not feeling so good.

When Ruthie comes home I can hear them talking and laughing at the table. I lay in our bed listening, and my stomach rumbling. I could smell Gram's chicken potpie. Maybe I'll just go in the kitchen and get some after Gram and Ruthie are asleep, unless they eat it all.

I lay in my thinking about what Ellsworth said, figuring he was probably right. With Mama having no money, and no one to take care of us while she tried to find a job, the farm probably was the best place for us to be, the only place.

While Gram and Ruthie finish their dinner and clear away the dishes I write a letter to Mama.

March 1924

Dear Mama,

I've been wondering about my father. What color was his hair? Did he have green eyes like mine? Could you send me a picture? I keep wondering if he'll ever come back. Sincerely, Louise

I didn't hear Ruthie come to bed, but in the middle of the night my growling stomach woke me up and I snuck into the kitchen. There on the stove, still keeping warm in the kettle, was enough leftover potpie to tide me over until breakfast. I finished it off with a piece of strudel, aim a thank you towards Gram's door, climb back into bed, and sleep 'til morning.

CHAPTER 29

Three days later, I'm sitting in our room writing what I remember about one of Gram's recipes, while Ruthie is off somewhere, probably getting into trouble with that Homer, when someone bangs on the door, shouting, "What have you been telling her?"

I shove the papers under our bed and peek through our door. Gram is standing over a steamy sink scouring her soup kettle. Mama stands in the doorway.

"What have you told her about Thomas?"

My ears perk up. *Thomas*?

Gram wipes soapy hands on her flour-sack apron. "Can't tell what I don't know." Her voice is calm compared to Mama's. "Maybe time is, you should tell us both."

"It's none of your business, *Muttie*. Look, I can't stay long. Someone's coming to pick me up. So you just listen to me, and listen good. I don't want you mentioning his name to her. I'll explain when I'm good and ready. All she has to know is that her father was a good man. That's all, you hear?"

I sit down so hard on the bed, it squeaks. Mama gasps. Gram hurries to slam my door.

"Now see what you've done, *Dummkopf*." Gram yells.

They're talking about my *father*. His name is *Thomas*. Mama's heels click across the floor. She yanks my door open. Without even a *'nice to see you, Louise'* or anything, she rips opens her handbag. "Read these," she says, shoving a long official looking envelope in my hand. "They're copies of our marriage license, your birth certificate, and a letter from the Government. Your father was listed as MIA. That means, missing in action, and don't listen to anything that old woman says about him or me, you hear?"

Her heels click as she heads for the door, with not even a nice-to-see-you, or a goodbye. I watch from my doorway as she stops to light a cigarette, then hurries up the road to wait for her ride.

The envelope is sealed tight, and weighs heavy in my hand. The corners are bent and wrinkled. I turn it over and over, and smile. She said his name, Thomas.

A car rumbles down the road, Mama jumps in, and is gone. She doesn't even wave good-bye.

Thomas. The name spins in my head, a nice name for a father. Somewhere in the shadows of my mind a long forgotten memory stirs. He has dark hair. My father has dark hair, and I remember now, he did have green eyes, the same color eyes as mine, and his name really was Thomas.

For a while I stare at the envelope. Should I open it? If I do, it might mean I doubt that she's telling the truth. I tuck the envelope in the bottom drawer under my old sweaters. I don't want Ruthie messing with it. Quietly I shut my door, lay on our bed, and wipe away tears. "I'm remembering him now, and Mama called him, Thomas.

Gram comes into my room and pats me on the shoulder, bringing tears again, but I'm not sad, and I don't feel like crying. I smile through my tears, because I'm happy. Gram knows. Someday I'll open that envelope, but not today.

"Your sister, *Liebchen*, she comes."

Without saying a word, we agree not to mention Mama's visit to Ruthie. She'd have one of her fits if she knew. I'm glad the envelope is my secret . . . my second secret.

I'll open the envelope someday, but not today. Someday I'll be walking down the city, not barefooted like now, but with proper shoes and a dress that fits. A pretty dress I've fixed up from one of Mama's old ones. My hair will be bobbed like the ladies in Ruthie's magazine, and Mama will introduce me to a handsome man named, Thomas, and she'll say, Thomas, say hello to your daughter, Louise."

I take out a piece of paper and write Mama a letter.

April 1924

Dear Mama,

> *I'm keeping the envelope safe. Next time I hope you stay longer. Gram made me a dress for my birthday. I'm fifteen now. The dress is not in fashion, but it's good enough 'til I move in with you. She baked me a cake, too. Sincerely, Louise*

Later, laying next to Ruthie in bed, I can't sleep for the moonlight coming through our window, thinking of my envelope, and hearing Ruthie's sleep noises. I'm old enough to leave this farm if I want to, and go on to high school. Mama must be thinking of that. What will Ruthie do if I leave? She hasn't even learned to milk Hilda proper. All she's good at is holding Hilda's tail out of the way while I fill the pail.

What am I thinking, I probably won't ever live with Mama again, especially now that she's got another husband and a new baby. Dottie, they call her. Wonder what her real name is? Can't be Dottie. Who would name a baby Dottie? If my father ever comes back, I suppose I could live with him. If he doesn't want me, I could always go to a convent like Mary Margaret from school. Then I'd be so close to God I'd be able to ask him about Ruthie, and how I could help her get her life in order.

Dark clouds drift over the moon. I slide down in our bed, sharing Ruthie's warmth, but I can't stop thinking up questions. Did my father really die in the war? Did he come home and run off because of me? Or was it Mama's fault. It's got to be somebody's fault. If I ever get married, my husband better not sign up for the army, at least not until he gets to know his children.

I doubt even Gram knows the truth about my father, but then, she wouldn't tell me if she did. Mama might know more than she's telling. I wonder if keeping secrets is something we get from our mothers and fathers, like weak stomachs and green eyes?

March 1926

Dear Mama,

What is going to happen to me? Will you ever answer at least one of my letters? I heard bad habits in the family get passed down to others. Please tell me if this is true. Sincerely, Louise

CHAPTER 30

I am bored. Ruthie and I have finished our chores and are in our room listening to the rain hammering on the roof, trying to find a leak, I guess. We still don't have electricity or indoor plumbing on the farm. We don't have music either, except for Gram's singing her German songs, and the nursery rhymes and dance records I hardly remember from when Mama played them on her *Victrola*. I tried to teach Ruthie to dance one time, but she was to young to learn, and now she thinks dancing is silly.

We've looked at all the advertisements in Ruthie's magazine until they're so wrinkled and streaked from her sticky fingers they're hard to see. I don't have any friends my age, except for Ellsworth, and he hardly counts, and the only books we have are cast off ones from school, and the one volume of *The Book of Knowledge* Mama sent years ago. The only time we see our neighbors is for church and funerals. Sometimes Ellsworth's mother stops by to ask if Gram needs anything from town.

Today I see her coming by in her buggy in the pouring rain, and Gram asks her in. She drips all over Gram's floor, but Gram says, "No mind. Louise can wipe up."

"I'm going to town for groceries," Mrs. Wolcott says. "You want I should bring you anything? It's no trouble, no trouble at all."

From our room I can see Mrs. Wolcott's eyes are puffy and she looks sad. Sometimes I get the feeling Mrs. Wolcott has more on her mind than she wants us to hear, and why did she pick such a stormy day to go for groceries?

They sit and drink Gram's strong coffee and sample her just-out-of-the-oven apple strudel, while they draw up a grocery list.

Mrs. Wolcott says something to Gram in a low voice. Right away Gram comes and gently closes our door, but not before I hear Mrs. Wolcott say, "I don't know where he got the money."

Ruthie grabs her pillow and plops down next to the door. "Must be something important if it's about money." She leans her ear to against the door.

"Let it be, Ruthie," I whisper.

"I bet it was Homer," she giggles. "Probably stealing again. Listen, Mrs. Wolcott is crying. Maybe someone's dead."

"Don't start, Ruthie," I whisper back, but I'm thinking, Mrs. Wolcott must have something important to say, or Gram wouldn't have closed our door. We shouldn't be listening, but if it's something about Ellsworth, I figure we have a right to know. I grab my pillow and hunker down next to Ruthie. The voices are muffled, but with one ear close, I hear snatches of what they are saying.

"I don't know what to do," comes through the door. "His mother can't . . . stealing . . . only staying for . . . thought we could . . . Mr. Wolcott don't . . . can't manage . . . sorry for my sister . . . her man . . . drunk . . . takes it out on the boy . . . money . . . bad influence . . . don't know how to handle him."

Ruthie leans over and whispers, "Who they talking about, Weez?"

I know right off it's that Homer, but if she can't figure that out on her own, I'm not telling her. What could he be stealing?

Right then Ruthie kicks the door by mistake, and quicker than lightening we jump on our bed as, Gram opens our door.

"This means no supper, you two," she whispers through her teeth. "You say a word outside, da strap you get." She closes our door tight.

"What are they talking about, Weez? I couldn't get what she meant."

"Just hush up, Ruthie. It's none of our business."

I wonder what could Homer have done to make Mrs. Wolcott cry?

"So what can we do now?" Ruthie asks. "It's still raining, and it's not time for supper. Wish she'd go home. Come on Weez, think of *something*."

She ought to be used to the rain by now. It's just about all the weather we've had for a month. "Think of something yourself, Ruthie. Look through that box of old stuff from Mama."

She leans over, peeks under bed on her side, handing upside-down 'til her face turns red and she drags out the box. It's filled with outgrown toys, a dried-out green turtle from Woolworth's that Ruthie tried to wish back to life, some of Mama's old make up, and party clothes, clothes you sure wouldn't see in church.

Quicker than I can stop her, Ruthie takes off her shirt, slides out of her overalls, and shimmies herself into an old slinky pink nightgown of Mama's, one with lacy straps and a slit up the side. She steps into a pair of old dancing shoes, pulls out a straw hat with the wrinkled red ribbons, some bright orange lip rouge, and an old bottle of Evening In Paris cologne with only a few drops in it. I know what she's planning, but once she gets her mind set on something, I don't even try to stop her.

She smears her mouth orange, pats herself with what's left in the perfume bottle, and pulls the hat down over one eye. With her hand on her one hip, she shuffles toward me in a pair of Mama's old shoes, and asks in a voice like Mama's, "How do I look, *Honey*?"

Without meaning to, I laugh. "You look like a goose, and smell like one, too, but you better not let Gram see you, she's mad already."

"I don't smell like a goose, I smell like Mama.

She does smell like Mama. She even looks a little like Mama. Before I can stop her, she rushes out of our room, right in front of Mrs. Wolcott and Gram. She skips round the table, bending and twirling, all the while singing the Christmas tree song, imitating Gram's German voice.

Mrs. Wolcott gasps and blows her nose. As I watch, Gram chases Ruthie around the room, then out the door into the pouring rain. I hear Hildie bawl as Ruthie runs into the barn. She's probably hiking up the nightgown and climbing up into the loft, where Gram isn't about to go up after her. I hope she doesn't trip and fall.

Gathering herself together, Mrs. Wolcott, pushes past me, runs out the door, and scurries toward her buggy. She climbs up, shakes her head, and drives away with not a thought to Gram's grocery list.

Back in the house I help Gram clear off the coffee cups and set out a tray for Grampa, one place for Gram's supper. She'll be eating alone tonight. Ruthie will come in when she's good and ready and, of course, I will get blamed just for not stopping her from barging in on Gram and Mrs. Wolcott. So now I have to worry about Ruthie being around that Homer who steals. He could hurt her too, or get her in real trouble, trouble I won't know how to handle. Darn Mama, anyway, Ruthie should be her worry not mine.

It isn't until I'm in bed listening to Ruthie's night sounds that I remember Gram's missing laudanum. Could that be what they were talking about? I thought it was Ruthie who took it. I creep out of bed, light our lamp, and find my pencil.

June 1924

Dear Mama,

Do you know our neighbors, the Wolcott? Well, Ellsworth's cousin Homer is living with them now, and he is big trouble. You need to know that he could be harmful to Ruthie. If you don't do something right away, whatever he does with her is going to be your fault, not mine. Sincerely, Louise

CHAPTER 31

It's been over a year since Ruthie cut my hair. Mama still thinks Gram did it. Gram never told on Ruthie. She didn't even make her tell me she was sorry.

I've about forgiven Ruthie by now, but I'll never *forget* what she did. It was her meanness that hurt. She knew it was my hair that Mama loved, and even though it's growing back, almost six inches so far, it'll never be like it was before Ruthie cut it. Sometimes I ask myself, what if it had been Ruthie who had the long, honey-colored curls, and I had done the cutting? I know what would have happened. I'd get strapped and have castor oil poured down my throat. Gram would've given me an enema to clean the badness out of me, and she'd send me to bed without supper for a week. Just because I'm the big sister, Gram would make me apologize twenty times over. Can't believe Ruthie got away with not even an ear pulling.

Guess I'll always be the one to say to Ruthie, *'keep away from the hot stove'* and *'it's not nice to pull wings off of butterflies.'* I wish I had a big sister to warn me about things and teach me what I don't know already. I wish I had a mother, too.

Sometimes at night when we're in bed and I can't sleep, that's when those wishes take over and I get so lonely. It's like there's a big hole inside me that never gets filled. That's when I get to wondering, will anyone ever love me for keeps? I thought once it might be Grampa, but he's gone now, and besides, he never did get around to teaching me to carve wood like he taught Ruthie. Ellsworth might love me a little, but since I don't love him back, he'll soon find someone else. It seems love has to be a two-way thing, to make it work.

While Ruthie sleeps, I brush a strand of hair off her sticky forehead. Sometimes her face can look so sweet and innocent when she's sleeping. That's when I figure it's my job to look after her, at least for a time. She doesn't have a father or a mother, hardly. All she's got is me and old Gram. There's a chill in the air, and with no moon, the night is dark. I cuddle up to her and kiss her cheek. I'll try to dream a funny dream, so I can tell it to her in the morning. It'll cheer her up. It's just one of the things I can do for her, as long as Mama's not around to do them.

CHAPTER 32

August 1924

Dear Mama,

> *Ellsworth's cousin Homer has the chicken pox. Did we have*
> *them before we came to Gram's? Gram says if we did, we won't*
> *get them again. Could you tell us? I'm not a bit sorry Homer*
> *has the chicken pox, but Ruthie sure is. Sincerely, Louise*

Fourteen days after that Homer got *his* chicken pox Ruthie breaks out
with hers. Gram fixes me a straw pallet in the kitchen so I won't have
to sleep in our room with her, just in case I didn't have them. Gram says
she's to stay in bed for a week and I should keep her from scratching.
If she won't let me in the room with her, how am I supposed to keep
her from scratching?

I set a chair right outside our window so we can talk. I'd rather be
up on the hill picking wild flowers, but I guess when you're scratching
you like company. I can tell Ruthie's enjoying getting so much attention,
and having me do her chores, but she sure hates the itching.

Gram keeps her coated all over with a paste of baking soda and
water. Makes her look like a ghost. I'm laugh except she's got a fever
and feels to sick to have me laugh at her.

"You scratch, you get enema," Gram tells her. Gram thinks enemas
cure everything, even warts.

"You ain't givin' me no enema. You try and I'll get out of this bed
so fast. I'll run away first chance I get and you'll never see me again."

She's making more of it than need be, but then she always does. Gram just shakes her head, mumbles something in German, and leaves the room.

"Stop scratching, Ruthie," I say, hanging over the windowsill. "Do you want pox marks on your face 'til you die?"

"I don't care a tar' nation darn if I do. It itches like crazy, and I'm gonna' scratch. Weez? Why did I have to get the chicken pox, and not you?"

"I told you to stay away from that Homer."

"I ain't staying' away from Homer. Besides, it ain't his fault."

"What do you mean it's not his fault?"

"I ain't tellin'."

"You've been smoking with him again, haven't you, Ruthie?"

"I have not! Anyway, you tell Gram, and you'll be sorry."

"Gram's going to find out, and don't try to lie your way out of it. I saw cigarettes under your side of our bed. Where did you get the money to buy them?"

Her eyes squint and she shakes her fist. "None of your damn-tar' nation business," she whispers as she makes scratch trails up and down her arm.

"You stole Gram's egg money, didn't you? After all Gram's done for you? Ruthie," I lean through the window. "Stop that scratching and tell me you didn't take the egg money."

"I didn't take the egg money." She chants the words out, in her black-lie voice, all the while scratching to beat the band.

"I'll have to think up a way to pay it back. If Gram finds out, leave your arm alone!"

She scratches more, just to rile me. "I'll say it was you that took it. She'd never think to blame me."

If she weren't sick I'd . . . but she's right. It would be just like Gram to believe her over me.

Ruthie flops back against her pillow, pretending sleep. I rest my arms along the sill and watch her. She doesn't care a fly's tooth for what she's done, lying and stealing from Gram, hanging out with that Homer. Someone's got to stop her before she gets into real trouble.

Chicken pox. Why are they called it chicken pox, anyway? More like mosquito pox to my way of thinking. I wonder what they do to girls in reform school? Mama would know. Maybe I could ask *her* for the money to pay back Gram. But then she'll think I stole it.

Ruthie's bubbling noises start. She's still scratching, even in her sleep, just like a chicken after corn. Maybe that's why they call it chicken pox, because of the scratching. Getting the chicken pox might be punishment for Ruthie. Maybe getting an enema is punishment, too.

I walk down to where Grampa is buried and gather a few late apples for Ruthie. As I walk back to the house, I see Ellsworth and his mother bringing a basket of flowers and a plate of fudge.

Ellsworth has to stay outside the window with me. His mother won't let him in, even though he's had the chicken pox. She's afraid he might catch them again.

Gram carries the basket in to Ruthie, who eats every last piece of the top layer of fudge and doesn't even think to say thank you. I could have told her she'd be sorry, and sure enough, she throws up all over our bed, while Ellsworth and I lean on the sill and watch. She's mad now, like it was Ellsworth and his mother who made her throw up. Now she won't even say good-bye as they leave.

Gram takes cleaning up after Ruthie in stride, and when she finishes changing the sheets and fixing supper, she sits on Ruthie's bed and sings German songs to her.

Outside I lean against a tree. Dusk is gathering and Gram's voice, soft and full of love, soothes Ruthie. She could have sung to me after my sledding accident, but she didn't.

Just as the sun slips into twilight, I catch a faint movement out of the corner of my eye. There, not ten feet from me are two deer, their ears perked.

We stand in the fading light, the three of us, the two deer, and me, listening to Gram's songs. The sweet smell of roses haunts the air.

If only Mama would come, she'd love seeing the deer this close. She'd love Ruthie, too, and maybe she'd even love me. And we would love her back.

Before he got sick, Grampa hung a rope hammock between two trees in the side yard. After her stay in bed, Gram allows Ruthie to lay in the hammock, as long as she promises she won't pick at her scabs.

Ruthie looks like a polka-dot scarecrow with her red scaly spots covered with calamine lotion, but I don't tell her that. I never wrote Mama about Ruthie's chicken pox. I figure if she came she'd bring little Dottie, and Dottie would catch them, too. I think I'm too healthy to catch them. Gram says it's because I must have had them when I was a baby, but I like to think it's because I'm so healthy.

I never wrote to Mama about Ruthie's cigarette smoking or stealing, either. Some things she just has to find out for herself. I never got to eat the rest of Ruthie's fudge, either. Gram said her pox-y fingers had touched every piece. I might have known.

October, 1924

Dear Mama,

Ruthie got over the chicken pox. I'm so healthy I didn't get them. Just thought you'd like to know. Sincerely, Louise

CHAPTER 33

I'll be sixteen in February. Gram says I'll be old enough then, to go to a Grange dance. I can hardly believe it. I'll be riding in Mr. and Mrs. Wolcott's buggy. I didn't know old people still went to dances.

By using my head and Gram's sewing machine, I finally fix up a couple of Mama's cast-off dresses so they are a little stylish. '*Save the yellow one for when you want to catch a beau,*' she had said. '*It's a knockout.*' I was only thirteen then, and the dress was three sizes too big, but when I tried it on last week, it fit. It didn't look good on me though; too many ruffles. It didn't look like any of the dresses on the magazine ladies, so I changed it. I removed the ruffles, rearranged the neckline, shortened the skirt, and put some starch in the collar. With my hair piled high, I looked almost grown up. I hope nobody notices Mama's old red shoes. They certainly don't match the dress, but they're all I have, unless I wear my farm boots.

March 1925

Dear Mama,

My birthday came and went, and now I can go to a Grange dance. Unless you get me a new one, I'm wearing one of the dresses you sent. I changed it a little and it looks okay. But I will be needing new clothes soon, clothes that are fit for a sixteen year old. And mama, I especially need shoes. Sincerely, Louise

"Teach me to dance, so I can go the Grange, too," Ruthie whines.

"Teach *you* to dance? You can hardly stand still long enough to have the tangles brushed out of your hair. Besides you're too young to go to dances."

"You think you're so swell, Weez, just because you're going and I'm not."

"I'll tell you all about the it when I get home. Now help me get into this dress. How does it look, Ruthie? It's one of Mama's old ones that I fixed up. Does it look okay?"

"It would look better on me."

"Don't be such a pill, Ruthie."

"If you say that again, I'll rip that hotsy-totsy' dress to pieces."

"Where'd you learn words like that? Did you steal another magazine when you were in town, or did that Homer steal it for you?

She bites her lip and shakes her head, and I know she's lying.

While I am waiting for the Wolcott's to come by in their buggy to pick me up, Gram calls me aside. I watch as she lifts the lid of her trunk. Again, a whisper of sweet lavender slips out. From under layers of yellowed cotton and frilly lace, she uncovers a small, blue velvet box, opens it, and lifts out a pair of tiny gold earrings. She presses them to her cheek as if they give warmth. Her moist eyes sparkle, and I can see she's remembering what it was like to be young.

"From my Herman, on our wedding." Gram smiles, as she hands them to me.

"For me? Oh, Gram, are you sure?"

She fastens them on my ears, screwing the stems just tight enough so they won't slip off, and then she steps back and smiles. Her eyes glisten with tears.

Ruthie stands by the door to our room, arms folded, chewing on a lock of her tangled hair. She glares at me and then, without a word, backs into our room and quietly closes the door.

"Don't get them lost, you hear?" Gram scowls. I put my arms around her and for once she doesn't pull away.

"Were you pretty, Gram?"

She brushes her hand across my cheek. "Pretty as you," she whispers.

My breath catches. She thinks I'm pretty.

Ruthie picks that moment to come charging into the room, dragging her quilt, which is spread out behind her like wings.

"Look at me, Gram." She whirls around in a puff of talcum powder. Gram pulls away from me. "I'm the cat's meow and I am going to a fancy dance," she shouts.

She has my lip rouge smeared across her mouth, and as she floats by, Gram scowls and mutters, "*Dummkopf*," but I can see she's holding back a smile.

I give my dress a final straightening. Ruthie can do whatever she wants, but I'm the one going to the Grange dance, and as soon as Mama sends me some decent dresses, we'll see then who looks like the cat's meow.

Mr. and Mrs. Wolcott pull up in their buggy, and there, big as life, is Ellsworth.

"Hi Weez. Bet you didn't know I was going to the dance, too, did you?" His grin about splits his face in two.

I reach up and whisper to him. "Duck down, Ellsworth, hide under the blanket. If Ruthie sees you, she'll make such a fuss Gram might make us take her with us."

I run back to the house to get Gram's strudel. "Gram, don't let her see Ellsworth," I whisper. "He's going with us." Gram nods, and sees to Ruthie while I grab the strudel and climb into the back of the buggy.

"I'll see you when I get home, Gram. Bye, Ruthie," I yell, trying not to squash the strudel or mess up my dress, or sit too close to Ellsworth. "Why in tar-nation did they let you come?"

Ellsworth grins, balancing his mother's angel food cake on his lap. I can tell he knows I am mad. Anyway, I'll bet Gram's strudel tastes better than Mrs. Wolcott's cake, any day.

All the way to the Grange, Ellsworth and his mother holler back and forth to each other. Mr. Wolcott smiles quietly as he drives the horse. I don't say a word, hoping they notice how disappointed I am that they brought Ellsworth. He can't even dance. If they think I am going to spend my first time at the Grange dance teaching him, they've got another think coming. It's a good thing that Homer is back visiting his mother, or they would have brought him, too.

The more I try to keep my hair in place, the more the buggy jostles it loose. How can I have a swell time if I look like Ruthie's half-stuffed cat when I get there?

The Grange Hall is lit up so bright I can see it even before we come within hollering distance. My cheeks smart from the chill in the air; I doubt I'll even have to pinch them pink tonight.

As soon as the wagon stops I step down, holding Gram's strudel careful, so it won't fall. I push the door open and the noise of the crowd and the smell of food draw me into a world of excitement. Everyone is bustling . . . young folks, old folks, mothers with babies, everyone in their fancy best clothes.

We pile our coats on benches against the wall with all the others. I duck away from Ellsworth as soon as I can. The food tables stretch as far as you can see, holding covered dishes and desserts, but I manage to put Gram's strudel in a prominent place where everyone can admire it. Women crowd around, checking the tables, shoving to find room for their covered dishes and cake stands. Children weave in and out between their legs like mice after crumbs. I've never seen so many desserts, bowls of applesauce and sauerkraut, deviled eggs and casseroles, and jugs of apple cider, even at funerals, or the Fourth of July picnic.

Men in buttoned down shirtsleeves and bow ties break out their accordions, and tune up their fiddles. Their wives gather in tight clusters, chattering like squirrels as they share the latest gossip. Young women in long skirts and high-necked blouses watch their husbands tug at stiff collars buttoned too tight. A swarm of noisy boys attack the piano. As soon as they are shooed away, another rowdy bunch takes their place.

My feet in Mama's red shoes are already starting to hurt something fierce, but I'm still going to dance . . . if anyone asks me. But what if no one asks me?

Suddenly a girl in a pink flowered dress walks toward me. "Hi!" she shouts, flashing a toothy grin. "You're Louise Guest, aren't you?"

"What?" I stiffen. I've never seen this girl before. Who is she, anyway, and how does she know my name? She looks to be about my age, but she shouldn't wear pink, not with that red hair. I know that from Ruthie's magazines. Her shoes do match her dress though, and she's pretty in a fashionable sort of way.

"I've met your mother," the girl continues. "You *are* Marie Guest's daughter, aren't you?"

My cheeks heat up. "Yes, I am, but . . . you know my mother?"

"Met her once, a while ago. Gosh, you look a lot like her. Maybe not exactly, but enough to be her daughter."

"You think so?" She's looking at my dress. She's probably seen it on Mama.

"I'm Eleanor Kamens. My mother told me to look for you. She said you might be coming to one of these Grange dances sometime soon. She said I should be nice to you, so," she smiles a toothy smile and shrugs, "I'm being nice."

"How do you do, Eleanor," I force a grin, but I'm not sure I like her. "I'm so pleased to meet you." I hold out my hand and she doesn't even take it. Did I do the wrong thing?

"Hey, kiddo," she grins again. "Don't be so formal. Just call me Ellie, everyone does. We'll be seeing a lot of each other, I'm sure."

Why is she being so friendly when I've never seen her before in my life? "How come you know my mother?" I ask, trying not to be too polite. If she notices I am wearing Mama's shoes, I'll just die.

"It's no mystery. Our mothers worked at the same nursing home. I met her there once. She said she had a daughter about my age. I've been looking forward to meeting you."

Mama never told *me* she worked at a nursing home. Ellie has lots of teeth. Her smile is wide but friendly, I guess. Her hair is stylishly close to her head. I feel one of my curls slipping free, and quickly re-adjust a hairpin to anchor it. I'll bet her hair never gets out of place. She must think I look awful, with these shoes and Mama's old dress.

"I come to these dances with my brother, Herb, whenever he's home from college," she says, flipping her fingers through her hair. "He's here now. Want to meet him?"

College! Before I can answer, she yells, "Herby," and waves frantically. "Herby, Oh, Herby, come over here."

A short, stubby boy swaggers toward us. He's wearing a white, checkered suit, with two-tone black and white shoes. His hair is redder than hers, and he flashes that same toothy grin. He straightens his yellow bowtie, looks me up and down, like he's guessing whether or not I can dance, and says "Hi, toots."

My face heats up. I fidget, pull at my dress, and with one foot on top of the other try to hide Mama's shoes.

"Herb. This is Louise, the girl I told you about, remember?" Just then the music starts up.

He lunges toward me and reaches for my hand. I quickly step back.

"Don't worry, I don't bite," he laughs as if he's told a joke. "You want to dance? I'm just okay-pretty-good, but at least I can fox trot you around the floor." He laughs again. "How about it, kiddo?"

I take a deep breath as he grabs my hand and pulls me onto the crowded dance floor. My very first dance with a boy, and he has to look like this. He spins me around once and we're dancing.

"What did Ellie say your name was?" he shouts above the twang of the fiddles.

Swell. If he thinks I am going to yell out my name, he's got another think coming. He's not half as good a dancer as I am. In fact he's not even "okay-pretty-good." But he asked me, and I'm dancing, just as if dancing happens every day of my life. I think a silent prayer for Mama's teaching me how.

When he finally catches the rhythm, we do all right. I try not to think about my tight shoes or my slipping-down hair. He laughs when our feet tangle, a loud, bigger-than-he-is, laugh. His hands are sweaty and he smells like Gramp's homemade beer.

I've never met a college boy before. I wonder if he thinks I'm pretty? Will he ask me for another dance? He might fall in love with me. He's got a lopsided little red smudge of a mustache. I didn't notice it right off, but I can see now he's not handsome at all. Mama would probably want me to marry him anyway. But I *absolutely* won't. It's who *I* want for a husband that counts, not who *she* wants.

The dance music stops, but the band starts right up again with a lively march. Herb grabs my hand and pulls me around the hall with all the others.

"It's the Promenade," he yells above the noise, as we circle around the room in step with the music. I don't care that my hair has sprung loose; I am promenading around the Grange Hall with a College Boy.

"Stand up straight, Herby," Ellie yells as we march past her for the second time. "You dance swell, Louise," she hollers right out so everyone can hear. "Better than that clumsy little pip-squeak brother of mine." She laughs, but I can tell she likes him, no matter how she teases.

"My mother taught me to dance a long time ago," I tell him, "Besides, you're not so bad," I lie, trying to be nice.

"Well, thanks a lot," he says, snorting like a little piglet.

I didn't mean to hurt his feelings. As the music stops, he's already looking past me for another partner. "Nice meeting you, huh . . . kiddo."

He doesn't even remember my name. Well, I'm not going to remember his, either.

"See you at the next dance, maybe," he yells over his shoulder, and he's gone. He'll probably never ask me to dance again, and I wouldn't say yes, if he did. I fight back tears, wishing I didn't care. Ellie walks over to me.

"Don't mind him, Louise," she says. "Oh, look who's here." She jumps up and waves as she runs across the room leaving me standing alone. Mama's shoes are pinching my feet like crazy. I feel tears coming, and I want to go home. Wherein tar' nation are the Wolcott?

Across the room Ellie stands talking to a young man whose pants aren't nearly as long as his legs. He's wearing a sleeveless sweater over a white shirt, a bright blue bow tie, brown shoes, and for gosh sakes his socks don't match. His slicked-back hair is parted in the middle and he has a pout-y mouth. I sort of like his looks. If Ellie brings him over, maybe he'll ask me to dance.

The young man has a glass of cider in one hand, and balancing a plate of food, in the other. He bends down so that his head nearly touches Ellie's, as if they have secrets. He looks up and laughs, nearly spilling his food. Ellie squeals behind fluttering fingers and waves at me. He looks at me, his face reddens, and he looks away.

They're talking about me. I just know they are. What can she be telling him? She hardly knows me. Is it the dress, or Mama's shoes?

Ellie throws back her head and laughs, almost as loud as her brother. My hand slips behind my back and I cross my fingers. The young man has a piece of Gram's strudel on his plate. Ellie points at it and then toward me. He glances up and catches me staring at him. His mouth goes pouty again, and he turns away. I turn away, too, pretending I didn't see him look at me. When I look back he's headed for the door. Ellie grabs his arm, but he pulls away, sets his plate of half-eaten food on the table, and he's gone.

My nose stings for wanting to cry. This is the last time I'm ever coming to a Grange dance. If I have to live to be an old maid, I don't care. I'd rather stay home.

Ellie pushes through the crowd toward me as I hurry in the other direction toward Mrs. Wolcott. When I look back, Ellie is dancing. She has forgotten me already.

"Oh, there you are, Louise," Mrs. Wolcott says. "We're going home, dear. Ellsworth is getting tired.

"Aw, come on, Ma," Ellsworth wines, "I ain't tired. I didn't even get a chance to dance."

"You can dance another time, Ellsworth. Now go find your father. Tell him we're leaving. Sorry we can't stay longer, Louise."

"I don't mind. I have a headache, anyway. It's all the noise, I guess." Another lie. I can't believe I only danced one dance and we're going home. I limp out of the hall following Ellsworth's mother.

As the wagon heads down the driveway we pass the young man Ellie was talking to. I duck down so he won't see me.

"What's the matter, Weez?" Ellsworth asks.

"Oh . . . I think I've dropped Gram's earring." The wagon bumps along leaving the lights of the lodge slowly disappearing behind us. "Oh, here it is. I found it," I lie again. I'm getting as bad as Mama. Ellie will never speak to me again after I ran off like that, but they were talking about me. Probably making fun of my clothes or my hair. Now I can add Ellie and that boy to my list of people who don't like me. And I thought she wanted to be my friend.

I slide down low in the buggy. If Ruthie ever does run away, I'm going with her. Maybe we'll both end up in reform school.

I wonder what his name is, that tall one, with the pout-y mouth and the mismatched socks. Guess I'll never know now.

May 30, 1925

Dear Mama,

I met Eleanor Kamens. She told me you and her mother used to work in the same nursing home. At least some people tell me what I'm supposed to know. And another thing, Mama, I will never go to a dance again, at least not until I have a proper pair of dancing shoes that fit. Sincerely, Louise

A week later I receive a letter, the first letter I had ever received. It is dated, *June the first, 1925*

Dear Louise,

I missed saying goodbye to you at the last Grange dance. I hope I will see you at the next one. We can play the field. And oh yes, there is someone I would like you to meet.

Your friend, Ellie Kamens

CHAPTER 34

"What are you getting all prettied up for, Weez?" Ruthie flops on our bed, almost on my dress.

"Move, Ruthie, you're mussing it up."

"You're not going to another dance are you? You said you'd never go again."

"Now, why would I say a thing like that?"

Ruthie narrows her eyes, and I can see her little mind wondering what to ask next.

"Want me to fix your hair, Weez? I can make it real nice."

"Do you think I'd let you touch my hair after what you did with Gram's scissors?"

"It's all growed out. Besides, I was just a baby when I cut your hair."

"You were not a baby. You were old enough to know better. Anyway, you can't come. I'm going with Mr. and Mrs. Wolcott again and I'll be meeting my friend Ellie when I get there."

"She wrote you that letter, didn't she, saying she was sorry?"

"You read my letter? Ruthie, how could you do that? Don't you know it's against the law to read other people's mail?" I don't have any privacy in this house. You want to end up in jail? Besides, it's not polite."

"I'll never do it again, Weez. I promise."

"Your promises aren't worth listening to." She's taking after Mama more every day.

"Besides, Gram said I could open it."

"That's a lie, Ruthie. Gram would never tell you to do a thing like that."

"Quit saying I'm lying. You're treatin' me like a baby."

"You do lie and that's just what you are, just a sneaky little kid, now button me up before I tell Gram on you." I turn toward her. "Do I look all right? Ellie said we should play the field tonight."

"I know. I read that part, too. But what did she mean, about the field? What field did she mean?"

"Oh, Ruthie. Don't you know anything? Ellie said if I know the steps all the boys will want to dance with me, a whole *field* of boys. Ellie thinks I'm pretty, even if Mama doesn't."

I open the box of half-used leftover makeup Mama gave me, and smear some rouge on my cheeks, but I can't see myself very well in the shiny piece of metal I have to use as a mirror. "Ruthie, did I put it on right?"

Ruthie steps close, wets her finger, and rubs at my cheeks.

"Quit smudging it. Just tell me if I put it on straight."

She squints. "It's a little lopsided, but it looks good that way. How come Mama doesn't think you're pretty, Weez? I think you're pretty."

She looks at me in such a straight-on way I think she means it. I go to hug her, but she shrugs me away.

"They're coming, Ruthie. I hear their wagon." I straighten my dress and take a deep breath. If Johnny is there again, maybe he'll ask me to dance. If not, I'll be stuck with Ellsworth all evening. "I've got to go, Ruthie. Be good to Gram while I'm gone, you hear? And don't go running off again with that Homer and get into trouble."

She gives me her I'll-do-whatever-I-please look. I am going to have to tell Mama about that boy.

The wagon pulls up. Mr. Wolcott is driving, Mrs. Wolcott is sitting next to him, and Ellsworth is sitting in the back. I wonder when they are going to get a motorcar? I'd feel much more important riding in a car instead of a horse drawn wagon. I wonder if Johnny has a car?

"Hello, Mrs. Wolcott. Hello Mr. Wolcott. I see you brought Ellsworth again." I don't even bother talking to Ellsworth as I climb into the wagon. He seems so young these days.

"Don't you look pretty tonight, Louise," Mrs. Wolcott smiles.

"Thank you, ma'am." I smile.

The wagon bounces along, as Ellsworth snaps his Black Jack chewing gum, breaking the silence. Gram won't let us have chewing gum. Says it's bad for our teeth.

Mr. and Mrs. Wolcott look like they're in the middle of a family upset, neither one talking or looking at the other. I'm sure glad they didn't change their minds about going tonight. I hope Ellie won't notice I'm wearing the same dress again, along with Mama's red shoes.

"There you are, Louise. Thought you'd never get here." Ellie takes my hand like we're old friends. She steers me toward the table. "Come on, let's eat," she says. "I'm starved. Did you ever see so much food? My stomach is about ready to meet my backbone." She hands me a plate and fills one for herself. Don't you with you could cook like some of these women?" she asks.

I smile to myself, thinking of my recipes. Then I remember I forgot to bring Gram's chocolate cake She'll be cross with me for that.

I want to thank Ellie for her letter, but she talks so much I can't.

"Try this, Louise. It's my mother's famous peach cobbler." She leans toward me and whispers, "She makes it with brandied peaches and it's *real* good."

"Brandy in her cobbler? Huh! I put some on my plate. It certainly looks good. Maybe I'll try to get her mother's recipe for my cookbook.

Ellie points across the room. "You see that boy over there? The one I was talking to last time you were here? We were rude to whisper the way we did, but we said nice things about you, Louise. If you had stayed, I would have called him back and introduced you to him. He signed up for the National Guard yesterday. He's going to look real spiffy in a uniform."

He's looking this way. I hold one hand over my mouth and look away so he won't think I'm talking about him. "Is he your boyfriend, Ellie?"

"Boyfriend? Gosh, no, Louise. Herb and I have known him forever. I went to school with one of his sisters. No. He's a swell guy, but he's not my boyfriend. He said he'd like to meet you, though."

"I thought you were you making fun of me."

"We weren't making fun of you, kiddo, it wasn't like that at all. I was teasing him. I bet him five cents he wouldn't ask you to dance. I thought it would be nice if he met you. He lost his nickel, because he was too shy."

"I thought you were laughing at my clothes."

"So that's why you ran out so fast. We weren't laughing at you, Louise, you shouldn't be so touchy."

"Well, it seemed . . . I was sure."

"You're going to have a hard time if you always think people are making fun of you. You've got to trust people, especially your friends."

I turn my head so she can't see my face pink up. "I'm sorry, Ellie. I just thought . . . well . . . with my dress and my hair coming loose and, you know."

"You'll never get anywhere if you think the worst of people all the time, Louise. Your dress was okay, a little country-ish, but then you *do* live on a farm."

"I can't help that," I snap back. "I don't have much else to wear right now. Didn't you notice this is the same dress?"

"But it doesn't look the same, Louise, what did you do to it?"

"Took some of the ruffles off, changed the neckline, and shortened it."

"You're more clever than I am. It sure looks different, and it's quite stylish."

"Thank you, Ellie, anyway, my mother is taking me shopping real soon, and so I'll have some new clothes. All I'll have to worry about is my hair."

Ellie stands back and looks me up and down, reaches over and tucks in a stray curl.

"Your hair is pretty, Louise, soft and shiny, but . . . to be perfectly honest, it does make you look sort of babyish."

I tighten my lips and slip my hand behind my back. She really doesn't like me at all or she wouldn't keep picking on me.

"Don't get me wrong, Louise. It's nice; it's just . . . well . . . it's old fashioned. Have you ever thought of getting it bobbed? I bet you'd be in a bob."

"The bees knees? I hope that means good."

"Yeah, you know. Nifty, swell, the cat's meow, a real humdinger."

"My mother is taking me to a beauty shop soon. Then all I'll have to worry about is my hair."

"The last girl Johnny carried a torch for had bobbed hair."

"Johnny? Is that his name?"

"Yeah, you want to meet him? He won't come over by himself because he doesn't know you. Just wait here. I'll go get him."

Before I can stop her, she hurries over, grabs him by the arm, and pushes him toward me. There's nothing shy about her.

"Louise, I want you to meet Johnny Paulsen. Johnny, this is Louise. Louise Guest."

"Hi," he says, pinching in the word.

"Hi," I say back, hardly loud enough for him to hear. I wonder if he really wanted to meet me.

Ellie folds her arms contentedly across her chest and smiles like a cat with a mouth full of feathers. If she had whiskers, she'd be cleaning them now. I hold back a grin at the thought.

Johnny reaches toward my hand just as the music starts up.

Does he want me to shake it or is he asking me to dance? I rub my sweaty hands down the sides of my dress and stare up at him. He's tall, with big hands and his arms are too long for his jacket. His after-shave lotion smells like pine trees, and his lips pout like he's thinking of something serious.

I stand there, staring at the floor as the music starts.

"I want to dance," his voice croaks. His Adams apple giggles up and down with each word.

"You mean with me?" The words come out before I can think, and he doesn't answer. He must think I'm a real country dumbbell.

Ellie bumps him with her arm. "Go on," she whispers. He nods at me and raises his eyebrows.

I guess that means he's asking. I smile and stand there.

"Yes," he smiles, "with you." He grabs my hand and we push through the crowd to the middle of the dance floor.

It's a waltz. We glide along with the crowd. He's so tall it takes a second to get in step. When we finally get started, I can tell he's a much better dancer than Ellie's brother. We dance through the crowd in silence. Is he ever going to say anything? We stumble, laugh, and recover.

"Guess I have two left feet," he mumbles.

"Oh, no. It's me," I say too quickly. "I'm the one with two left feet."

He stops dancing and stares at Mama's shoes.

"Hey, I think you're right. Your shoes are both pointing in the same direction."

I look down and stumble again, and he laughs. We both laugh. He's teasing, and I feel my face heat up. Maybe teasing means he likes me, a little anyway. The music changes speed and the promenade begins. We do the high-step march in time to the music, holding hands.

"Ellie said you brought that apple strudel to the last dance. Did you make it?"

I shake my head. "My grandma made it, but I have the recipe, and mine tastes as good as hers, maybe better." Why did I say that? He'll think I'm bragging.

"Maybe you can bring yours next time and I'll tell you if it's as good as hers."

My heart skips. That means there'll be a next time. We both smile as the music changes to a two-step. I like the way his hands feel, not hot and sweaty like Herb's, but warm and strong. Herb's felt like wilted lettuce.

He goes quiet again. If the music wasn't so loud we could talk. If he asks me for a date, what should I say? Will Gram even let me go? If he ever kisses me, I wonder if I'll hear bells and see stars, like it says in Ruthie's magazine.

The music changes rhythm. This time it is a fast-moving fox trot. Mama taught me to fox trot, and I fall into step perfectly.

"You really are a good dancer," he says.

"And so are you," I tell him.

"My sisters taught me how to move my feet. I've got three of them."

I smile up at him and raise one eyebrow. "Three feet?"

"No, three sisters," he says, and we burst out laughing, because we both know we are teasing. He holds me a little closer as we weave through the crowd, and I wonder if he can hear my heart pounding.

Then, quicker than an owl can blink, Ellsworth Wolcott is pushing between us. He bows a stiff bow and says in his high miss-matched voice, "I'm cutting in for this dance, Weez." He nods so hard his teeth click. "Ma said I could."

But Ellsworth, can't you see . . . ." but before I can finish, Johnny lets go of my hand, backs away, and stalks off the dance floor, leaving me with Ellsworth. He puts his hand on my back, grabs my hand, and struggles to get his feet working in the right direction.

"Ouch," I squeal as he steps on my foot.

"Now see what you've done, and I don't mean denting my shoe." Hot tears sting my eyes. "Whoever told you *you* could dance, Ellsworth?" My question breaks into his one, two, three counting. "You're no more ready for a Grange dance than Ruthie is. Let go of my hand. I'm getting out of here. I want to go home."

"But, golly darn, Weez, it's the waltz! It's the only one Ma showed me."

"It is *not* a waltz, *dummkopf*, it is a fox trot. Can't you even tell that? And don't swear."

"Aw, gee, Weez."

I hear his disappointment, but all I can think of is, I'll probably never see Johnny again, and I was going to bring him my strudel.

"When you get home, Ellsworth, you tell your ma you need more practice. I'm getting my coat. Tell her I'll be waiting in the wagon."

I look back at the dance floor and there is Johnny, smiling and dancing with a very pretty girl. I run quickly to the wagon. I don't care how long I have to wait. I won't go back in there and dance. I just want to go home and try to forget all about him. Why don't things ever work out the way I want them to, and what am I going to tell Ruthie?

July 1925

Dear Mama,

If you knew how unhappy I am you would at least answer this letter. I can't stand Ruthie. I can't stand the farm anymore, or our neighbors, and I can't stand the way I look. I need to get away from this place. Why do you hate me so? Sincerely, Louise

P.S. What does it feel like to fall in love?

CHAPTER 35

It's Sunday. I wake to an overcast morning heavy with dew, and the smell of rain in the air. Ruthie doesn't say a thing all through breakfast. After milking and feeding the chickens, we dry off, go to our room, and close the door before Gram can think up any other chores for us to do.

I continue brushing my hair even after all the tangles are out, waiting for Ruthie to ask about the dance. She keeps thumbing through her tattered magazine, humming to herself in her off-center way, stringing out my patience.

I pace back and forth still brushing. Rain splatters against our window, until I can stand it no longer.

"Well, pip squeak, do you want to hear about the dance or not?"

"What dance?" she asks, squinting into her magazine.

"Suit yourself," I shrug, put my brush down, and wrap curls around my finger.

"Okay, Weez. Leave your hair alone. Just get to the telling of it. You didn't talk about the dance last time, so this time it better be good." She settles back against her pillow, shifting over to make room for me. I inch close and begin a story to please her.

"Well, it was like this," I say, sinking down next to her and clearing my throat. "We get to the hall and it's all lit up brighter than the eastern sky at daybreak. Mr. Wolcott parks the buggy and we walk inside. The tables are fairly slumping over with the weight of all the food. Hams and turkeys, scalloped potatoes, and every casserole you'd ever want, and Jell-O salads and pies and cakes and homemade ice cream, and bottles of Coca-Cola."

Ruthie's eyes close and she smiles, savoring the tastes. "Don't stop, Weez. What happened next?"

"Well, when the music starts, I see a field of young men on one side of the room waiting to dance, and all the girls on the other side waiting to be asked. Those boys must have thought I was the prettiest, because they crowd around me and I dance every dance with every one of them, until the music stops and there . . . standing right in front of me, is a very special young man."

Ruthie's eyes widen. "A special young man? Then what?"

"Well, after seeing this young man, the rest of the boys fade away. I look up at him and he looks down at me, and suddenly lights turn on in my heart and I hear bells ringing."

"Lights and bells," she smiles and nods. "Just like the magazine says."

"That's right, Ruthie, just like it says." I look over to make sure she's getting the full effect. "His name is Johnny."

Ruthie jolts up, letting her magazine slide to the floor. "How did you know his name?"

"Ellie introduced us at the last dance, didn't I tell you?"

"What happened next, Weez?" Her eyes spark, and she pulls on my sleeve. "Tell more about that Johnny."

"Well, stop interrupting and I will."

I slide down next to her and wrap my quilt around us. She smells like fresh-cut grass. She must have used some of Mama's left over soap for her bath last night.

"Well," I continue, lowering my voice to a whisper. "Right away I can tell he has that same light turning on in his heart. He swings me onto the dance floor and we dance until the bell in the church spells out midnight." Ruthie turns to me, and scowls.

"Suddenly I stop dancing," I continue, racing through the telling, "and remember Gram told me if I wasn't home by midnight my hair would turn as straight as yours, so I dashed out of the hall and ran all the way home, leaving that special young man in the middle of the floor, and me wondering if I would ever see him again.

Ruthie bolts upright, folds her arms across her chest and glares at me.

"You're lying, Weez! Quit teasing and tell me the true part, not what you made up, or I'll tell Gram you are a lying son-of-a . . ."

"Quit that, Ruthie. It's Sunday."

"Just tell me, Weez."

"Okay. This is the true part."

"Cross your heart?"

"Cross my heart. Ellie introduced me to him, and I knew right away I liked him a lot. He is very shy, and has three sisters." I straighten the quilt to cover my feet. "He's joining the National Guard. That means he'll be wearing a uniform."

"Did he tell you that while you were dancing?"

"No, Ellie told me. He hardly said a word while we were dancing, except to tell me I had two left feet."

She leans back and stares at the ceiling. "I've never seen anyone in a uniform up close, I'll bet he'll look real handsome."

I know she is picturing him in her mind already.

"He'd looks handsome even in regular clothes," I tell her. "Anyway, when we danced, I didn't even care that I had on Mama's old shoes, though they pinched something fierce."

"You're going to take me with you to the next Grange dance, aren't you, Weez, if Gram says I can go?"

"If Gram says you can go, yes, I'll take you." No use arguing with her when she gets this far into wanting her own way. Besides, I know Gram won't let her.

"I only want to see if he's like you say he is, that's all. So tell some more about what really happened, and don't lie this time."

"Well, there I was in Mama's shoes, and him so tall he's looking clean over my head while we dance, and I knew for sure he was about to ask me if he could take me to the next dance, when something happened."

"Something like what?" Ruthie asks and I tell her all about Ellsworth cutting in.

"He really did that? What did that Johnny say when Ellsworth cut in on your dance?"

"He didn't say a thing. He just hightailed it out the door."

"Because he was mad, huh?" She smiles and nods her head. "I bet he was real mad, and jealous, too."

"I just know his face was beet red and he was gone, and I'll probably never see him again." My voice catches.

"I thought this was going to be a *good* story, Weez. That's not the way a *good* story is supposed to end."

"Well that's the way this one ended."

The rain has stopped and thunder echoes through the dark sky. We lay back listening, and my tears start up.

"He's got the nicest pout-y mouth," I sigh, pulling my quilt over my face. "I'll probably never see him again."

"Tell more, Weez?"

"The story is over, Ruthie, now leave me alone." She wiggles, and I can practically hear her brain wheels turning again, thinking up more questions. "Anyway, I don't need him. When I go live with Mama, I'll have my own shoes and all the pretty clothes I want. I won't need Johnny. And at college, I'll have plenty of boyfriends."

She pulls away and sits up on the edge of our bed. "You ain't never going to college, Weez, Mama won't even let you go to high school."

I push her shoulder. "Ruthie, you don't know what you're talking about." But she's right. Mama's promises don't mean a gosh-darned thing. She'll make me get a job doing something I hate, like working in a factory or scrubbing floors, or I'll be staying on the farm, under this old quilt, forever. Just leave me alone, Ruthie. I hate everybody."

"Don't cry, Weez, he ain't worth it."

"He *isn't* worth it," I yell from under my quilt. "How many times do I have to tell you?"

"See? You said it, too. He's not worth it."

"Get off this bed, Ruthie, and get out of this room."

To my surprise, she goes. She thinks its Johnny making me cry, but it's Mama. She's the one making me wear her cast-off clothes and not letting me finish school. If I can't believe my own mother, who can I believe? Ellie was right. I don't trust anyone, and why should I? I lay back against my pillow. Someday I'll find someone special. Just wait. I'll show Mama. I'll show everyone. Someday I'll be special myself. Then maybe someone will love me. I need to know what it feels like to have someone really care for me, someone to fill the aching in my heart. I know I have lots of love to give, but no one wants it. No one really cares if I live or die, not even Mama . . . especially not Mama.

I close my eyes and pretend I am living in a warm house filled flowers, and supper smells so good, and children are laughing. I am their mother, and I have a husband who loves me. But what's the use? I can dreams up stories, and none of them will probably ever happen.

When I open my eyes, the rain has stopped, and the sun is just dipping behind the far off hillside. The trees shimmer their greenness against the orange-purple color of the sky, and I can smell supper. Chicken soup, made from the one I killed yesterday, I guess. Poor rooster.

Ruthie come running and stands over me. Her shrill off-key voice cuts through the quiet. "Gram says it's time for you to set the table. And you know what, Weez? I'm going to the next dance with you. I want to see that Johnny person. Now hurry up, before I tell Gram you got a boyfriend."

CHAPTER 36

August 1926

Dear Mother,

I can hardly believe it, but Gram said you are coming to take me to your house. I won't be any trouble, you'll see. I'll help with Dottie. I gave all my outgrown clothes to Ruthie, so I'll need some more. They can be your outgrown ones, because I'm learning to fix them up so they fit me and are a bit more stylish. l will be needing shoes, and a brassiere, Mama. I really DO need a brassiere. Sincerely, Louise

P. S. Please forgive me for not writing for so long. You see, I met someone at the Grange dance and he is all I can think about. His name is Johnny.

"Gram says Mama is coming for you on Sunday, Weez. Do you think she'll really come? I hope she forgets."

"You don't mean that, Ruthie, besides I'll only be gone for a month. I'll be back before you know it." I can't believe I'm leaving the farm. Maybe after Mama sees what a help I can be, she'll want me to stay with her for good and bring you too.

"Why is she taking you and not me? It ain't fair. I won't let her." Ruthie balls up her fists. "If you stay away for a whole month, I won't be here when you get back. I'll run away."

"You're too young to run away. Wait 'til you're fourteen or fifteen. Then you can earn your own money."

"I won't have to. I'll have someone with me to earn money."

"You're talking nonsense, Ruthie."

"Just wait, you'll see," she grins and I know who she's thinking will go with her.

"Gram needs you, Ruthie. If you left too, who'd milk Hilda or feed the chickens?"

"I don't give a tar' nation damn for that stupid old cow or those chickens."

"Calm down, Ruthie, and quit swearing."

"I hate you, Weez. I can't wait 'til you leave."

She won't know me when I get back. My hair will be different. I'll have all new clothes. All my old farm ways will have washed off me like spring snow, and I'll be ready for a life in the big city. "Just think, Ruthie, while I'm gone you'll have the whole bed to yourself"

She snuffles and kicks at our bed. Her tears certainly aren't for me leaving; they're for her not going, too. Guess I shouldn't let my excitement show so plain.

Somehow Gram's chicken potpie doesn't taste as good as it usually does, and I go to bed feeling empty. There are things I must tell Ruthie before I leave, things she should know. I wiggle her knee from the middle of my back. It's really Mama's job to tell her, but if *I* had waited for her to tell me those things, I wouldn't know anything. All my learning about becoming a woman, and having babies came from a book at school, and by watching the animals. I just want to make it easy for Ruthie.

"Ruthie. I need to tell you some things about growing up." She wiggles around in bed like it's full of ants.

"I know everything, Weez. You learned me how to milk Hilda, and I already know how to wash my own hair. I suppose you're taking your hair brush."

"Course I am. Mama gave it to me."

"Anyhow, I know how to stay out of Gram's way when she's having a spell and how to look up words in your dictionary. You aren't takin' that are you?" I shake my head. "So what else is there for me to know?"

"I mean personal things. Like, well . . . I mean like . . . 'the monthlies'."

"You mean 'the rag' thing?" She rolls her eyes. "I already know all about that."

"Who told you? And don't call it 'the rag'."

"Everybody calls it that, even the boys at school. Becky French told us months ago, after she got it. I'll be getting it soon, too. Becky says then I can have babies."

I am not ready to hear this from my little sister. "Becky French shouldn't be talking about such things, especially not with the boys around. There's a book I want to show you."

She looks up at me like I'm some stranger instead of her sister who's trying to help her.

"I'll bet it's that silly Kotex book about Dumb Dora and her silly mother. I've seen it. It's sappy. Becky showed us. She showed us where babies get born, too, and . . ."

"Okay, Ruthie!" I can't believe what she's saying.

"I used to think it was from kissing," Ruthie giggles. "That's why I kissed Homer behind the barn." She looks up at me, waiting for me to be shocked, I suppose. "I wanted a baby then, but when Becky said kissing isn't all you have do, so I decided to wait, at least 'till I leave the farm."

"If you don't stop hanging all over that Homer, you might not get a chance to wait. And who do you think will care for your baby when you leave?"

"*Leave* . . . Why would I leave?"

"Maybe when you grow up you'll probably run off and leave your kids, just like . . ."

Before I can say I'm sorry, she rushes at me with fists flying.

"Ruthie. I didn't mean it. I'm sorry."

"I hate you!" she screams, balling up her fists, punching me, reaching for my hair. "I hate you!"

I try to grab her hands to make her stop, but she lands a solid punch at my nose. Blood runs down my face. We roll around, hanging on to each other. Gram comes out waving her arms. She yanks us apart and marches into the kitchen.

A bunch of my hair is twisted in Ruthie's fist, and she's limping. Gram wipes the blood off my face. She doesn't ask who's to blame, just helps clean us up, dabs our scrapes with iodine, and sends us back to bed.

I'm too old to be sent to bed without supper, but Gram says we both asked for it and she doesn't even bring us leftovers. Ruthie makes a quilt-nest on the floor. Guess I'll have the bed all to myself tonight.

After a while I lean over and ask, "You going to stay there all night? I said I was sorry."

She shoves the bed with her foot. "I don't want you for a sister anymore."

"You act like a wild cat when you're mad, Ruthie, an ornery little wild cat."

"You shouldn't say that about me."

"I'm only telling you what you sound like."

"I don't mean about the car, I mean what you said before. About leaving babies, like Mama did. If you say it, it might come true."

"Things don't come true just because someone says it, even if it's *me* doing the saying." She sniffs and wipes her nose down her nightshirt sleeve.

"If I say I'm sorry again, will you come back to bed?"

"Sorry's not good enough." Her voice gets quiet and she leans up on her elbow. "I don't want to be like her, Weez. You got to undo what you said, so it won't come true."

There is a mean bruise on her cheek. "Come back to bed, Ruthie, please?"

"Not until you take back what you said."

I lay still, wondering if I really did mean it.

"Say you take it back, Weez, about leaving babies."

"All right, I take it back, now come back to bed before a spider gets you."

She makes me shake out both our quilts, and I'm sorry I mentioned spiders. She snuggles up against me.

"Weez, Becky said her sister in Bridgeport got rid of her baby. Did she mean she killed it?"

"For pity sakes, Ruthie, don't say a thing like that." That can't be true. I know Becky's sister. She'd never do a thing like that. Never.

"Becky tried to make a baby with a boy."

"Ruthie. She did not. She's only eleven."

"Did too. She let us watch."

I sit up quick. She must be lying.

"When I do it, I'm not going to let anyone watch."

"Ruthie! Stop saying things like that..." It's that Homer, he's getting her to talk like this.

"I don't think I'll have any babies" Ruthie says, and starts laughing so hard she can't stop. "Hey, Weez," she blurts out between high squeals, "wouldn't it be funny if... if I had a baby and left it with Mama?" She stops and turns to me, fear shining through her laughing tears. "And what if she won't let it stay?"

I lay still, letting the quiet night creep over me. I can't help her. I don't know what to say. She needs me and I don't know what to do. I sit up in bed and turn toward her. She looks so young with her face all blotchy from crying.

"Ruthie, are you going to be all right when I leave?"

"Don't worry about me, Louise," she sniffs. "I can take care of myself."

I have to believe that, because I'll be leaving soon.

"Remember what Mama used to say when we lived with her?" Ruthie asks and mimics Mama's voice. '*Life goes by quick. You got to live fast or you won't catch the brass ring*.'"

"I don't remember her saying any such thing, Ruthie."

"Well she did. And I ain't letting any brass ring get by without me grabbin' it."

"How about if you write to me when I'm gone? And if you ever really need me, I'll come home."

She's asleep, or at least pretending. I don't guess she cares if I'm around or not. I straighten her quilt over her. Sometimes she reminds me so much of Mama it's scary. She shifts against me. Her half-stuffed cat falls from her hand and slides to the floor.

The moon spreads it's colorless light across the bed. The wild flowers I picked this morning give out their sweet, damp smell of spring.

Why can't moonlight be warm like the sun? What will happen to Ruthie while I'm gone? Is it my fault the way she is? God, whatever happens to her, please don't let it be my fault.

I haven't lived with Mama since I was seven. She doesn't know anything about me and I don't know her anymore. What will we talk about? And how will I get along with her new husband? Maybe Ruthie is right; maybe I should stay on the farm.

Louise and Mama

CHAPTER 37

Mama's city apartment is small and crowded. My bed is the living room sofa. I don't get much sleep because Dottie is teething. I take over the minding of her while George, Mama's newest husband, takes Mama out every night to restaurants and picture shows.

I thought I'd be the one doing those things with Mama, but it isn't working out that way. She says she doesn't trust anyone but George or me to stay with Dottie, not while she's teething, so my being around gives them a chance to go out together. Every morning she tells me about all the fancy foods they ate and the picture shows they saw. I don't feel much like her daughter, more like a housekeeper and someone to listen to her talk.

I don't much care for Mama's new husband, George, either. He's short, bald, and nervous as a rabbit. Not someone I thought Mama would want for a husband. He has a sour smell, like milk too long off the ice, probably his shaving lotion or some special soap. It bothered me at first, but I'm getting used to it. My father's soap smelled better than that.

Mama's kitchen is bright with morning sun shining through frilly half-curtains in Mama's kitchen. The wallpaper is yellow striped, and she sets a yellow rose-patterned dish of cold cereal in front of me each morning, with a pitcher of milk in the same design.

"We've got to do something about your hair," she says, drinking her coffee. "And those shoes. Where did you ever get those shoes?"

"You gave them to me, Mama."

"Well, we'll have to get you some new ones, a pair for every day and a pair for dancing. I hope you remember how to dance, Louse."

I nod and she smiles, and I know she's remembering, too. She lights a cigarette and blows the smoke straight up to the ceiling. "We'll go to Gertie's and get you all fixed up, then go look at shoes. You'll look like the cat's meow. We'll have lunch at a fancy restaurant. But first I have to get Dottie settled."

Dottie sits in her wooden highchair banging her cereal bowl with a spoon. It clatters to the floor, splashing milk all over Mama's black and white linoleum. Before she can get out of her chair, I'm on my feet.

"I'll do it, Mama."

"No. Never you mind. George will do it. We've got to get going. I made an appointment and we don't want to be late. He'll mind Dottie while we're gone. GEORGE? GEORGE! Come here."

Gertie's Beauty Shop is in the rear of her apartment. We enter through an alley and walk up a pair of narrow stairs to her kitchen. A sink and a hair dryer are against one wall, a table piled high with well-used magazines stands next to a sagging overstuffed chair, and a big black, swivel chair sits in the middle of the room, waiting. The sharp smell of ammonia makes my eyes water. Gertie opens a window and sits me down in the black chair, admiring my hair, letting it waterfall across my shoulders.

"I used to be able to sit on it when I . . ."

Mama interrupts, "Just cut it, Gertie, she's not a baby anymore. We're turning her into a young lady, a real city girl. Cut it all off, and give her a henna rinse while you're at it."

Mama primps at her own hair in front of the mirror. Seems like she can't pass one without looking at herself.

"Please Mama, I don't want dye in my hair. Anyway, it's getting darker on its own.

"Oh, come on, just a little won't hurt. It'll add some life to it," Mama says, thumbing through a magazine.

Gertie puts her finger to her lips and shakes her head. She understands.

"You'll look like the berries when Gertie gets through with you," Mama says, exchanging one magazine for another. She flips it open and settles into the brown chair. "She wants a Marcel wave Gertie."

That's what Mama wants. They could ask me what I want. I don't even know what a marcel is.

Gertie tosses a flowered sheet around my shoulders. "Ready?" she asks, clicking her scissors. She grins and spins me around in the beauty parlor chair.

Snip, snip, snip. My curls begin falling to the floor, like dead things. Snip, snip, snip. "I'd like to save them, Gertie," I whisper.

"Save them?" Mama laughs. They'll just get eaten by moths."

"I'm giving them to Gram. She'll hang them on a tree for the birds for nest building. At least the robins and blue jays will appreciate my hair."

Mama shrugs and rustles through another limp magazine, while Gertie shampoos what's left of my hair. My head feels light as a breeze. She pours on flax seed oil and rubs it in.

"Makes it shine real pretty, doll face," Gertie smiles.

With sharp, metal clips and styling gel, I watch as she crimps and fusses my hair into deep waves.

"Here," Gertie says, draping a hair net over the clips. "This will keep your hair from being sucked up into the fan of the dryer." She wheels my chair over to a squeaky electric hair dryer, turns on the switch, and the big machine comes to life. I can see her and Mama talking, but I can't hear what they're saying.

I sit hunched over from the heat, and just when my ears are about to sizzle, Gertie comes over, flips the hair dryer off, pushes the swivel chair in front of the mirror, and removes the net and hot clamps from my hair.

"Now, we're almost there," she boasts, as she combs and pushes and prods my hair into what will be my new style. My eyes smart and I stare at my lap. I don't want to watch.

"Okay, Louise, open your eyes, honey, we're all done." The words flow from her mouth like sweet syrup.

I don't want to open my eyes. Will I look like the cat's meow or a skinned rabbit? Ellie said I'd be a humdinger with short hair. What if I look like an old lady? I'll never be able to face anyone again.

Gertie pats my shoulder. "Come on doll, open your eyes,"

Mama tosses her magazine toward the table. It slides to the floor.

I open my eyes and stare at my reflection. Who is that looking back at me? I've never noticed my eyes before. I've always seen just my curls. With them gone, my hair looks darker and my eyes are green. My neck looks long, like a chicken's neck. I turn my head and raise my chin, and before I know it, I'm smiling at my reflection. Not like a chicken's neck, but like the smooth neck of a lady in Ruthie's magazine. I squint my eyes. Can that be me?

Gertie beams, leans toward me, and smiles. "Well, what do you think?" She lowers her voice. "You know, Louise, you should wear Lilly of the Valley fragrance. It would suit you real nice."

I can see Mama in the mirror, too. She's staring at me. She hates it. I know she does. If she had let me keep it long, I could have managed it myself. My cheeks heat up. Why doesn't she like it?

Gertie spins my chair around, looks at me from all sides and whispers, "You really are pretty, you know that, Louise?"

Did she just say I was pretty? Maybe I heard wrong.

Gertie turns to Mama. "Your girl looks pretty swell, don't she?"

Mama keeps her eyes glued to my reflection in the mirror.

Why doesn't she say something? She knows it's her fault. She said to cut it short, and now she hates it.

Gertie hands me a mirror so I can see the back. I sit up straight, letting my head tip from side to side, trying to make my neck look even longer. I look at the back, then at the front, then the back again. I suck in my lips, making my cheekbones stick out. I don't care what Mama thinks. I like the way my new hairdo makes me look. I look older. When I get some new clothes, Ellie won't say I look like a kid anymore, or a country girl.

Am I really pretty? Maybe Mama won't say so, but Gertie did. I heard her, and she should know. It's her business to make people look pretty.

If Gram hates it, I might be in trouble. And what about Ruthie and Ellie? It *is* short. I'll die if Johnny doesn't like it.

"Well," Mama finally says, in a cramped voice. "It certainly came out short, all right, and you certainly do look . . . older . . . much older. I'll say that much." She pushes at her own hair, fluffing it out. Compared to mine, Mama's hair looks mousy and thin.

"Well," Mama says again, turning to Gertie. "I guess it's time to schedule an appointment for me, don't you think?"

"Any time," Gertie says, with her chin pulled in tight. "I'll get the book. Just tell me when, and we'll mark you down."

Mama slaps money on the table and heads for the door.

With a broom and a dustpan Gertie sweeps my curls into a pile and stuffs them into a paper sack. She hands it to me when Mama isn't looking, and I slip it into my pocket. I thank her and she gives me a quick hug and we wave good-bye.

"Maybe with some decent clothes," Mama mumbles as her heels click down the stairs, "you might just look . . . well, we'll see."

She stops walking and turns, lifts her eyebrows at me, and says, "Something came up. We won't be doing any shopping on this trip."

"But Mama, you said we could buy . . ."

There's been a change in plans," she says in her singsong voice. "There's something important we have to tend to first.

I glare at her with my new green eyes. "I suppose this means no new clothes?"

Another time, I promise."

"Promise? Mama doesn't know a promise from a cow pie. I know what Ruthie will say in her, 'I-told-you-so,' voice.

Mama turns and smiles brightly. "Right now we'll get a quick bite, and then, oh, we have another appointment, and we don't want to be late now, do we?"

The fancy restaurant Mama promised turns out to be a corner diner, bright with harsh lights. It's long, like a railroad car. We sit on high, cracked, plastic stools at the counter. Solitary men sit hunched over plates of food, their elbows resting on the counter as they breathe in steamy mugs of coffee. A man about Mama's age doesn't give her the time of day but he winks at me and smiles right out so everyone can see. My cheeks burn and I turn away, but inside myself, I'm smiling.

She promised a fancy restaurant; well, I won't say a word. I won't even tell her what I want to eat. I want her to see how angry and disappointed I am, but Mama doesn't even notice.

She hails the counter man and orders us corned beef on rye, without even remembering I don't like corned beef.

She spreads a paper napkin in her lap, erasing the creases with her thumb. "I realize you can't stay with George and me, Louise, there just isn't room. It isn't going to work out the way we planned. I guess you'll just have to stay on the farm for a while longer. "You know, it hasn't been easy for me."

I know no such thing. Mama keeps talking like she wants to dig me under with words. I turn away from her.

"Now listen here, young lady, she says leaning close. "I know you can't stay on the farm forever. I'll get you settled somewhere."

She pulls out her scented handkerchief. Chanel N⁰ 5. A rush of memories floods over me, and I reach up to pull down a curl but it isn't there.

"I'm doing the best I can, what with Deedee needing me, and George losing his job."

"George lost his job?" The perfume fades.

"Yes, and it wasn't his fault. A lot of people got laid off at the plant, and he was one of them. Now *I'll* have to go back to work."

I know what she's getting at. I won't be included in her life, ever. She hasn't even asked about Johnny.

"It's just too small an apartment and, well, you wouldn't be happy living with us. You understand, honey. Maybe when George gets us a real house. You know I want you with me, but I have to think of what's best, you know, what's best for all of us."

"That means no more school, doesn't it?"

She shrugs and nods. She probably has a job already picked out for me.

As if she can read my mind she says, "Oh, I almost forget." She squints up at the clock on the wall. "Come on. We'd better hurry. We have an appointment with Mr. Middleton in a few minutes. His candy store is right down the street. Oh, didn't I tell you? He has a job for you."

"You want me to work in a candy store?" A hollowness fills my heart, and I pinch hard to hold back tears. Why not a dress shop or a bakery? I won't let her see me cry, I won't, but *a candy store!*

CHAPTER 38

A man greets us at the door. It must be Mr. Middleton.

"Marie, nice to see you again. This must be your daughter, Louise. Come in. Come right in, both of you."

He ushers us into his shop. The sweet smell of chocolate wraps around me like a warm blanket. I can hardly breath for the smell. So this is what Mama has planned for me instead of school. She just doesn't understand. Can't she see I want to make something of my life? She got me a hairdo, now I need clothes so I can start school and continue on to college. She promised, and now she wants me to waste my life working in a candy store.

A glass case filled with chocolates, all shapes and sizes, runs up one side of the shop and down the other. A work center and cash register sit across the back wall. The floors are glossy white and spotless. Two girls about my age are waiting on customers. One girl wraps a small white box, the other stands waiting for a woman and her little boy to make up their minds. She glances over at me and raises her eyebrows. I can tell she's looking at my dress, one of Mama's cast offs. At least my hair is stylish.

The cash register dings, and Mr. Middleton smiles. His black, patent leather shoes tap reassuringly as he slicks back his shiny black hair. His stomach pushes out so far the buttons on his suit jacket won't button, and I can see the wide red suspenders that are hold up his sharply creased pants.

"My two girls are going off to college and I need replacements," he tells Mama. He turns to me with a proud smile. "I treat my girls real good, Louise. I trust you will like working here once you get your living arrangements settled."

Living arrangements? He must think I'm going to live with Mama.

"She'll love it here, I'm sure," Mama nods, eyeing the chocolates.

The cash register dings again. Mr. Middleton drums the tips of his plump fingers together and smiles, as one of his girls busily polishes sticky fingerprints from the glass cases, pretending she isn't listening. How does Mama expect me to work in town if she won't let me live with her? It will take two hours to get here from the farm. She must be plum crazy if she thinks I can do that.

"Girls," Mr. Middleton says, "Make up a little bag for the ladies. It's on the house," he grins, waving off Mama's weak protest. "No one ever leaves The Peter Paul Candy store without a taste of our famous chocolates."

He hands the bag to Mama and shakes my hand as we leave. My fingers smell like chocolate before I've even taken one out of the bag.

Mama isn't crazy after all. She has one more surprise for me before she sends me back to the farm.

Mama hikes Dottie up on one hip while she wipes off the tray of her highchair. "You'll love it at Clara Kamens' house, she's Ellie's mother, you know. She's going to take you in. She'll tell us when you can come. It will be sometime after the first of the year. You'll stay at the farm until then." She blots her bright red lipstick with a paper napkin while I take in what she just said.

How can she do this to me, her own daughter? Farm me out like a sack of dirty clothes, giving me to someone I don't even know. I could stay with her until I can get my own place. I wouldn't mind sleeping on the sofa.

"She's a nice lady. You'll love her," Mama says, smiling into my face. "Come on, honey, she's got a big house and you'll have your own room, and Ellie to pal around with. She can help you pick out your clothes.

Maybe Clara will teach you to sew and you can make your own. You know I never had time to teach you all that."

When did she ever have time to teach me anything? She doesn't even know I've taught myself to redesign her old clothes so they fit me and look up to date, and to cook as good as Gram. "Don't worry about me, Mama. I'll be all right. I'll live anywhere you say." My smile comes hard, through clenched teeth. "I just hope Ellie's mother likes me."

"She'll love you, honey, just as much…" For a second her smile softens, and she runs her hand along my cheek. She reaches her arm around my shoulder, but instead of the hug I long for, she musses up my hair.

"You just be packed and ready when I come to get you on Saturday."

"I'll be ready, Mama. Don't worry. I'll be ready."

"I fixed you a jelly sandwich for you to eat on your way back to the farm, in case you get hungry. And the chocolates, they're fattening you know. Don't eat them all at once."

We take turns lugging my valise to the bus station. I wave good-bye until she's out of sight and open the lunch sack. She forgot the chocolates. The bus moves slowly along the city streets toward the country, stopping at every corner. At this rate, I won't get there before dark. I never thought I'd be going back to the farm like this. I can just imagine what Ruthie will say about my hair. I can see my reflection in the window. Even though I'm still wearing Mama's remodeled cast-off dress, I don't look bad.

The bus driver watches me in his mirror. He smiles. I lower my eyes to hide the flush of pride that creeps up from my heart to color my face. Mama never really said she didn't like my hair, but she sure didn't seem happy when Gertie finished with it. I hope Gram and Ruthie get used to it real quick. Maybe now with my hair short, I won't remind Gram of Mama so much.

My bringing the curls for the birds will please Gram, but I'll still have to reckon with Ruthie.

CHAPTER 39

"It's ugly, Weez. Just plain pig ugly." Ruthie pokes her finger at my hair. She shrieks and pulls back as if she's teasing a snake.

"Stop being silly, Ruthie. You're just jealous, that's all, and quit messing it up. Anyway, Gram likes it. She says it makes me look like her when she was young."

"Guess I can't think of you as *Weez* no more. Maybe I should call you, 'Miss Louise,' like you're my teacher or something. What's Ellsworth going to think?"

"I don't give a you-know-what for what Ellsworth thinks."

I won't tell her, but it's Johnny I'm worried about. If he thinks its pig-ugly, I'll never speak to Mama again, ever.

I needn't have worried. Johnny can't seem to take his eyes off me. If he wasn't sure about how he felt about me before, he is sure now. He even opens the car door for me whenever we go out. I didn't think my hair could make such a difference. Guess I'm growing up fast, even without Mama's help.

It seems strange doing the farm chores, now that I'll be leaving soon. I won't be doing the milking now that Ruthie can do it without Hilda tipping the pail over.

"Ruthie, you're going to have to learn to churn the butter, too. Gram's arms are giving out. Think you can do that?" She's still not talking to me. She thinks it's my fault I'm leaving. She should be blaming Mama. She's the one pulling all the strings.

September 1926

Dear Mama,

The early bus comes at noon. I'll be waiting. It comes twice a day now. Ruthie would like you to stay for lunch. Sincerely, Louise

"Come on, Ruthie, answer me so I know you're listening. Do you think you can you learn to do the churning?"

"I already know how. I'm not stupid, you know."

"Look, I'll be leaving in a few days. Can't you be nice for a change? How about giving me one of the wooden animals you carved so I can remember you?"

"I'd stomp them to bits before I'd give you one." Her words sting, but she's only mad because I'm leaving.

"Don't worry, Ruthie, Mama will come to get you soon."

"Don't *you* start lying to me too, besides, I don't want to live with her. I want to go with you and live in Ellie's house."

"I'll come back to see you and Gram." I reach toward her. "Come on, Ruthie. I know you love me."

She pulls away. "I never said that. I just want to live in Ellie's house, too, so I can play the gramophone and . . . I hate you, Weez."

I can see by the look on her face the word *love* never entered her head for a minute.

"If you're going to help me pack, Ruthie, hand me those red shoes and that sweater. I've just about got room in my valise."

"Why are you packing now? You ain't leavin' for another whole week."

"I just don't want to forget anything."

"You shouldn't be leaving me here alone with Gram. What if she has another spell? What am I supposed to do then? She's gettin' so she don't even love me no more."

"Of course she loves you, Ruthie." I reach toward her but she pulls away. "Just don't act up when I'm gone."

"Ever since you come back from Mama's, and she got you all dolled up with a new hairdo, you think you're so smart. And besides, it ain't a job that's making you leave the farm, it's that Johnny person you're always thinking about. Look at you," she says, eyeing me up and down. "Just because he's coming over to give you a ride in his car, you're getting all spiffed-up. I can tell you're stuck on him. You probably love him, don't you?"

With her arms crossed and scowling, looking so much like Mama it's scary. She marches out of the room as if she's leading the whole United States Army.

But she's right. Every time I think of Johnny, my heart jumps. He's sweet and shy, and he likes me, at least I think hope he likes me. Why else would he be coming all the way out here to give me rides in his car? He looks so handsome in his National Guard uniform, with those serious brown eyes and pout-y mouth, and when he's near me, I *do* hear bells ringing in my heart. I've got him so burnt in my memory I doubt he'll ever fade away. I just wish I knew how he felt about me.

CHAPTER 40

"He's here, Weez." Ruthie yells as she grabs Johnny's hand, like she's parading a prize pony at the county fair. "You told it right about the uniform." She grins up at him. He pulls his hand away. I could wallop Ruthie. She has no business dragging him in like that.

"Hi, Johnny." I blink and fluff up my hair. I believe he's looking at me as if he wants to kiss me. If Ruthie weren't gawking at us, he just might have.

"That's my kid sister, Ruthie."

"Hi, kid sister, Ruthie," he says.

Ruthie beams. She flutters her eyelashes, and gives him her, 'see-how-cute-I-am,' look. "Johnny," she says, just as if she knows him all her life. "How about giving me a ride in your jalopy?"

He pays her no mind, just looks around the yard, taking in the house, the chickens scratching in the dirt, and the sagging barn. Probably wondering where Gramp's resting place is.

"Louise, I thought you said that Ellsworth kid lived right next door."

"He does live next door," Ruthie says, pushing in close, fingering the buttons down the front of his jacket. "Around here, next door means a half mile down the road."

"He hasn't been around today," I tell him as I nudge Ruthie out of the way. "Haven't seen him since yesterday when he came over to buy some eggs."

"Well, he's got some unfinished business to account for." Johnny says, sounding jealous.

"You're talking about Ellsworth cuttin' in at the dance, ain't you, Johnny?" Ruthie says, smiling her big grin.

Johnny pouts and looks down at her. She smiles up at him again, like she's forgotten I'm the one he came to see.

"Can I pick you up for the dance next week?" Johnny asks, ignoring Ruthie.

I feel my cheeks pink up. "Do you really want to?"

"No trouble. I just don't want you riding with that kid."

As we walk into the house, Johnny takes off his hat. Ruthie giggles and stares up at him. "How come your forehead goes back so far?"

Johnny blushes and puts his hat back on.

I grab her arm. "Ruthie, if you don't stop being such a smart aleck, I'm going to . . ."

"You got to catch me first," she shouts as she runs past me.

"Pay her no mind, Johnny. She hasn't the sense of a snail."

I can see Gram standing down where Grampa is buried, and her mouth is moving. She's talking to him again. I walk Johnny toward the car so he won't see her. He can meet Gram some other time.

"About the dance next week." His voice still smarts from Ruthie's remark. "What time should I pick you up?"

"Oh, about, but Johnny wait, I forgot. I can't go; Mama's coming to take me to Ellie's house. And we'll be busy all day Saturday."

He pouts, and I wonder if that pout means I'm his girl now?

He hurries to his car and I wave as he drives away. I hope he doesn't think I'm being hard to get.

September 1926

Dear Mama,

> *The early bus comes at noon on Saturday. I'll be waiting. It comes twice a day now. Ruthie would like it if you stayed for lunch. Gram says it's all right. Sincerely, Louise*

CHAPTER 41

It's Saturday and Mama is taking me to Ellie's house today. I'm all packed and ready, in fact I've been ready for days.

"Don't let Ruthie get away with anything while I'm gone, Gram. I'll be back to visit before you know it."

Her arms cross against her chest and she stands tight-lipped. I can see my reflection glistening in her eyes. She turns towards the house before I can hug her. I give a final look toward Gramp's resting place and say a silent good-bye.

"Ruthie, can you help me carry my things to the bus stop?" Wouldn't you think she'd offer?

We stand and wait, and my heart is torn between sadness and expectations. What will it be like living in town? No blueberries, no nuzzling up to Hilda, no Ellsworth, and no Ruthie. It's the *no Ruthie* that causes my eyes to tear up.

I sit on my sagging valise, blow my nose, and brush at flies. I watch for Mama's bus while Ruthie stomps ants.

Turkey buzzards soar overhead, rocking slightly from side to side, holding their wings in a shallow V and we wait some more.

The bus comes and the bus goes, leaving a trail of dust behind, but no Mama.

"She must have meant the afternoon bus," I lie. Ruthie raises her eyebrows with her I-told-you-so look on her face.

We drag my things back to the house then back down the road again, to wait for the four o'clock bus. It comes and goes. Ruthie blows a horselaugh with her mouth.

"Shut up," I say, stamping my foot.

"I didn't say nothin', Weez," she croons with a big smile plastered across her face.

All the way back to the house Ruthie whispers in her off-key voice, "*I told you so, I told you so.*" She can be so mean sometimes.

Back in our room, Ruthie flops on our freshly made bed, getting the dirt from her shoes all over my quilt.

"I suppose now you want me to help you *unpack*," she scowls. "You know, at this rate, you'll still be living on this farm long after I'm gone, 'cause I'm not depending on Mama. I'll run away before I ever depend on her. You should know better, Weez. You're the oldest."

"If you don't shut your mouth, Ruthie, I'll . . ." I shove the valise under the bed again.

Someday I'm going to make things turn out the way I want. No one will ever catch *me* lying to my children. I'll love them with my whole heart. Sometimes I wonder if Mama t even has a heart. No wonder my father left. Some day I'm going to look up and see *him* getting off that bus. I won't recognize him, but he'll know me. He'll say, 'Hello, Louise.' And I'll say, 'Was it my fault you left, Papa?' Crazy thinking. Of course it's not my fault. And he's probably dead anyway.

It's nights like this that I can't sleep, because everything seems so hopeless, and I fall into my lonely black hole of questions. What if I turn out like Mama? I'm her daughter. What if it *was* my fault my father left? What if I really fall in love with Johnny, and he doesn't want to marry me? What if I never get married at all? Maybe when I live Ellie's house, I'll be able to forget my black hole of loneliness. One thing's for sure, Ruthie's bubbling won't keep me awake anymore. Funny thing is, I'll miss her soft night sounds.

The next day everything turns out right. Mama *is* on the bus. She says I got the date wrong. I'm sure I didn't, but, anyway, she's here, and now that I'm really leaving, Ruthie cries. There are tears in Gram's eyes, too, even though she tries not to let them show. I let her see mine. I want her to know how much I'll miss her. I do love her so.

My world is changing. I guess Mama is going to have a part in it. After all, she *is* my Mother. She must love me a little, no matter what Ruthie says.

CHAPTER 42

Mrs. Kamens is as nice as Mama said she would be. I've never known anyone like her. She is a round little roly-poly wisp of a lady, like someone in a storybook, and she smells like vanilla flavoring.

I stumble over her name and she tells me to call her, Mrs. K. "Everybody does," she says.

Her small head is covered with tight little white curls, and instead of walking through the house she bobs along with her tiny pointed feet barely touching the floor. Her dresses are like tents, her arms are short and stubby, and her laugh sounds like church bells on a clear day.

"Dear Louise," she says in her high singsong voice. "It's so good to meet you. Don't you look pretty? Ellie told me about your hair. It's lovely. Would you like some tea? Some lemonade? I do make good lemonade, lots of sugar and lime slices floating on top. The secret's in the lime," she whispers. "Anything your heart desires, dearie. Just ask. Cinnamon toast, maybe?"

I've never heard anyone talk like she does, and I've never had cinnamon toast. Although she is quite round, Mrs. K is as light on her feet as a hummingbird, and it seems as if the slightest breeze might whisk her away.

"Shall we visit the library? Have a picnic? Walk in the park?" she asks. I have to turn my head for fear she'll see me smiling at the way she is. She shows me through the house and helps me unpack. When I tell her about my cookbook, she is thrilled and says I can try out my recipes in her kitchen any time I like.

"I must give you my recipe for my brandied peach pie," she winks. "It's positively scrumptious!"

The house has a parlor, a separate dining room, and what Ellie calls a powder room. I wasn't sure what a powder room was until I looked inside. The kitchen in the back of the house is homey and warm, with a gas stove, an icebox, and a large round table for meals.

"The iceman comes twice a week," she says, "unless we forget to put the 'ICE TODAY' sign in the window. She asks me not to use the powder room unless it's a real emergency. We hardly ever use the parlor either, so it can stay clean for company. We eat in the kitchen, so the dining room doesn't get dirty either. It saves on the housework, you know."

Upstairs there are four bedrooms with lots of closets, and three bathrooms. One of the bedrooms is mine, and I have my very own bathroom. I can take a bath every night if I care to. Wait 'til Ruthie hears that. I'm going to get me some lavender soap.

September 1926

Dear Ruthie,

Mrs. K's house is swell. I have my own bedroom. There is a three-way mirror on my vanity. Seems I can never pass by without looking to see if my hair is in place. Yesterday I caught myself looking to see if I had any corn from dinner stuck in my teeth, and for a minute I thought it was Mama staring back at me. Gave me a real fright. Remember the picture of us when you were little, you on Mama's lap and me standing close with her arm around me? I hung it on my wall. At night, if I leave my window open, I can smell Mrs. K's garden of roses. My wallpaper has roses, too, yellow roses, like Gram's. I pretend the ones on my wall are real, and I let their sweetness put me to sleep. Isn't that silly? I hope you are being good for Gram. I miss you, Ruthie. Sincerely, your sister, Louise

CHAPTER 43

Johnny kissed me last night. It was nothing like Ellsworth's kiss back on the farm. My heart just about leapt into my throat. And I practically did hear bells ringing, I actually did. I could tell he was going to kiss me before he did, he got so nervous.

Ellie says all her boyfriends kiss her the first time they go out. I'm glad Johnny waited. I don't want him thinking I'm *easy*. But what if it was because he didn't want to kiss me before? I'd die if he didn't want to. Ellie says I'm stuck on him. 'Just don't let him go too far,' she says, 'don't let him get you in the back seat of his car and have his way with you. He hasn't tried anything, has he?'

When she said that, my hand flew behind my back. We *do* sit in his back seat, but he hasn't tried anything. It's none of her business, anyway.

'What if he did go too far, Louse,' she said, 'and then decides to break up with you? He might tell everyone you're a hussy, a real vamp. What would you do then?' Johnny would never do that. Besides, I hope we're not going to stop seeing each other, ever.

Last night before Ellie went to her room, we sat on my bed polishing each other's toenails and talked. She told me I'm too young to get serious. "For crying out loud, Louise,' she said, 'I'm just trying to warn you. Has he ever talked about his father to you?"

I frown at her. "What do you mean? What's wrong with his father?"

"They don't get along at all. According to what he used to tell Herby and me, they almost come to blows sometimes. I guess his father is real hard on him."

Ellie knows more about Johnny than I do, but anyway, she's probably exaggerating. Ellie noses into other people's business too much, and she asks too many questions. Just because she's two years older than I am, she thinks she knows everything. She doesn't even have a steady boyfriend. Johnny knows I like him, and I'm sure he feels the same about me. He only said it once, but still . . .

I think Ellie's jealous. She's already jealous of my cooking. She wrinkles her nose at everything I fix, but seems she still always asks for seconds. It makes me smile to think she's just plain, green-eyed jealous, . . . of me.

That's why I was so surprised then she said, "Louise, I'm planning a party for you."

"For me? A real party?"

"I'll invite everyone I know, and we'll play twenty questions and charades, and we'll dance 'til the wee hours."

"Can I invite Johnny?"

"Oh, I've already invited him."

"*You* invited him?"

"Of course I did, Louise. He's goofy over you. Besides, Johnny comes to all our parties. You don't think I'm trying to steal him away from you?"

"Well . . . I thought . . . you . . . I mean . . . Yes, I guess I did."

"For crying out loud, Louise, I'm your friend. Friends don't steal each other's boyfriends." "You slay me. Don't you trust anyone?"

"I'm sorry, Ellie, I just thought you might . . ."

"Herb's coming home from college, and he's bringing a couple of school chums with him. I may even have my own boyfriend by the time the party is over. Don't be such a worry wart."

"I'm sorry, Ellie."

"Let's just forget it, Louise. Johnny probably won't look at another girl if you're at the party. Don't you know he's stuck on you?" She smiles, and I breathe easy again.

"He used to bring his old girl friend, Helen, when he was stuck on her."

She didn't have to tell me that. She looks down at my dress. Her eyebrows hike up a notch.

"Louise, you know you look swell with your new hairdo?"

"Do you really like it, Ellie? It's nice of you to say."

"Yeah, but, well . . . what dress are you planning to wear to the party?"

"Oh, don't worry about me. I'll find something."

January 1927

Dear Mother,

We had a party at Ellie's house. It was swell. I wore your old lavender dress, but I took off some of the ruffles, fixed the hem, and it looked real spiffy. When I get my first paycheck, Ellie and I are going shopping. I'll be eighteen next month and Johnny is taking me to a picture show. Isn't that swell? Did I tell you my bathroom has a tub with lion's feet holding it up? I am going to bye some scented soap. By the way, I like my new hairdo. It makes my eyes look big. You never said if you liked it or not. You won't have to worry about me anymore, Mama. I'm learning to take care of myself. Sincerely, Louise

CHAPTER 44

The best thing about working at the candy store is I get to see Johnny most every day. He stops by on his way to night school. The next two best things are, I can eat all the chocolates I want, and I get a paycheck every week. Since Mrs. K won't take any money for rent, I can spend it all on fabric to make my clothes, and anything else I want. Ellie and I went shopping the other day. I used up all three paychecks. I bought shoes, three pairs; one for work, because I have to stand most of the day, a pair to match a new green dress I'm making, and another pair to go with the rest of my clothes. I think Mama will approve, *if* I decide to show them to her. I was surprised that Ellie was so helpful. She says green is my best color, too.

I haven't met Johnny's family, but he says they're sure to like me. At least now I have something decent to wear. He says he's going to give me a special present for my birthday. I hope it is Evening In Paris cologne.

I like it when we sit in the back seat of his car and he holds me close. It seems I haven't been held close, ever. He hasn't said he loves me yet, but I'm pretty sure he does. I can't think of spending the rest of my life without him. What would he say if he knew I hug my pillow every night, pretending it's him? He'd laugh, but it's like being in his arms, and when I wake up in the morning, I'm smiling.

Mama promised when I turn eighteen she'd buy me six pairs of silk stockings. It will be nice if she remembers, but like Ruthie used to say, I won't hold my breath. Anyway, I already bought two pairs myself.

Sometimes I think Johnny needs glasses. He never notices my new clothes. He never notices when Ellie uses a henna rinse on her hair either. She thinks it looks stylish. I like her original color, but she hardly listens to me. She probably still thinks of me as a country girl.

I'm getting a studio photograph taken so I can give it to Johnny for his birthday. It's May twelfth. I can't guess what he will give me on my birthday. Maybe I shouldn't have told him that my birthday was coming up. He'll think I'm hinting for a present, but I'm not. It better not be a box of chocolates.

March 1927

Dear Ruthie,

Thank you for your handmade birthday card. It was swell. It's the best card I ever got. Mrs. K gave me this writing paper and Ellie baked me a cake. It fell in the middle but it still tasked swell. Johnny took me to dinner and gave me a pair of brown gloves. They are swell, but I wish they were black. Mama forgot again. Good thing I didn't hold my breath. Ha, ha, ha.

Did I tell you I got a raise? Ever since my boss found out I'm good at numbers, he lets me do the accounts.

Tell Gram I miss her. I'll come to see you both one of these days. Want me to bring you some peppermint chocolates? Ha, ha, ha. I guess I'd better, or you'll have one of your fits. Be good for Gram and don't give her any trouble. P. S. I like being eighteen. Sincerely, Louise

March 1927

Dear Johnny,

    Thank you for my swell birthday present. I've always wanted a pair of brown gloves. I hope they didn't cost too much. The dinner at the Railway Diner was swell, too. Sincerely, Louise

CHAPTER 45

Tonight I'm cooking for the whole family. Herb is home from college for a couple of days, and I've invited Johnny over for dinner. It's sort of our anniversary, but I doubt he'll remember. It's been a year and six months since we met, and I'm making his favorite meal, pot roast with brown gravy, mashed potatoes, and green beans. For desert I'm serving Gram's chocolate cake, which I improved. That will be one of the recipes in my book, *if* Ellie ever gets around to typing my recipes.

Everything is ready. The table looks so nice with candles and roses from Mrs. K's garden. She's letting me use her good china and silver, too. Johnny's coming early to choose the right records for the *Victrola*, so we can dance after dinner.

Ring! Ring!

"I'm coming," I yell as I hobble across the floor with my shoe straps dangling.

Ring! Ring!

"Hold your horses." I head down the stairs as fast as I can.

Ring! Ring! Ring!

"For crying out loud, Johnny, I'm coming!"

The next thing I know, I'm curled in a heap at the bottom of the stairs with Mrs. K's afghan over me. If I squint, I can see Johnny and the others hovering over me.

"What happened?" I moan.

"You're okay, Louise. You fell." Johnny's voice is soft and his face pale, paler than the others looking down at me. "Hold still, Louise, don't try to move. The doctor's on his way." He holds my hand and bends close, so close I can smell his Old Spice. I close my eyes.

"Stay awake, Louise. Can you hear me?"

"I think we should move her to the sofa," Herb says, reaching toward me.

"Don't touch her," Johnny pushes him away. "She may have broken bones." He strokes the side of my face with his hand, gentle as a kiss.

Johnny? I ask inside my head. *You* will *marry me, won't you*? I open my eyes.

"He's right, Herby," I hear Mrs. K whisper. "We shouldn't move the poor thing until Dr. Burrows gets here. Dear sweet Louise, so pale, so pretty." She pulls the afghan up under my chin and smooth's my forehead. "Are you in pain, dear?" she asks. "Can we get you anything?"

I try to smile, but it doesn't work. I'm numb, but happy. They're caring for me. Even Herby. My eyes spill over with tears and everything blurs.

"My, God, she's crying," Ellie gasps "She must be hurt bad. I promise I'll finish the typing for you, Louise, honest," she whispers, "but please don't die on us."

Ruthie said that to me once, in the snow. I smell the roast and the carrots. I want to say, "*Don't let it burn*," but I don't really care about the dinner. They love me. That's all that matters.

Two days later I lay propped up in my bed surrounded by six of Mrs. K's sofa pillows. A huge vase of roses sits on my dresser. They're from Johnny's father's garden.

"How long will my leg be in a cast, Dr. Burrows?"

"Not long, Louise. The x-ray machine shows you broke the fibula bone in your lower leg, but it's a clean break. It'll heal nicely. It'll be about six weeks."

"Six weeks. No dancing for six weeks? I'll forget how." Johnny might find a new partner by then.

"I want you to stay in bed for a few more days, and keep the leg elevated. If everything goes as we expect, you'll be up and on crutches before you know it." He reaches in his bag. "Take one of these in case there's any pain." He hands me a small bottle. "It's a simple fracture. You were a lucky lady."

Lucky to break a leg, that's a funny thing for him to say.

"When the cast comes off, we'll get you used to walking again. You'll be able to go back to work in a couple of weeks after that, if you take it easy. For now, Louise, just rest."

May 1927

Dear Mother,

> *I guess you didn't know I broke my leg a couple of weeks ago. The doctor says it's mending fine. I'm getting better with my crutches. The doctor says I can go back to work soon. Mr. Middletown came by and brought me a giant chocolate cat. Ruthie would go crazy over it.*

> *Mrs. K just brought in tea and cookies. She is so good to me. Goodbye for now. Sincerely, Louise*

If I hadn't broken my leg, I would never have had the time to test all my recipes. I've refined them so everything will taste even better than Gram's. Well, maybe not better, but at least as good. I'm getting used to my crutches, too. I can manage without any help at all.

If only Gram could taste what I've done to her turkey-bone soup and her blueberry pie. It's all in my own special adding's, like cayenne pepper and cinnamon and lemon juice. She's sure to notice the improvements. Ruthie told me writing down Gram's recipes without asking was stealing. No mind. Wait until my cookbook gets printed. Gram will be so proud of me. She won't care. As soon as Ellie finishes the typing, the manuscript will be ready. All I need is a title. Then I can get it published.

I sit with my leg propped up on a pillow. Let's see . . . *'Recipes From Gram's Kitchen',*

'Things I Learned from my Grandmother', 'Cooking with Louise', or maybe just *'Louise's Cookbook'.*

It will be in all the downtown bookstore windows in Hartford, maybe even New Haven, and I will autograph every one. I'll be famous. I'll send a copy to Gram, even if she can't read it. Mama might not want to buy a copy; I'll just give her one.

Who am I kidding? Maybe nobody will. I flop back against the pillows, sending the pages scattering to the floor. What makes me think I could ever get a book published? I've only been through the eighth grade.

My leg is all pins and needles. I hope it's not a bad sign. Mrs. K comes in with a lunch tray.

"Oh mercy me," she sings out, stepping over the pages on the floor. "Looks as if we've had a little accident. I'll get Ellie to pick them up. Don't think I can bend down that far myself," her singsong voice hesitates, "but I suppose I could try."

"It's all right Mrs. K, I can get them with my crutches."

"You're such a clever girl, Louise, and brave, too. See what I've brought you? A nice cup of hot soup and a tasty sandwich." It's a thin tomato soup and American cheese on white bread, with the crusts cut off.

I sigh, remembering Gram's red potato-leak soup and liverwurst and onions, heaped high on open-faced slices of pumpernickel.

"Thank you, Mrs. K, but I'm really not very hungry. I think I'll just take a little nap."

I pull the covers up and close my eyes. I can see it now, *Gram's Best Recipes, by Louise E. Guest.* If I'm married by the time it gets published, I guess I'll have to use my new name.

June 1927

Dear Mother,

> *This cast is driving me crazy. Can't wait to get it off so I can go back to work and go dancing. Did you ever break any bones? Sincerely, Louise*

It's been five weeks, and I am as cranky as a caged squirrel. My leg itches me to screaming, and Johnny hasn't been around in two days. Probably seeing someone else. Well, let him. I don't care. I don't care about anything.

I lie back and close my eyes, remembering Ruthie and her chicken pox. With the faintest sound the door opens, and Ellie sneaks into my room. Slowly she tiptoes to my closet, opens the door and slips my new green sweater from the shelf.

"Put that back," I whisper, scaring her half to death. "I never said you could borrow my sweater. It's brand new." I grab my crutch and wave it at her.

"Oh, come on, Louise. Don't be such a spoilsport. You aren't going to wear it, at least for a while, anyway. Let me borrow it, please?"

If she wears that sweater, she'll fill it out better than I do. When Johnny comes over I don't want him to see her in *my* sweater.

"Come on, Louise, just this once?"

I suppose I'll have to say yes. It *is* her house, and she promised to type my recipes. I just don't want her to look better in it than I do. "Just be careful, I haven't even worn it yet."

"Thanks, Weez." She runs out of the room then sticks her head back in. "I'll get at that typing real soon. Got to run. My new beau is picking me up at seven. Don't worry, Louise, I'll have it done in a week or two."

A week or two, I thought it was almost finished.

"Isn't Johnny coming over tonight?" Ellie asks.

"Yes, but don't bother waiting for him. He probably won't be here 'til way after eight, and . . ."

"Got to go. Thanks, Toots. Toddle-do!"

I get out my notebook. There are three more recipes I want to write down. Johnny took them from his mother's Danish cookbook: Roast turkey stuffed with apple and prunes, Bread and beer soup, made with pumpernickel bread and dark beer, and something called, *leverpostej*. He said it is a liver paste of some kind. It sounds awful, but he said it's good and he loves it. Ellie will have to type these, too.

The doctor never told me my leg would itch this bad. I want to scream. Mrs. K's knitting needles help a little, but there are still places I can't reach. Mama would never have thought of using knitting needles to help this way. She didn't even knit. I guess Gram never taught her. She never taught me either. It's Mrs. K who is teaching Ellie and me. Her knitting style is so different from Gram's. Grams needles are fast. Tick-a-tick-tick. Like woodpeckers storing nuts in a tree stump, but Mrs. K's needles don't make a sound, like they're made of cooked noodles.

Gram used to spin out scarfs lengths quicker than we could wear them and yet, even though Mrs. K plods along turtle-slow, her afghan seems to grow almost as fast as Gram's scarves. She must sit up in her room all night knitting. Every morning it's a foot longer than it was the day before. She says I have the patience to knit. She doesn't say that about Ellie. Guess I could teach Ruthie to knit, too, except she's got about as much patience as a hungry pup whining for it's supper. I reach into the knitting bag Mrs. K gave me and pull out a ball of yellow yarn and the potholder pattern. Now how did she say to cast on these stitches? I try eight times and never get it right. Maybe the directions are wrong. Each time I rewind the darned ball of yarn, I can feel the itching start up again in my leg.

It doesn't take me long to figure I need another lesson. Guess I'm just as much of a ninny as Ruthie is when it comes to patience. I lean back and stare out the window.

Mama finally sent flowers, but no visit. She didn't even sign the card 'Love'. Takes more than a broken leg to get her to come around. Johnny stops by most every day on his way to night school, bringing me records and books and candy bars.

I hear him coming now. His car is pulling into the driveway. I straighten my dress and primp at my hair.

"Come on up, Johnny." He bounds up the stairs.

"You're looking pretty hotsie-totsie sitting in that chair," He kisses my cheek. "Brought you a liverwurst and onion sandwich."

"My favorite. How did you know?"

"You told me once, in one of your more romantic moments."

He's teasing and I love him for it. "You've got to eat some, too, so I won't be the only one smelling of onions."

"Don't worry. I made plenty."

"*You* made them?"

He pouts. "Did you think they made themselves?"

"If you want to play cribbage, we can take the board out on the verandah. Ellie's got a date and Mrs. K's at a neighbor's house."

"You mean we're alone in the house?" He wiggles his eyebrow and puts on a silly grin. It looks out of place on his face; he usually looks so solemn.

"No funny business, Johnny, she'll be home any minute."

"When's your cast coming off?"

"Soon, I hope, the doctor's coming again tomorrow. This tastes so good, Johnny. It was swell of you to bring it. Want a bite of my chocolate cat? There are still oodles left."

"I'd rather have a bite of you."

My face reddens. "Fresh. Come on; help me downstairs. Can you carry me, or am I too heavy?"

"Heavy. You must weigh all of ninety-five pounds. If you lived at my house, Ma would fatten you up, but quick."

"I don't want to be fattened up, thank you. Last time I saw my mother, she could hardly button her dress up the side. I don't ever want to get like that.

He carries me down the stairs, nuzzling my neck. He stumbles once, I squeal, and throw my arms around him. "Be careful, Johnny, I don't want to break the other leg, too," but I can see he did it to tease. We sit at the table, finish the sandwiches and I deal the cards.

"You look nice tonight, Louise, Even prettier than usual. What are you so happy about?"

"Shouldn't I be happy? I'm getting my cast off soon, I just ate a wonderful sandwich, and I'm sitting here with my favorite beau."

Johnny blushes and pouts. Maybe I shouldn't be so forward. He counts up his points and we continue, scoring up after each hand.

"By the way, I brought you a record for the *Victrola*. Do you like operettas?"

"Operettas? Why, ah . . . I guess so. I hardly ever, I mean, I don't think I've ever heard one, Johnny.

"It's Gilbert and Sullivan's, *Pirates of Penzance*. You'll love it. It's swell. The story is told in words and music, sort of like an opera, but so you can understand it. My sister Agnes listens to it all the time.

"We didn't have a *Victrola* on the farm. We didn't even have electricity." I never told him that before. Now he'll probably think we were poor. I don't think we were poor. We just didn't have much extra money.

"I'll play it for you," he said, winding up the *Victrola*. He told me he wasn't musical, said he couldn't sing like all his brothers do.

"Don't think I learned about operettas all by myself," he says, as if he knows what I'm thinking. "Agnes explained it to me. She's sick a lot, and when she isn't feeling well, she stays in her room and reads and listens to all kinds of music."

"I like jazz and popular songs and dance music," I say, so he won't think I don't know anything at all about music.

"Agnes likes jazz, too, but I thought you might like to hear something different. I'll keep it low, like background music, 'til you get used to it. Think you can stand it?"

"As long as it's in English. They didn't teach other languages in my school in Coventry."

There are so many things I still don't know. He probably thinks I'm a dumb bell.

"Yeah, it's in English. Agnes saw *Pirates* on stage once in New York. Maybe someday I'll take you."

New York? He wants to take me to New York?

"You'll like Agnes. She's a couple of years younger than me. Guess she's my favorite in the family. She's the one I talk to most, her and Lorry. Lorry works at the Aetna Insurance Company. She's on their women's basketball team. They call themselves, 'The Crimson Tide'. But the newspapers refer to them as the '*Hotsy-Totsy*' Girls. Yup, that's what they called them. Lorry, my youngest sister, keeps all the clippings in a big scrapbook. Did I tell you, she's looking for a place of her own? But I think Agnes will probably always live at home with the folks."

All this talk of family hurts because I feel I don't have one. He doesn't know how lucky he is, even if he doesn't get along with his father.

"My three brothers are just a bunch of rough-and-tumble kids," Johnny laughs. "Sometimes they don't know their . . . well, never mind. I can't sing, but I've got the ambition; the others got the musical talent. I just sort of yodel and let the rest of them carry the tunes when Lorrie gets the notion to play the piano for us."

He's talking so much, must be the liverwurst. I love it when he talks like this, as long as he doesn't start up about his father. My leg itches. Darn! I left the knitting needle upstairs.

The screen door to the kitchen squeaks. "Yoo-hoo. Is anybody home?"

"It's Mrs. K," Johnny whispers, wrinkling his nose. "Now we can't have any fun." I shake my head and hush him.

"Hi, Mrs. K, we're out here on the verandah. I just beat Johnny in a game of cribbage."

The cast finally comes off. "Dr. Burrows, it's ugly!" I grimace. "My leg is all scaly and white. Look at it! It smells too, like . . . like dirty socks; like Gramp's room before he died. I think I'm going to be sick to my stomach."

"Take it easy, Louise."

"It won't be like this forever, will it?" He moves my leg. "Ouch. Oh, God, it won't even move." Now I know I'm going to be sick.

"Just give it time, Louise. It'll be as good as the other in no time. Just keep rubbing it with oil and do the exercises I've prescribed. It healed nicely. In a day or two you'll hardly know it was ever broken. You'll be fine, don't you worry."

Mrs. K hovers near the bed. "Oh, but, Louise, isn't it just wonderful having that nasty old cast off? Just think, in a twinkling you'll be dancing around the room and running up and down the stairs. Well, maybe you shouldn't *run* down the stairs. You don't want the same thing to happen all over again, now do you?" She worries her hands. "Oh, my, wouldn't that be terrible, another broken leg? My, oh my." She wobbles away shaking her head.

"Now, don't you fret, Mrs. Kramer, she'll be just fine," the doctor says, as he follows her down stairs.

"Good-bye, Dr. Burrows, and thanks for everything."

"Remember, Louise, call me if you need me. Bye, now."

I do the exercises and my leg gets a little better every day. When Johnny walks me around the block my broken leg works as well as the other one. We look like an old married couple out for an afternoon stroll.

"Anytime you want to take off into a run, let me know," He teases, as he reaches over a fence to pick a daisy for me. "Race you to the corner."

"Just give me another week or so, Johnny, then ask me again." I take hold of his arm. "The doctor says . . . ."

"You still can't tell when I'm kidding, can you?"

"I'm sorry, Johnny." But he's right. I never know when he's kidding or making fun of me. He pulls away and shakes his head.

"And quit saying you're sorry all the time. *Jeez,* Louise. Let's just go back to the house. I've got to get going."

"Johnny? Will I see you on Saturday? I'll be able to go to the dance by then. The doctor said it would be all right, if I sit most of them out."

"Not this Saturday. A friend's coming to town."

"A friend? Oh." My hand slips behind my back.

"Don't worry, it's a buddy from the Guard. You sure do keep a close track of me, don't you? Look. I'll see you in a few days. Just keep doing your exercises. Why don't you listen to that record too? You might even like it."

I wonder if his friend is really someone from the Guard? He's never lied to me, but he's not being very nice, either. We walk back to the house in silence.

"Okay, Johnny. I'll see you when you get back, next Saturday, maybe?" I wave as he walks to the car. "Call me, if you want to, Johnny? Oh, and thanks for the daisy."

He waves as he drives away, forgetting I'll have to manage the stairs by myself. I'll be fine, but if I fall it'll be his fault. I toss the daisy on the grass. It was starting to wilt anyway.

CHAPTER 46

Well he's back, and he never said a thing about his friend or what they did. I guess he has a right to keep secrets from me. I just hope he's telling me the truth about his friend.

I'm planning a picnic for us, anyway. I'm fixing tuna salad on rye bread, deviled eggs with chive, fresh blueberries, apple cider, and my chocolate cake.

"I know you will have fun, Louise, dear," Mrs. K says as she helps me pack the picnic basket. "And see that Johnny drives carefully. Oh, by the way, I almost forgot. There's a letter for you on the dining room table."

"A letter for me? Who could be writing to me?"

From the barn where I'm hiding. September 1927, I think.

Dear Weez,

Bet you're surprised my writing you? You should be. Gram is acting more crazy than before. Remember her talking to Grampa? She's doing it again and he talks back. Her craziness is rubbing off on me because I think I hear him, too. She lights matches. She'll burn the house down if she's not careful. I'm running away if she don't kill me first. I hate living on this old farm. Hilda's drying up, chickens scratching for feed that ain't there. We're running out of food too. One good thing, Gram won't let me finish school. I don't need no schoolin' anyway. I know everything about everything. She tries to send me to

Sunday school. Don't need that neither. If you care at all for me you better come home or you might not ever see me again. Your sister Ruthie."

She should have written to Mama, not me. Gram can't be as bad as she says. Go back to the farm now? But I did tell her to write if she needed me. I don't guess she'll really run away. I'll have to answer her letter when I have time. Maybe tomorrow? Maybe Monday? Some time next week for sure.

Louise with cat's meow dress

CHAPTER 47

The picnic basket and blanket are in the back seat. We drive along in silence, edging toward the Connecticut River. Johnny never mentioned his friend's visit, and I won't ask. Let him keep his secrets.

I keep thinking of Ruthie's letter. She can sure spoil my life even when she's not around. Johnny's not saying a word. The car scatters leaves as it plows through them, red, yellow, orange. I remember when we used to make great piles of them under the eaves of the barn and jump in, squealing and shouting, loving the leaves, loving Ruthie and Gram, forgetting about Mama.

I want to tell Johnny about the leaves, but no, he's in a mood. That's what he is, moody. Makes me nervous when he doesn't talk. Will he ever have things to say to me? He's probably wishing me to be somebody else. I smooth down the pleats in my new skirt. Ellie thought I should take the blue, but I chose the green. Green matches my eyes. I thought Johnny might notice my new outfit, say something nice, but he doesn't.

He taps his fingers on the steering wheel and stares at the road. I should have chosen the blue. We come to a grassy knoll along the edge of the river, and he pulls over.

"This is perfect, Johnny, shady and nice. Don't you love the way the sun sparkles across the water? Like tiny diamonds."

He looks out at the water. "Yeah, I suppose," he says, as we spread the blanket under the trees. I open the basket and set out the sandwiches and the thermos of lemonade.

"Oh, look, Johnny, quick." A blue and white Kingfisher darts from a branch above the river. He hovers in midair, plunges in, and flies up again, water drips from his mouth as he angles away.

"Did you see that?" I whisper.

"Yeah. Nice," he says, around a mouthful of sandwich.

I watch as the water rippling out in ever-widening circles. "Don't you love it when something like that happens when you're watching? Like it happened just for you? It's like a magic sign, don't you think?"

"Sign? Yeah, sure, I guess." He finishes another sandwich. I'm still on my first as he reaches for an egg, two halves at a time.

"Good eggs," he says.

"Thanks. You picked a nice spot, Johnny. On the farm we had to walk five miles to see a lake like this." He coughs. I pour him some lemonade. "Can you swim, Johnny?"

"Swim? Sure, I can swim," he says, wiping his mouth on his sleeve. Darn. I forgot napkins. "I can't swim. Never learned."

"Everybody can swim. Good cake, Louise. You make it?"

I nod. I want to tell him about my recipes but I doubt he's in an interested mood.

"I'll have another piece if you don't mind."

"You want more lemonade, too?"

He shakes his head. "Brought something better. Let's pack up. I'll drive us where no one will see us."

"I hope it's not whiskey, Johnny." He grins and wiggles his eyebrows.

"What if we get caught?"

"Don't be such a worry wart, Louise. I'll find us a good place."

I gather our things and climb into the car. He pulls onto the highway and drives to a dirt road that edges back from the river. He'll want me to drink, too.

"I hate the taste, Johnny." Once Ellie and I got into her mother's peach brandy, and even after a small glass full I had a headache all the next day.

We park. He reaches in the back seat, pulls out a pint-size bottle about half full, unscrews the cap, and takes a strong gulp. He gasps and his eyes pinch shut as he runs his sleeve across his mouth.

"Ah, that was good," he whispers. "Want some?"

I shake my head. He's showing off, trying to impress me.

"Come on, Louise. Have a snort." I shake my head again.

"Just one?" he holds the bottle out to me.

"Okay, but just one." I tip the bottle, swallow, shudder, and hand it back. He takes another swallow, settles into the seat, and shuts his eyes.

"If Pop could see this he'd have my hide for sure. Do you ever do things just to spite your Mom or your Gram?"

Things I've said in letters to Mama flash through my head and I cross my fingers. "No. Is that why you're drinking, to spite your father?"

"Well, what do you think, angel face?" He grins a silly grin.

"I think you've had enough," I say, as he takes another long swallow. "What's he like, anyway? Your father, I mean."

Johnny's hand tightens on the wheel. I wait, but he just sits there. "Well, what does he do? What's his job?" He looks at me as if it's none of my business.

"He paints houses," he says with a shrug. 'He's just an old house painter from Denmark. His partner's a real artist when he takes the time, but all day long they just paint houses, inside and out, Monday through Friday. Don't know how they stand it."

He offers me the bottle. I shake my head again. "Doesn't sound too bad to me," I say. "Let's walk a while, Johnny." But he's back to his own thinking and doesn't even hear me.

"Ever since I was a kid he's had it in for me. Always picking on me. I can't ever please him. I used to try, but I finally gave up. Found it was no use. Maybe it's all those kids. Seven's a lot, you know, to feed and bring up. Ma had two that died before we were born."

"How horrible, Johnny. What happened?"

"Nobody ever said, really. I just heard them talking once when they didn't know I was listening. But I'm the one he's got it in for. Oldest son, I guess. He thinks the girls are special, Agnes, Anna, Lorry. He can't do enough for them; always bringing home presents, and giving them pennies. The boys can get rowdy, but he pretty much leaves them alone. 'Just let 'em be,' he says, 'they'll grow up to be good painters, some day. You'll see,' he says. But that's not the life for me. No sir-ee. And I told him so. That's probably why he's got it in for me. Pop's already got arthritis in his hands. Crazy way to spend a day, hanging onto a paint brush, painting ceilings, getting arthritis." He shakes his head. "If he thinks I'm going to follow in his foot steps, he's crazy. No sir-ee, not me."

"I always thought living in a big family would be . . ." but he interrupts.

"Just because I can't handle a brush without spattering all over everything but the walls. He thinks I'm stupid. Stupid and clumsy." He shakes his head.

"Well, he's wrong, Johnny. You shouldn't listen to him." He looks down at me and grins his pout-y grin.

"Ah, Weez, somehow I knew you'd feel that way."

"Please don't call me, 'Weez!'"

"Isn't that what they call you on the farm?"

"My name is 'Louise,' and that's what I want you to call me." He laughs.

"Wonder what Pop will call you when he meets you? He's not keen on Germans, you know. Your grandparents came over from Germany didn't they? That makes you a kraut. Hi, little kraut."

"You think your father might not like me because grandparents are German? I can't help where they came from. Besides, You're drunk, so quit calling me names! I don't call you a 'dumb Dane' do I?

Maybe my father was German, too. Mama never told me. He might even be Danish. Why are we fighting? "Let's go outside. I want to walk."

He screws the top back on the empty bottle and heaves it into the river. We walk along the path in silence, watching the bottle bob up and down until it gets stuck on some twigs along the shore.

"Pop hates Germans, 'cause of the war. He might call you, *Heini.* That was another name they had for German soldiers during the war, *Heini.*"

My face reddens. "He'd better not." I stop and look up at him. "You've got a mean side when you've had a drink or two, Johnny, did you know that?" But I doubt he's listening. "The war is over and I wasn't a soldier, and I can't help it if my ancestors came from Germany! What about your mother? Does she hate Germans, too?"

He softens and he smiles. "Her name is Laura. Pop calls her, *Louw-ah.* Don't worry about Mom. She won't care if you're German."

"I'm not sure I want to meet your family, and if you ever bring whiskey along when we go out, I'm staying home. And furthermore, you're to call me by my right name, 'Louise, and maybe I'd better walk home, alone." I start walking. Right now I think I could easily hate him.

"Gosh, Louise, don't be a spoil sport." He trots after me. "I'll call you 'Louise,' don't worry, and so will Pop. Don't worry about Ma either, and it's too far to walk from here anyway." He hands me his handkerchief.

"Just don't forget," I say, blowing hard.

"Come on, I'll beat you to that tree."

He reaches the tree first and we sit on the grass facing the water. A soft breeze ruffles the river birches. Somewhere nearby, someone is burning leaves. I breathe in the sharp smell and close my eyes. In my mind I can see the farm. It is about time for milking Hilda, if she is still fresh. Johnny picks up a leaf and begins pulling it apart.

"I don't know what's the matter with me, Louise. I guess thinking about Pop sets me off."

"It can't be so bad, Johnny."

"Well, it is."

He drops what's left of the leaf and picks up a stone, sending it skipping five times across the water. "Pop's nice to everyone else, it's me he picks on. He's from the Old World, you know. And Danes are strict, especially with their fir sons, strict as hell. You get out of line once, and POW, you're in for it. He's got strong hands. Must be from all that painting."

"What about your mother?" I ask.

"Ma's all right. She has diabetes. Has to shoot insulin into her leg every day."

"Every day? How awful. How does she stand it?"

"She's used to it. She never complains. Not to us anyway. It's making her old before her time. She might even loose a leg eventually. He shakes his head as if to clear his thoughts, "but never mind. Let's not talk about my family anymore."

Poor Johnny. He's like a hurt little boy, and I love him for it. We walk along in silence and then he stops.

"Did I ever tell you about Helen?"

I step back, as if he'd hit me. "Helen? Who is Helen?" I lie, because I know who she is.

"She was a friend of Agnes's. Used to come to the house all the time. We got sort of friendly and started going out." He fidgets, tucks his shirt in, smooths back his hair. "She asked millions of questions, made me feel important. Made me feel I might amount to something, no matter what Pop thinks." He skips another stone across the water. "Besides Helen, I haven't known any girls I could talk to, except my sisters, and they don't count. You know what I mean, they're just sisters."

I want to shout, *What about me? Don't I make you feel important?* What makes him think I want to hear about his other girl friend? He's not even looking at me. Why doesn't he shut up about this what-ever-her-name-is?

"Helen was the first girl I ever thought serious about." He leans back and looks up into the trees. I can see he's picturing her in his mind. "She said she loved me. Guess it went to my head."

If he doesn't stop, I'll die; just die. He's kissed her. Probably thinks of her when he's kissing me. She must be pretty, pretty as a movie star. I want to jump into the river and disappear forever. If I did, he wouldn't even notice. Why did I ever think . . . .

"Then Agnes told me Helen was really serious about someone else all the while she was seeing me. She was just stringing me along to make him jealous. Then it was over then, just like that."

Does he expect me to be sorry for him? What am I supposed to think when he talks like this? What am I supposed to say?

He sighs. "After that, I began to think Pop was right. That's when I signed up for the National Guard."

"Do you still love her, Johnny?" I whisper. "Oh, never mind. I don't want to know." Please, God, make him say no. "Do you?"

He takes a second too long to answer.

"Not sure I ever did. What is love supposed to feel like, anyhow? Oh, let's just not talk about her any more."

I lean back against the seat. Pretty soon he'll start comparing me to her, and I won't stand a chance.

"Gee, Louise. I probably shouldn't have told you all that stuff about Pop.

It's Helen he shouldn't have told me about. Doesn't he know that? "Can we go for a soda now, Johnny? I'm thirsty."

"Look, Louise, I'm sorry. Talking about Pop sets me off, and the booze, well. Never again, I promise. You know how I feel about you."

I don't know how he feels about me. How am I supposed to know if he never tells me?

He steps off the path and picks a single wild flower, root, and all, and hands it to me. "Will you still be my sweetheart?"

Always, I want to say, but instead I take the flower. It's a jack-in-the-pulpit and it doesn't smell good. I dig a hole with my foot and lay it back in the dirt.

"Look, I tell you what. I'll invite you over to the house, and you can meet the whole family. How about that?"

I look up to see if he's teasing.

"Come for dinner," he says. "With all of us at the table they'll hardly know you're there." He runs a finger down my cheek. "I'm sure they'll all think you're swell. Now, how about that soda, or maybe a chocolate frappe, or a triple banana split? Just name it, kiddo. Whatever you want."

He takes my hand and we head back to the car. I lean back and watch the bare branches race by. Something is bothering me, and if I'm ever going to feel right about him again, I've got to tell him. We pull into Mrs. K's driveway.

"Johnny, it's your business if you want to take a drink once in a while, but it makes you talk mean, and I don't like it."

He stares out the window. I settle back against the seat.

"You've never talked to me like this before, Louise. Is this a side of you I should watch out for?"

"Maybe it is. I hate it when you get mean. It scares me, Johnny."

"Okay. Stay where you are, Louise. I'll come around and let you out."

I sit up tall while my heart sings. At the top of the stairs we stand in front of the door and he kisses me, a long, tender kiss.

"I love you, Louise."

Did I hear him right? Did he say he loves me? He pushes his fist tenderly against my chin. "But don't tell anyone I said it."

He *did* say it, I heard him. He said he loves me. I stood up to him and he said he loves me.

Lying in bed in my room, I smile and wonder what our children will look like. Our children, Johnny's, and mine. I hope they all have his dark eyebrows and his funny, pout-y mouth. But please don't let our children take after Mama.

October 1927

Dear Mother,

Gram is giving Ruthie trouble. Someone has to help her. I can't leave. You got me this job, you know. You should do something about Gram before Ruthie runs away. It might be too late already. Sincerely, Louise

CHAPTER 48

January 1928

Dear Mother,

What's going on with Ruthie? I haven't heard anything for a while. Guess you would let me know if anything was wrong. Things are fine here. I'm seeing a lot of Johnny. Hope you and your family are well. Do you remember the name of the perfume Gertie said I should use? I would like to get some. Sincerely, Louise

I can hardly believe it but next month I'll be nineteen. None of the things Mama promised have happened, but my life *is* changing. I'm away from the farm; I have a place to live, a job, and someone I love. So what if my mother doesn't care about me, and my father left before I even had a chance to remember what he looked like, and I never had a chance to go beyond the eighth grade? What do I care? I'm going to quite working at the candy store and get a decent job in a dress shop. Now that Mrs. K will let me use her sewing machine, I'm going to be designing all my own clothes, and maybe selling some dresses to shop in town. Everything is turning out fine. My leg is as good as new. I can even run and it looks perfectly normal.

And tonight Johnny is taking me to a picture show and, if Ellie gets around to finish the typing, my cookbook will be ready soon, and I can send it to a publisher.

I'll wear Mama's old dress that I re-did. It turned out real nice. Ellie says it makes me look like the cat's meow. Guess that can't hurt. It even matches my green eyes, too. My ankles are trim like Mama, one of the good things I inherited from her. Ellie's ankles are just okay; at least they're not like her mother's. Mrs. K doesn't have any ankles at all.

"Going out again tonight, I see," Ellie scowls her disapproval.

"Yes, I am. Johnny is taking me to a picture show."

"Seems as if you're seeing a lot of him lately. You think he's pretty swell, don't you?"

She's jealous. I can tell. When she's between boyfriends she gets this way. I can't help it if she doesn't have a date. "They're showing Al Jolson," I tell her." She gives me a blank stare. She doesn't even know who Al Jolson is. "The show is called, *The Jazz Singer.*" I like it when I know something Ellie doesn't. Shows her I'm not the dumb country girl she makes me out to be. Wait until I learn something more about operettas.

"Anyway, don't suppose you'd like me to tag along?" she asks.

She must be teasing. "How about if I tell you all about the show tomorrow, okay?"

"Sure. I was only pulling your leg, Louise, about going with you. Oh, by the way, my mother said to give you this. It came in the mail."

Inside the package is a small bottle set in a velvet-lined box. It is labeled, Lilly of the Valley. It's from Gertie. What a nice thing for her to do. I must send her a thank you note.

A car rumbles into the driveway and honks. It's Johnny. My heart beats a little faster.

"He's pretty early isn't he?" Ellie says. "The moving picture show doesn't start 'til around seven."

I shrug my shoulders and open the bottle of cologne, splash a good amount behind each ear and on my wrists, and down the hollow of my neck.

Ellie coughs. I knew she would. I put the bottle on the table and check my hair in the hall mirror. The horn honks again.

"Don't be too late, now," Ellie smiles.

She's acting like she's my mother. She'd better not use any of my cologne while I'm gone. It wouldn't be suitable, us both smelling the same.

"Bye, Ellie. See you when I get home, and don't wait up."

I dash out to the car. Someday I want to have Johnny come to the door when we have a date, and not make me walk out to the car alone. I read in a magazine, it's the proper thing for a gentleman caller to do. I guess Johnny doesn't read those magazines.

"Hi, Johnny, I smile as I climb into his shiny new model 'T' Ford.

"Hi, yourself, kiddo," He says, wrinkling his nose as as he rolls his window down. He isn't even going to say anything about my new cologne. I adjust the pleats I ironed into Mama's old dress so they fall into place, and settle into the front seat next to him.

"You should have heard Ellie tonight," I say, trying to start a conversation. Sometimes he needs a good push to get him talking. "She got mad, just because we're going to a picture show and she isn't. She even wanted to come with us. Can you beat that?" He pouts and doesn't say a word.

"She doesn't have a date tonight." Still silence. I shiver; slide closer to him, wishing his car had a heater. "Don't you think that's funny, that she wanted to come with us?" He shrugs. "Really, Johnny, sometimes talking to you is like talking to the broad side of a barn."

"Nice perfume," he says, not even looking at me. He doesn't like it, I can tell. Maybe I over did it a little.

"Do you really like it?"

"I like it so much my eyes are watering."

I slide away from him and he doesn't even notice.

The crisp January air gives a frosted feeling to the whole world, like it's setting up for more cold weather, maybe snow. The smell of apples comes through the open window and I wonder if Gram has gathered the apples from the tree down near Gramp's resting place.

We drive along in silence for what seems like an hour, and Johnny eases the car down a dirt road, a good ways from the movie theater, turns off the motor, and rolls up his window. We often stop like this before a dance, if we're early. It's a habit I've grown to like.

"Thought we'd park for a while. That okay?"

"Sure," I say, glad my cologne is wearing off a bit.

"Since it's your birthday next Tuesday and I'll be at the Guard, I thought we'd celebrate tonight. I got you a present."

"A present for me?" I smile. He did remember.

"Yeah, well, it's a pre-birthday present."

Pre-birthday. That means he has another one for later. I just knew he'd remember.

"Nothing much," he says, handing me a flat package.

I rip off the paper as fast as I can.

"Hey, be careful," he scowls, "you don't want to wreck it."

"Oh, Johnny, it's wonderful. You look so handsome in your uniform and everything. When did you have this taken?"

"A reporter came by our Guard meeting and took a photo of each of us with his Speed Graphic camera. Someday I want to get into photography myself. Do you really like it?"

"It's swell, Johnny, I'll keep it, always." I reach over and kiss his cheek.

"You really do smell good, Louise." He moves closer and tries to get his hand inside the top of my dress.

"Hey, watch out," I laugh, pushing his hand away.

"Come on, Louise. Don't be like that. Look, we've been going on like this for months." His hands are busy again. "You feel so good. You drive me crazy. Let's not wait any longer."

"Johnny, no, for Pete's sake. You said we were going to wait."

"Forget what I said. Let's do it now. Come on. It's all I can think about. It's killing me."

"But what if something happens?" His hand inches up my leg, wrinkling my dress.

"Nothing's going to happen, Louise. It's okay. I promise."

I can feel his heart beating as fast as mine; feel him harden against me.

"But . . . I don't know. Shouldn't we wait?"

"I told you, nothing is going to happen."

"Johnny, tell me you love me. Say it, please." He did say it once, the first time he kissed me. What if we *do* it, and he decides he doesn't love me? Ellie said that happens to lots of girls.

He kisses me again, a hard, open-mouthed kiss. Part of me wants him to go ahead, the other part . . .

"Come on, Louise. Like I said. Nothing's going to happen."

"But, Johnny, are you sure?"

"Course, I'm sure." He moves closer and pulls up my dress. "I'm real sure," he says close to my ear, sending a shiver down to my stomach.

I want to ask him, did he do it with Helen, but I bite my lip. "Johnny, say it, just say it. Tell me you love me."

He struggles with the buttons on his pants then looks down at me, serious-like. I doubt he even heard me. "You sure it's okay, Louise? We won't do it if you say no."

I do love him so, how can I say no? He kisses my neck sending a chill through my whole body. Maybe if he does it, then he'll tell me he loves me. I pull him close, letting him know it's okay.

"Johnny," I whisper, and he kisses me again. I can hear his heart beating fast, and I kiss him back. I can feel my trembling flowing from my body to his.

"Oh, Louise, baby. You're so great."

We should stop, I know we should stop, before it's too late, before, but I don't want to hurt him; I don't want him to stop. He hesitates again, and I say to him, "It's okay, Johnny, just tell me you love me."

"Oh, just a damn minute," he whispers, tugging at his trousers. We giggle as he struggles his pants loose. If only he'd say it. Why is he so afraid to tell me he loves me? Maybe he's thinking of Helen instead of me?

He covers my face with kisses and reaches under my clothes, inching himself inside my panties, as my body takes over my thinking. His National Guard hat on the seat jabs me in the back, but I hardly notice. He pushes his way inside me. I stiffen and cry out as a sharp pain shoots through me. I bit my lip and hold back tears. Now he's the one making noises, breathing hard. He groans, loud rhythmic groans, and the car sways, back and forth. God, help me.

He falls heavy against me, and it's over. As quick as it started, it's over. Slowly, I pull away. Breathing hard, he leans back against the seat. His eyes are closed.

The pain is still there. I look up at the stars. They seem so close I can almost reach out and grab them. A sliver of a silvery moon mocks what we have done. Oh, why did I let him do it? My tears set the stars dancing in wavy circles.

"You okay?" he asks, pulling at his pants and buttoning them.

I blink, forcing the stars into their familiar pattern. I sink down into my corner trying to be invisible. It's over and I'm not feeling anything except shame and a dull pain inside me.

"Wow," Johnny lets loose with a sigh that fills the car.

Wow? Is that all he can say after what we just did? I couldn't say no to him. He should have known I couldn't say no.

Mama's face flashes across my mind. I shake her away, yank my damp panties to where they're supposed to be, and straighten my wrinkled dress. People are going to know, Gram and Mrs. K, and Ellie. It must show on my face. And what will Mama say? I feel so ashamed and I hurt.

Johnny's body tenses and he grabs me. "Quick, Louise. Duck down. I think someone's coming." He shoves me down as fear replaces my pain.

Two figures walk toward the car, their feet rustle through the dry leaves. My heart is beating so loud I'm afraid they might hear it. "What if they see us?" I whisper.

Johnny puts his hand over my mouth and I smell the loamy wetness of what we've done, a smell oddly like dried figs. My body tightens against him. We mustn't get caught. Please God don't let us get caught.

The footsteps come close then gradually fade. Johnny wipes a spot from the steamy window and whispers, "It's okay, they've gone. They didn't even see us."

He looks cow-eyes at me and says, "You were swell, Louise. You okay now?"

I nod, but I'm not okay at all, and I'm not ready to talk. He must think I'm a pushover. What if he brags to his friends; spreads the word around about what we just did in the back seat of his car? Angry tears sting, and I brush them away with my fist. Why did he have to go and do it before we were married? Ellie will probably guess right off when she sees me.

After a stretch of silence, Johnny says shyly, "There's still time for that picture show."

Time for the picture show! How can he say that, after what just happened? I slowly shake my head. "Please, just take me home."

He whips his head around. "Suit yourself, Louise." The gears grind and the car leaps ahead, leaving a fountain of crushed gravel behind.

Silence hangs like a damp sheet between us, and he pouts all the way home. Well I can pout too. I sit back, arms folded across my wrinkled dress. Anyway, what was so swell about that? Was I supposed to like it? I didn't know it would hurt. Maybe something's wrong with me. I must have scared him when I cried out. Ha. I'm glad for that. I won't let him do it again, not ever, at least not until we're married. But maybe, now that we've done it, maybe he won't want to marry me. Ellie says young men think about doing it all the time, and they do it whenever they can. This certainly wasn't Johnny's first time. He's probably done do it lots of times with Helen. What if he wants to do it with me again? I hold back tears again. There's just so much I don't know about these things.

I move closer, but he doesn't respond. His feelings are hurt, or maybe he feels guilty, too.

I move away. He doesn't say another word until we get in front of the house. He stops the car and looks at me.

"Louise?"

"What," I say, spitting the word out like a cherry pit.

With one of his rare smiles, he reaches across me, opens my door, and brushes his lips across my forehead. "Pick you up on Saturday?"

He's not mad, and probably not feeling guilty, either. I shrug so he won't know if it's a yes or a no, and ease myself out of the car. I walk slightly stiff-legged up to the front porch and let myself in without saying a word.

The only light in the house is in Ellie's room. She has her radio on so loud I can probably sneak past her door. I don't want her seeing me. She'll know in a minute what happened.

Ellie could have told me it would hurt. Mama never would have. She never told me anything about love, or life for that matter. If Ellie asks about Al Jolson tomorrow, I'll make something up. All I want to do is take a warm bath, snuggle into my nice clean bed, and sleep.

The next day, fifteen minutes before I'm due at work, I telephone the candy store.

"Mr. Middletown? This is Louise, speaking. I won't be in until eleven this morning. I had an urgent message from my mother." I cross my fingers and slide behind my back. "She has a bad toothache and I'm taking her to the dentist." At least on the telephone he can't see my face redden up.

That evening when Ellie and I return from work, there is a florist box on the front steps.

"Must be for me,"Ellie says as she grabs the box. She reads the name on the card shrugs and hands the box to me. "What kind of a swell time did you have last night, that calls for flowers?"

"Don't be silly," I say. "I just mentioned to him, he had never sent me flowers. I guess he decided to do it."

"By the way, how was the picture show?" she asks, sounding as if she knows darn well what happened last night.

"I didn't care for it much. How about next time let's you and me go to see that Charlie Chaplin one. Okay? I hear he's pretty funny." I can see she's trying to read my mind. Lying gets easier the more you do it, doesn't it, Mama?

March, 1928

Dear Mother,

> *You're going to like Johnny when you meet him. We go dancing whenever we can. For my birthday he gave me his picture. You might want to see it sometime, or maybe not. He gave me a pair of gloves, too. Did I tell you Mr. Middleton gave me a raise?*

> *It must make you feel old to have a nineteen-year-old daughter, Mama. Sincerely, Louise*

CHAPTER 49

"You mean you really want me to come to your house for dinner, Johnny?

"Not until next month, Louise. It's Pop's birthday and Ma's going to cook a goose. She'll do it up with all the trimmings, a real Danish feast. I think you'll like it, Louise, and you said you wanted to meet my family."

"I don't know, Johnny. I'd like to, but I may be coming down with something. Did your Mother say it was okay? I'd be nervous, you know. What if you family doesn't like me?"

"They'll think you're swell. I know they will."
    "Johnny, I'm not sure. Do they know how long we've been going together? Have they ever said anything about me being German?"

> *March 1928*
> Dear Mother.
>
>   *Johnny invited me to his house for dinner. He wants his family to meet me. Do you know any Danish people? Did they like you, even though you are German? What do they eat? Please answer. Sincerely, Louise*

It's teatime in the parlor. I have just set out a plate of my special ginger cookies. Mrs. K brings the cups and her favorite teapot.
    "Smells good, Louise. Shall I pour?"

I nod, "Mrs. K, can I ask you something?"

"Of course, Dearie, what is it? Is something troubling you?" She removes the flowered tea cozy, pours the tea.

"No, well . . . yes."

"Two lumps or three, dear?"

"Oh, two, please, Mrs. K. Sometimes I feel so stupid, like I don't know anything. You see, Johnny wants me to meet his family, and I don't know what to do."

She hands me my cup and replaces the tea cozy. "What do you mean, Louise? Don't you want to go?"

As she settles next to me, her feet swing out and the sofa sinks. She reaches for her knitting bag, as lengths of colored yarn trail across the floor.

"It's not that, Mrs. K, I want to go. I really do, but shouldn't I bring his mother a present or something? Isn't that what I'm supposed to do? They're Danish, you know, and I don't know their customs."

"Well, let's see, Dearie. Seems like bringing something would be nice, no matter what culture they come from, as long as it isn't too personal or too expensive. Louise, will you hold this ball of yarn while I try to untangle it. Have you thought of bringing some of your nice cookies?"

I put my cup on the coffee table next to the sofa and start winding the yarn as she untangles it. "Johnny says his mother is a good cook. She might think I'm trying to outdo her with my baking. What do you think about flowers?"

"Flowers would be nice." She digs into her kitting bag again, muttering, "Can't imagine where I left my glasses. I'm sure I put them in this bag.

"But I don't know," I shrug. "His father gardens. He grows grapes right in their backyard. Don't know what all else, probably vegetables, flowers, too. It would be just like me to bring them daffodils or roses and find they have a yard full."

"Can't you ask Johnny what his father grows? Oh here they are. I knew they were here somewhere."

"I could ask him, but he doesn't know a daisy from a dandelion. Johnny's color blind, you know, red-green, I think."

She turns and stares at me. "I didn't know that." She takes another ginger cookie and fans herself with her hankie.

"Yeah, it's hard for him to see apples in a green tree unless he's up real close."

"Choosing ripe tomatoes must be challenging, too." Mrs. K mumbles as she shakes her head. "Almost impossible, I'd say." She makes clucking noises and shakes her head. "Such a nice young man, too. You know, if you marry him, all your boys will probably be color blind too."

I stiffen and feel my face heat up. Why did she have to say that? Does she know? But she goes off in a safer direction.

"Think how difficult it must be, when it comes to choosing a socks or a tie that matches what he's wearing, but then . . . he doesn't wear ties, does he?" She puts down her cup.

I wish I'd never brought Johnny's color blindness up. She's right, though. I take another cookie. "That's why his socks don't match sometimes, Mrs. K."

"That poor boy," she says, shaking her head. "I wonder if it runs in his family. I wonder if it runs in *my* family. Oh, my-oh-my. I don't know what I'd do if I had that problem."

"I doubt that you're color blind, Mrs. K," I say, but she isn't listening. She stares at her knitting.

"Why I do believe I've picked up the wrong color." She squints and adjusts glasses. Do you suppose I'm colorblind and don't know it? My, my, wouldn't that be dreadful. Maybe I'd better check to see if I've made other mistakes, but then I wouldn't know it, would I? Even if I do have that affliction."

"But Mrs. K! What about my present for Johnny's mother?"

"I'm sure you'll think of the perfect thing, dear. Ask Johnny, he'll know. Color blind. Poor thing." She struggles up from the sofa just as Ellie walks in.

"What's going on in here? Are you two talking about me?"

Ellie helps herself to a cookie, then another and another. If she doesn't watch out she'll be as round as her mother.

"Louise was wondering what present to take to Johnny's mother when she goes there for dinner. Maybe you can help her, Ellie. I've got to go get my glasses. Did you know Johnny was colorblind? And there's a chance I might be, too?"

"I wouldn't worry, Mrs. K," I tell her. "Everything you knit looks perfect, doesn't it, Ellie?"

Ellie shrugs and takes a fourth cookie. "I always thought he was trying to start a new trend when his socks didn't match. So, he's invited you to dinner, has he? You two are getting pretty thick."

"Come on, Ellie, help me. What should I take?"

"Louise, you make things so complicated. Get Johnny to ask his mother what she'd like. Gosh. It's only dinner. She'll probably say something easy, like a jar of pickles or olives. I don't know. Nothing baked or cooked. You know Danes. Certainly wouldn't want anything you made yourself. She wouldn't want you messing with her dinner."

There she goes again, saying things about my cooking. She really *is* jealous of my cookbook. The idea, that any recipe of mine would 'mess up' a dinner!

I wonder when, or if, she is going to finish typing my recipes. I could offer to pay her, or try to do it myself. What if she gets the amounts, or the ingredients mixed up?

Late March 1928

Dear Gertie,

Thank you for the Lilly of the Valley cologne. It's just what I wanted. I love what you did to my hair. I think my boyfriend likes it too, although he doesn't say much. I guess that's the way with boys. I'm looking forward to my next appointment. By the way, do you know anything about Danish people? Do you think a Danish woman would like Evening In Paris cologne? Sincerely, Louise

Next Sunday is dinner at Johnny's. If my stomach is still upset by then I won't go. All I want to do is sleep. Whenever I think of meeting Johnny's mother, my throat tightens and I feel like throwing up.

His father will hate me because I am German, and his mother will think I'm just a silly shop girl, because I work in a candy store. Maybe I should stay home. Johnny could tell them I'm sick.

April 1928

Dear Ruthie,

I am going to meet Johnny's parents on Sunday and I'm scared. Bet you never thought I'd say that, did you? Well, I am. There are so many things I don't know, and this muggy weather doesn't help my stomach. Sometimes I wish I'd never left the farm. Can you believe that? Life was so simple back there, with you and Gram. You aren't being trouble for Gram, are you?

Remember she isn't getting any younger and be careful of that Homer. You mustn't hang around with him are you? I miss you, Ruthie. Be good. Sincerely, Louise

CHAPTER 50

This is my first time on a city bus and it's crowded; so many people. Where are they all going?

Johnny gave me directions. You'd think he could have arranged to pick me up if he really wanted to. He said coming all the way from the Guard to Ellie's house would make us late for supper. He said he knew I could manage by myself, but I'm not so sure I can, with with my stomach acting up. Maybe I should have worn another dress. His mother might think this one is too fancy. Johnny said, get off at his street, turn left, then walk three blocks to the house. I don't like walking in the city alone. Nothing to be afraid of, I suppose. I think the next stop is where I get off.

"Sir?" The bus driver doesn't even turn his head. "I think I get off at the next stop." He shrugs and continues driving. "Are you going to stop for me?" I yell over the engine noise. He sighs like his world is coming to an end.

"Jeez, girlie. Just pull the cord, and I'll stop!"

"Thank you so much. I just wanted to make sure." He didn't have to be so rude. I pull the cord and at the next stop he cranks the door open. "This is my first time, you know, on a city bus, I mean." He shrugs and rolls his eyes. Maybe I'm not supposed to thank him, or even talk to him.

Johnny better be there when I arrive. From the way he talked, no telling what tricks his brothers might try. Johnny calls them clowns. I've never even seen a real clown. Never been to a circus. Johnny said he'd take me someday.

It's a pretty street, verandahs, gardens, and lots of trees. Wouldn't mind living here. Hopscotch lines on the sidewalk. Must mean kids live around here. Mustn't walk on their lines.

I reposition my purse and the box of candy I brought, pick up a stone, and toss it into the '8' square. One two three, four five, six seven . . . pick up the stone . . . eight, turn and jump back to home.

His sister Peggy must be young enough for hopscotch. I've never eaten cotton candy, either. Johnny says it's spun sugar. Wonder how they make it? If I knew, I could put that in my cookbook, too.

I come to number 279 Capon Street. No, Johnny said his house was 276. He said on the left. He must have meant if you were coming from the other direction. I cross over. That's funny. There's no number 276 on this side either. All these houses have odd numbers. That house across the street looks like the one Johnny described, gray, next to a vacant lot, front stoop three steps up, two wicker chairs. I cross over again. These are the even numbers, except for number 279.

Will you look at that? The number 9 hangs crooked. Someone turned the 6 upside down. His brothers I'll bet. Either it's supposed to be a joke, or the whole family hates Germans.

I should walk right by, go around the block, and take the bus home. I don't feel well, anyway. But what will Johnny tell his parents if I don't show up?

The house looks pretty small for nine people. 'Everybody gets in everybody's way', Johnny said. No wonder.

The steps are loose. They could use a sweeping, too. Wonder who's job that is. Should I ring the bell or knock? I can't just walk in. Now my hands are sweaty.

Something crashes against the door from the inside. I step back. There is a loud slap and a yelp, followed by silence. I back away as the door cracks open.

A blond head appears. It must be his little sister, Lorry. She looks to be about twelve. She looks a lot like Johnny; same dark eyes, same pout-y mouth.

She looks as lonely as I feel. Why isn't she smiling? With four brothers and sisters, a mother *and* a father, people who care about her, she doesn't know how lucky she is.

"Hello, I'm Louise."

She looks me up and down and scowls. Maybe Johnny didn't tell her I was coming. Maybe it's my dress. My shoes? She hates me already, I can tell.

The bow in her hair jiggles as she shakes her head.

"You don't look anything like Helen."

Helen again. My fingers find their familiar place behind my back. I'd forgotten about Helen. Johnny said she was practically part of the family. My stomach tightens.

"Isn't Johnny home yet?" I ask. She has no right to compare me to someone I've never met. Besides, Johnny said he was through with Helen. The door opens wider and Johnny pushes in front of his little sister.

"There you are, Louise. I thought you got lost."

"Thanks goodness you're here." I lean against him. "I was afraid you wouldn't be home."

"Told you I'd be here, didn't I. You've met Lorry?"

She stares up at me through half-closed eyes. "I thought Helen was coming," she says, with a loud sigh.

"Okay, kid, that's enough," Johnny says. "Get in the house. Go on before I tell Ma you're running around without shoes. Come on in, Louise. Sorry I couldn't come to get you, but I told you why." He puts his arm around my shoulder. "You okay, Louise? You look pale."

"I'm fine, now that you're here. I'm just nervous about meeting your folks. Especially your father," I whisper. "Is he home?"

"Yeah, they're all here. Come on in. Didn't you hear one of the boys get whacked just now? That was Pop. Ma's in the kitchen with the girls, fixing up dinner."

The thick smell of cooked cabbage hits me, and my stomach tightens. It smells different than Gram's and I swallow hard.

The living room is stuffed to bursting with deep sofas and overstuffed chairs, each with tightly crocheted doilies covering their backs and arms. Assorted paintings crowd the walls. Country scenes, cathedrals, old men, making the room shrink in size. Foreign-looking knickknacks and family photographs cram every available surface, and potted plants are everywhere.

Lorry sits at a scarred upright piano in the hall, fingering the notes to Mary had a little lamb. A stack of sheet music means somebody else must play, too. Johnny said he wasn't musical so it can't be him. A clock on the mantle gives out with hollow chimes, telling us it's six o'clock. Soon I'll be eating a big Danish meal at a table full of Danish strangers.

In the dining room two girls about my age clear stacks of books and piles of papers from a huge dining table, skillfully toss a lace tablecloth over it, and begin to set out ten places of flatware, dishes, and glasses.

Without even stealing a look my way, the girls scurry back and forth to from the kitchen. Maybe I should offer to help, even though we haven't been introduced. I catch a glimpse of an older woman passing by the door to the kitchen. She's tall, with snow-white hair, and walks with a slow, deliberate step, almost a shuffle. It must be Johnny's mother.

A slight, not very tall man with a friendly face and piercing blue eyes comes up behind us. "You are Louise? The one we hear about?"

"Mr. Paulsen?" I stick my hand out. "I'm pleased to . . . I mean . . . I'm glad to . . . make your acquaintance." Damn! I've rehearsed it enough times, why is it coming out wrong? He'll think I have no manners at all.

He smiles, showing a gold tooth part way back in his mouth. He takes my hand and his blue eyes scrunch up like a kitten's. Johnny's brown eyes don't do that. He seems friendly, not like I thought he'd be. Should I say happy birthday to him or did Johnny say it was his mother's birthday?

"*Goot* to meet you." His accent is heavy but not like Gram's.

"Boys," his voice gains a gruff tone, "Come, say hello to Johnny's friend."

Three awkward boys in various sizes crowd around, making sure not to bump their father. They must be Lou, Fred, and Sven. They grin, and I smile back, letting them know I'm wise to their trick of mixing up the address. They don't look any more harmful than Ellsworth did at their age. I won't tell Johnny about the house numbers. Better to be on the good side of these three, since I may have difficulty dealing with his three sisters and his mother. If only I could sit down. My legs feel weak.

"Girls, *Lauw-ah?*" Johnny's father bellows. "Come. We have company."

His two other sisters come in from the dining room, first Agnes, the oldest, then Anna. We smile awkwardly and say hello. Lorry slinks in behind Agnes. They're thinking of Helen, comparing me to her.

We wait as Johnny's mother maneuvers into the room. Her eyes meet mine, and she steps back as if I've slapped her. Didn't she know I was coming? Didn't Johnny tell her?

For a second she staggers, and her face turns pale. She glares at her husband and gasps, "*Ah Gud, huner gravid.*"

No one is close enough to hear except me, but I can't understand her Danish words.

"Johnny's girl?" she asks, not even taking my outstretched hand. Johnny's father's eyes narrow, and they both stand frozen, staring at me.

What have I done? Did they just remember I'm German? I shouldn't have come. I grab the box of chocolates I had set on the arm of a chair.

"These are for you, Mrs. ah . . . . I brought you chocolates."

"I don't eat chocolates. I have the diabetes."

"I didn't know. I mean, I knew about your . . . well, I mean, but I didn't know you couldn't eat chocolates." Johnny should have told me. "I'm sorry. I'm so sorry."

She waves me to silence. "No trouble. The rest can eat them. Come." She turns toward the dining room. "We must start."

Johnny's father takes her arm and leads her to her place at the foot of the table. The girls walk quietly to their chairs, while the boys scramble to theirs. Johnny shows me where I am to sit, right next to him. He even holds my chair for me.

"Sit now, before it gets cold," his mother snaps as she scowls at Johnny.

Johnny squeezes my arm and whispers; "She's not at her best tonight."

His mother hears and gives him a stern look. How can she dislike me when she doesn't even know me? It's Probably because I'm German, and *not* Helen.

If this family eats Danish feasts this size often, why aren't they all fat? Roast pork and a goose, two kinds of potatoes, carrots, green beans, yellow squash, creamed onions, and dark heavy bread. A whole pound of butter makes it's way up and down the table before disappearing totally. Pickled herring is passed around, Johnny warned me about that, but I eat some anyway. Red cabbage, stronger than Gram's but tastier, many dishes I don't recognize, and two kinds of pies on the sideboard, waiting. I can hardly look at it all and keep my stomach from heaving.

Johnny's father reaches beside his chair and pours a clear liquid into a small glass near his plate. No one says a word while we eat. The boy's manners are perfect and I watch mine closely.

Everyone is served a small crystal glass of blackberry wine, even Lorry. Between her sips she scowls at me from under thick blond lashes. I keep getting that cold stare from Johnny's mother, like I've got some disease and am not welcome at their table. Lorry and Agnes seem shy and don't give me so much as the time of day, but I catch them nudge each other when I choke on the pickled herring.

After what seems like hours, the meal is finally over and, as if by a miracle, I've managed to keep everything down.

Good-byes are awkward. I say my thank-you, and wish a happy birthday to everyone at once, hoping it reaches the right person.

Johnny's car is parked in their driveway. The number 6 is back hanging the way it belongs. I nod at the boys, and they hide behind each other trying to look innocent.

Halfway home I yell to Johnny, "Stop the car." I crank open the window and throw up down the side of his car.

"I suppose it was the food," he says, his words wrapped in disgust. He hands me his handkerchief. "Or maybe you just can't stand my family."

"It's not your family," I wipe my mouth and lean back against the seat.

Realization weighs heavily on me, as my stomach heaves again, and I know. How did his mother know even before I did? Johnny said nothing would happen. He lied. What will Mama think of me now?

"Must have been the herring," Johnny says.

"Just take me home, please."

I sag into the furthest corner of the front seat and don't say a word all the way home. Silence widens the space between us, and he doesn't even kiss me good night. Maybe he's wishing Helen *was* here, instead of me.

Inside the house I rush to the bathroom. It could be all that rich food. There certainly was a lot of it.

But one look in the mirror tells me it wasn't the food. I didn't know whether to laugh or cry.

April 1928

Dear Mother,

I went to Johnny's for dinner. I think the pickled herring was bad, or I drank too much blackberry wine, but I can't keep anything in my stomach. I'm taking a few days off from work. I don't think I can stand the smell of chocolate until I feel better. Do you suppose I'm coming down with something? It could be the influenza? Sincerely, Louise

April 1928

Dear Mrs. Paulsen,

Thank you, for letting Johnny invite me to your house for dinner. It was delicious, really. I had a lovely time. I hope I wasn't too much trouble. Sincerely, Louise Guest

CHAPTER 51

Mrs. K stands next to my bed fussing over me, fluttering her lace hankie like she's flagging down a streetcar. She's waiting for me to say something. I just wish she'd go away and leave me alone.

"Are you sure you don't want a nice cup of tea, Louise? You look a little . . . peak-ed. You have to keep your strength up, you know, . . . I mean, . . . even if you aren't feeling well."

"Must be something I ate." I reach for the water glass by my bed.

Ellie leans against the door, arms folded, fingers tapping aimlessly on her arm. She doesn't believe I'm sick. I can tell she's mad because her mother is making such a fuss over me. She has on the new sweater her mother knitted. I like the one she made for me, better.

"You're not contagious, are you?" Ellie backs away, making a dramatic gesture by covering her nose and mouth. She's making fun of me.

"Don't be silly, Ellie. Of course she's not contagious." Mrs. K turns to me. "Are you sure you don't want some nice cinnamon toast, Louise? I can make it in a jiffy."

The thought of food makes me shudder. "I just want to lie down for a while. Have you ever eaten pickled herring?" I try to quiet my stomach with my hand. "I had to try it to be polite. Maybe it was the wine." I lay back against the pillow, thinking maybe if I look tired they'll go away.

"Poor dear," Mrs. K sighs, as she leans over me, placing her cool hand on my forehead. I close my eyes, remembering Mama how used to do the same thing when I was little.

"Mrs. K? Could you telephone Mr. Middletown at the candy store? Tell him I won't be in for a couple more days."

"Of course, Louise. You just rest. I'll take care of everything." She lowers the shade and maneuvers herself and Ellie out of the room.

Johnny hasn't called for three whole days. His mother must have told him. By the look on her face I bet Ellie knows, too.

I lay half asleep. It could still be the influenza. I'm not the kind of girl who gets herself into trouble. Ruthie was always the one who did that. I close my eyes and gradually all thoughts fade from my mind and I drift toward sleep, feeling more content than I deserve.

The front door slams. I wake with a start, pull the bedspread up over me, and sink into a pool of remorse. A sharp voice comes from downstairs.

Where is she? Where is that girl? *Louise*? *LOUISE!* Are you up there?"

"It's Mama!" I gasp, brushing sleep from my eyes, pushing my hair in place. Frantically I try to smooth out the wrinkles in my bedspread, as her heels click up the stairs. My door flies open. She stands in the doorway, her hands on her hips, her eyes glaring at me.

"Oh, Louise, it's true," she blurts out. "I can see it in your face." She rushes to my bedside, reaches toward me, and puts her arm around my shoulder. Her perfume invades my room. Not the familiar Evening in Paris, but something new, something that makes my eyes smart.

For a fleeting second, there is a gentle look in her eyes, but before I can wish for her to stay like this forever, she pulls away and she is *Mama* again.

"You foolish girl. You've gone and gotten yourself . . . *per-egg-nant*?" She spits the word out in three syllables. They bit into me like sharp, teeth.

It is the first time I've heard the word said out loud, except in Danish, and I realize it's true; I *am* pregnant. I'm going to have Johnny's baby. I'm going to be a *mother*.

The thought wraps around me like a warm quilt and I feel transformed. Me! A mother, with a baby of my very own. I don't have to tell Mama it's true. She knows, just like Johnny's mother knew.

His mother must have told him. That's why he hasn't called. He's afraid to talk to me. He's feeling guilty. Well, he damn-nation better feel guilty. It's more his fault than mine.

"We'll have to do something about this," Mama mutters pacing up and down, rubbings her hands together, nodding her head, planning my future again, talking, not to me, but to herself.

"We'll send you away. Yes, of course, to a place for silly young girls who are too stupid to wait until after they are married. There are places like that, and that's just where you're going."

"Mama, what are you saying?"

She shakes her finger in my face. "For unwed mothers, Louise. Yes, you will go there and we will put it up for adoption."

"Stop talking like that, Mama! I'm not going to any home, and don't call my baby, '*it*'! I don't care what you say. It's my baby and I'm going to keep it. Nothing you say will change my mind. I'll manage by myself. I don't need you or Johnny."

"Honey, listen to yourself. You don't know what you're saying. You just leave everything to me. I know what's best for you."

"When did you ever know what's best for me?"

"Listen, young lady." She grabs my shoulders. "You just let me handle this, I said I'll take care of everything, and I will."

I pull away from her. "You can't tell me what to do. I can manage my own life now." Doesn't she see? This is my chance to have something of my own. Someone I can love; someone who will love me.

Mama paces. "Don't be foolish, Louise. People will talk. They'll start counting. It takes nine months you know, and besides," she laughs and primps at her hair. "You know I'm too young to be a grandmother."

"That's all you ever think about, isn't it, Mama, how it will affect you. Do you ever think about *anyone* but yourself?" I see tears in her eyes. She turns away and shakes her head.

"You don't understand anything, Louise."

"I understand I'm not going to give up my baby, no matter what you say. I'll be fine. So please, Mama, just go away and leave me alone."

"Now, Louise. Be sensible." She pulls out her scented hankie and blows her nose. "What if whoever-he-is won't marry you? Does he even know about the baby?"

"Of course he knows," I lie, but I am going to tell him. "You don't have to worry, Mama. His name is Johnny, and he'll marry me. We'll move away. We'll take our baby with us and you won't have to tell anyone, or even see me or my baby ever again."

"And if he won't marry you?"

"You haven't heard a word I've said, have you, Mama? He loves me, he wants to marry me."

"I'll bet his parents won't approve of you. They probably think you are some sort of a . . . I don't know what. "She sighs, "I'm only thinking of what's best for you, Louise."

She takes my hand, but this time I pull away. "Don't say any more, Mama. You've said enough. Besides, you don't know his parents. You don't even know me." I pound my fist on the bed. "You don't know anything about me!" I turn away and hide my head in my pillow. What if she's right? Johnny said his parents hated Germans. They won't want a *kraut* for a daughter-in-law, much less a German grandchild.

"Didn't I warn you?" Mama picks imaginary dust off the bedspread.

"Warn me?" I snap, raising up to face her. "When were you ever around long enough to *warn* me about anything?" You haven't spent a Christmas or birthday with us for, for as long as I can remember."

She steps back as if I'd struck her, and that's just what I feel like doing.

We stare at each other. Our breathing slips into a rhythmic unison. Same nose, same eyes, flashing daggers, and hair that once was the same, but is so different now. I've never stood up to her like this before, ever. I don't really mean to hurt her, but what I say is true.

Mama has never been in this room before. Does she see how clean and bright it is? Does she even notice the vase of daffodils on my dresser, the framed picture of her with Ruthie and me, when Ruthie was just a baby? She must see I have a comfortable place to live now, and I don't need to live with her to be happy. We glare at each other, and I wonder who will speak first.

As if she has always done it, she puts her arm around my shoulder. It is warm and soft and triggers my tears.

"How far along are you?" she asks, close to my ear.

I see her through a blur of tears, knowing exactly the night it happened.

"Four months," I whisper.

"Four? Are you sure?" She reaches in her purse and hands me a flowered hankie reeking of her perfume. I blow hard and hand it back.

"Yes, I'm sure. We only, we only did it once." Why am I telling her this? It's none of her business.

"You're sure it's Johnny?"

"*Mama!* If you knew me, you wouldn't have to ask that. Of course I'm sure." I slide off the bed and walk to the window. I want her to leave me alone.

Down on the lawn, a black cat slinks low in the grass, stalking a robin. The neighbor's dog, a large, shaggy, brown thing, watches eagerly, waiting for his chance at the cat. If I make a noise I can warn the bird and the cat. Nothing is safe in this world. The only thing you can do is, protect yourself. Will Johnny marry me? He'll have to marry me. Our baby will need a father. The cat creeps closer.

"Have you set a date?" Mama asks.

"What?" I say. The sharpness in my voice alerts the bird. The tension in the grass below disappears, leaving the cat cleaning her paws, and the dog sulking off.

"When is he going to marry you?"

I wonder myself, but I'm not telling her. "Right away. As soon as we can." My fingers cross behind my back.

"Does he love you, Louise?"

I can see her planning again, wanting to send me away 'til it's over, so she can continue her life as if I didn't exist. Well, she can just forget that. She *is* going to be a grandmother whether she likes it or not. "Yes, he loves me. Johnny said he would marry me," I cross my fingers again. "And if his mother and father object, we won't invite them to the wedding. We're both old enough, you know."

Mama stares at me, purses her lips, and for the first time I notice her eyebrows are gone. She has drawn in arches above her eyes, giving her a permanent look of surprise. I raise my eyebrows and stare back, hoping she'll notice I'm mocking her.

"Where is this person?" she asks. Why isn't he here with you and why haven't I met him?"

I turn away, showing her I'm dead set against answering any more of her questions. She shakes her head and struts out of the room, still wearing her surprised expression. If there ever is to be a wedding, I'm not inviting her.

June, 1928

Dear Johnny,

By now, your mother has told you. I thought you would have come to see me right away. I guess you are mad or disappointed, or maybe scared. I guess I should be sorry. I was at first, but not anymore. I want to have our baby. We should have waited, but since we didn't, I'll be fine, even without you. And you can tell your mother her grandchild will have a wonderful mother, even if I am German. I am four months along. If I never see you again, have a swell life. Sincerely, Louise

Two days later I receive a reply with no return address. I can tell it's from Johnny by the straight, perfect lettering on the envelope.

June 14, 1928

Dear Louise,

Yes, my mother told me. It wasn't the happiest news I ever got, but if you will give me a little more time, everything will work out. Be patient. There will be a wedding. There has to be, no matter what my mother says. Don't worry, Louise. You know how I feel about you. Everything will be okay. I promise. Yours truly, Johnny

YOURS TRULY??? I want to rip his letter to shreds. Why didn't he come and tell me all this himself? *Yours truly?* He can't even put the word love on paper. What's the matter with him, anyway? What's the matter with me? Maybe I wish he *wasn't* the father of my baby.

CHAPTER 52

"Louise," Ellie shouts from the bottom of the stairs. "You've got a letter. It looks like it's been sent to the wrong address twice. Didn't you tell people you live here now?"

"Would you mind bringing it up, Ellie?"

"My mother said you should come downstairs and read it," she yells. "You've been spending too much time in your room. She says it's not healthy."

Someone is always telling me what to do. It can't be from Johnny, he knows this address. "Just leave it on the table in the hall," I yell. "I'll get it later."

As soon as I hear her go into the kitchen, I slip downstairs and bring the letter back to my room. It's wrinkled and stained, and I know before I open it, it's from. Ruthie.

July 1928

Weez. Mama came and took Gram. Said I should clean out the house she would come for me soon. Do I believe her? No. By the time you get this I'm out of here leaving with Homer. He says he can get us factory jobs in another state easy. If we can't get jobs we go south and work in the fields. Do not worry. I can take care of me. I hate Mama for leaving me here. I guess I hate you for the same reason. Mama never loved me. Neither did you. We're going and you can't stop me. Don't try. I took

Gram's egg money again. Homer took her medicine. Not me.
Tell Mama if you want. I don't care. Your sister, Ruthie.

P. S. Who will clean the chicken house now? Ha, ha, ha.

Her letter lays limp and wrinkled beside me on my bed. I run my fingers along the grimy pages. Her words sting; I shouldn't have left her. How will I know where she is or if she needs me? *'Don't try to find me,'* she said. How could she leave Gram and run off with that Homer? I told her he was no good and now I've lost her for sure.

Oh, Ruthie. You should have let me know sooner. Mrs. K would have taken you in. You could have real baths in a real tub, and slept in a real bedroom. You're too good to be with someone like that Homer. I tried to keep you out of trouble, sneak food in to you when you were bad, help you grow up proper. Even with your lying and cheating I still cared for you. You are my sister.

Tears sting. She never even learned how to say thank you but I still loved her, she must have known that. Straightening the corners of her wrinkled letter, I wonder what the stains are. Dirt? Tears? You never know with Ruthie. It's my fault; I tried to tell Mama. Maybe reform school will be the only way to straighten her out.

I read the letter again. If she's thinking of a factory job, it must be in a textile mill. Massachusetts and New Hampshire are full of them. Johnny said they are always looking for under-aged girls to work the machines. If I try to find her, where would I start? Johnny could find her. He can do anything. But what if he decides not to come back to me just like my father?

It's been a month since Johnny answered my letter. He promised we'd be married. If he meant it we need to make plans in a hurry. I'm getting bigger every day. What if I never hear from him again? I'll have to manage on my own. I always dreamed of having a big wedding, like in the magazines, me in a frilly white dress, with a veil from Gram's trunk. I will be holding a bouquet of pink roses from Gram's garden. Ruthie would be my maiden of honor, her hair combed, and a smile on her face. Mama would be there, too, all gussied-up in a flashy mother-of-the-bride dress.

There won't be a father of the bride to walk me down the isle, unless I ask Mama's newest husband, or maybe Mr. Middletown, from the candy store. Certainly not Johnny's father; he wouldn't do it anyway, not when he'll too soon to be a grandfather.

But it isn't going to be that way. I'll end up being Louise Guest, an unwed pregnant mother. I pick at the tuffs in my quilt. Not *my* quilt, Mrs. K's quilt. Everything in this room belongs to Mrs. K. She's been more of a mother to me than Mama ever was. Maybe I'll have two mothers of the bride, even if one does wobble when she walks. I blow my nose. I don't guess crying can be much good for my baby.

My baby! "Hello, baby. Your daddy said there'd be a wedding. Ha." I pat the roundness of my stomach. "If there is one, you'll forgive me if I hide you under a bouquet of flowers. You see, you really aren't supposed to be in the picture yet."

I've got to stop thinking about this or I will make myself sick. All I want to do is sleep. Sleep and eat everything in sight. If I don't stop eating, this baby will get so big it'll never come out.

Mama hasn't come back. If she didn't hate me before, she certainly hates me now. I doubt she'll ever want to see me again, or my baby. Have it your way, Mama. You're going to have a granddaughter or, if Mrs. K is wrong, a grandson. Whether you like it or not, you are going to be a grandmother.

August 1928

Dear Mother.

By now you must know Ruthie ran off. If you know where she is, please tell me. What are you going to do with Gram? If you see Ruthie, tell her I love her, because I do and I always will. Sincerely, Louise

CHAPTER 53

"Louise, Dear? Are you asleep?" Mrs. K pushes the door open with her ample body and tiptoes in carrying a tray.

"I'm awake, Mrs. K, just being lazy. Seems I need a lot of sleep these days."

"I brought you a nice cup of hot tea and a cardamom muffin. Your recipe, you know. Ellie typed a few up this morning. Those muffins sounded so good, I just had to bake up a batch. You don't mind, do you, Louise?"

But I do mind. She should have asked. They are *my* recipes, and they aren't even in a book yet. She should have waited.

"If you wish I can bring you coffee, but in your condition coffee isn't the best thing for you, now is it?"

I sit up and rub stiff tear tracks from my face. "Hot tea will be fine, Mrs. K, Thank you."

She sets the tray on the table next to my bed, "Let's have some sun in this room, shall we?" she asks, adjusting the shades to let the sun come streaming. "It's a beautiful morning. Now, isn't that better?" She pours my tea, stirs in two lumps, and places a muffin on the saucer.

"Thank you, Mrs. K, but you shouldn't have bothered, I could have come downstairs."

"No bother at all, Louise, dear. I see you've had a good rest." She's pretending not to notice my red eyes. I sip my tea, letting its warm sweetness seep through me.

"Mrs. K, can I ask you something?" The edge of the bed sinks as she settles close to me, nearly upsetting my tea.

"What did you want to ask, child?"

"Well, do you think I am a horrible person because of the fix I've gotten myself into?" I glance down at my rounded stomach.

"Of course not, Louise. What a silly question to ask."

"Really?"

She takes my hand. "Now don't you go worrying yourself, what's done is done. As long as you and Johnny love each other, I'm sure everything will work out just fine. A little more tea, dear?" She asks, and before I can answer she fills my cup and adds two more lumps of sugar. The muffin sits untouched.

"Of course it would have been better if you had waited until after you were married to get . . . ah, well . . . you know . . . to start a family. But as I said, what's done is done, and now you must get on with your life."

I steady my cup as she shifts her weight.

"Is there anything I can do to make things easier for you, Louise?"

I nibble at the muffin. "Well, I hate to ask, but I doubt I'll fit into any of my dresses for the wedding. If there is a wedding, I should wear a nice dress, don't you think? It'll be a small wedding, just family, but still . . . it *will be* a wedding."

"And you *shall* wear a pretty dress, Louise, dear. I'll see to that. We don't get married every day, now do we? Well, I mean, most of us, well, you know what I mean." She blushes, and I know she's thinking of Mama.

"There's something else, too," I say lowering my voice.

"What is it, dear?"

"Do you think, well, you know my Mother, do you think I'm at all taking after her ways?"

She studies me as if she's measuring how much she should say. She straightens my quilt, picks up a crumb, puts it in my saucer, and clears her throat.

"Louise, we all have bits of both our parents in us, in fact, all our ancestors. Did you know that you might be related to a famous poet named, Edgar Guest? He used to write for a big newspaper in Michigan. He's had books of poetry published, and he's quite well known."

"A poet? Really, Mrs. K?" Wait 'till I tell Johnny.

"But no matter who we're related to," she continues, "we have to live our own lives, you know, make our own choices and learn to live with them. We are individuals, children of God, if you will. We can choose what we want to do with our lives, and with His help it will happen. At least that's the way I see it. Of course I *do* see some of your mother in you. You have her eyes and, if I can guess, you probably have her hair, too, at least when she was younger, but I don't see you having her wild streak. What if you *do* take after good old Edgar, and go on to write something more than just a book of recipes?"

I stiffen. It is not *just* a book of recipes. They are *my* recipes, Gram's and mine, but maybe she didn't mean it to sound that way. "I guess I could be a poet someday, if I wanted to, couldn't I?"

"That's the spirit, Louise, dear, but I think I know what you're getting at. Your mother is a . . . well, she *has* had a rather unconventional life. From what you've told me about your sister, Ruthie, she may be headed in that direction, too."

"Mrs. K, I used to think I could change Ruthie, but I don't know anymore. I just don't want her to get into any serious trouble."

"She'll have to figure out her own life, Louise, just like the rest of us. She has choices of your own, but you can't make choices for her. It's what *she* chooses, and what she does with those choices that count. We each live with our own consequences."

I set my teacup on the tray and lean against my pillow. "Ruthie told me once I worry too much about my hair and what people think of me. I've never forgotten that. Sometimes I look deep inside myself and all I see is someone with pretty green eyes, a long neck and nothing else, and I wonder if I will even know how to raise a baby."

"Oh, Louise, you're bright and creative, smart too, and you're going to be a wonderful mother to your little girl."

She adjusts herself on the bed, causing it to sag again. "Just think, she'll have some of your traits, some of Johnny's and maybe . . ."

"You keeps saying, *she*, Mrs. K. How do you know it's going to be a girl?"

"Oh, I can tell by a lot of things, your eyes, the shape of your stomach, how your face looks."

I have my doubts until she tells me her last six predictions have been right.

"In fact I've been right for the last ten times," she says, "if you count two sets of twins. I'm never wrong. So don't worry, you'll have a girl all right. You can count on that. And she'll be her own person, just like you are.

"Look at Ellie and me, Louise. Aren't we just about as different as any mother and daughter can be? She is a lot like her father, my late husband. The dear man had red hair like Ellie's, and he was just as outspoken as she is."

"Well, I hope I don't have *all* my mother's traits."

Mrs. K rubs the corner seam of her napkin into a tight role. Our tea has grown cold, as she looks at me and bites her lip.

"Mrs. K? Are you all right? Is something bothering you? Can I get you more hot water?"

She shakes her head. "I'll just take these tea things away, and later we can talk again, dear. I can see you're tired."

"I'm not tired, really I'm not." I am tired but I can see something is worrying her. She sighs. "What is it, Mrs. K?"

"Well, there *is* something I think you should know about your mother."

"About my Mama?" My heart sinks. I'm not sure I want to hear any more about Mama today.

"I don't know how much you know about your mother, Louise, but she had a difficult life when she was young." She shakes her head. "A lot of pain; a lot of pain indeed. When you know the whole story, you may think differently about her."

Something in Mrs. K's voice makes the hair on the back of my neck prickle.

"It's a hard story, Louise. She told it to me soon after we met. Guess she sensed I was a good listener, and she needed to tell someone to get it off her chest. But in your condition, it might not be the right time."

"I already know what kind of a person she is, but in my heart, I love her anyway. It's just that I don't want to hear any more bad things about her live. Tell me about my father, Mrs. K. He's the one I want to hear about. Did you know him?"

"No, dear, I didn't meet your mother until long after he was gone. I don't know what happened there, I just know she loved him very much, and she said for the short time they were together, they were happy."

I wait, thankful I had veered her off the subject of Mama's past. But I can practically see the gears in Mrs. K's head as she shifts into talking about the person that was my father.

"Well," she settles and continues, "this is what I know. Your Grandmother made her life so unbearable on the farm, your mother ran away to New Haven when she was fourteen. She worked as a waitress in a restaurant near Yale University and met Thomas, a starving young student. I don't believe she planned on falling love so soon. She was only sixteen then, you know. I think she wanted to make something of herself and try to undo the feelings of worthlessness she'd felt before she left the farm.

"They were married and Marie, your mother, supported him with her meager earnings and the healthy tips she received with her customers. Thomas became jealous when he saw her flirting with her customers. He didn't realize she was only thinking of the tips she would be able to take home.

"She was just seventeen when they married, too young, really, but she said they were happy and when you were born, she thought their family would live happily ever after. He stayed for a few years and then he ran off.

"Your mother was devastated. He might have re-enlisted, or met another woman, or just been jealous of her; she was never sure which, but he never come back.

"When you were born she was left with little money and a young child to care for. She said her friends helped for a while and then she remarried and had Ruthie. When her second husband left, she couldn't take care of both of you and work at the same time. There were no baby-sitters then, so she did the next best thing she could think of, and that was to leave you with her mother and father on the farm. It almost broke her heart but she didn't want either of you to know how bad she felt.

"She could have put the two of you in an orphanage, you know. Louise, I hope my telling you all this will make a difference between you and your mother. You judge her too harshly, you know. She did the best she could under the circumstances. We all have to live with what life gives us."

In spite of myself, tears run freely down my face. Poor Mama. "I'm glad you told me, but she should have told me herself. She could have explained. It might have made a difference in our lives. It doesn't seem fair, does it?"

Mrs. K reaches in her apron pocket and hands me a clean hankie. "Well, Louise, I . . ."

"It's as if she was trying to live the past over," I interrupt. "Every time she has a new baby, she gives the old one away. If only I had known. Don't you see? It isn't fair, Mrs. K." I bury my head in her lap and she strokes my hair.

"Now don't fret, Louise, look on the bright side. You're strong and healthy. You're going to have a sweet little girl of your own soon, and deep down in your heart you know your mother loves you."

"Right now I don't want to think anymore."

"Oh, mercy, have I said too much?" She gives a nervous laugh and flutters her handkerchief.

It isn't until I am in my bed for the night that I suddenly remember the photograph from Gram's trunk. Who was the baby in Gram's arms? Was that Mama's baby, too? No, she was too young to have a baby at least I think she was. Mama's baby? It couldn't be, but if it was, what happened to it?

I slump down not knowing if I'll ever want to get up again. Somehow I still can't put this whole story of my mother together.

Mama. I've always thought of her as a happy-go-lucky, think-only-of-herself kind of person. It was what life handed her that made her the way she is, but it still doesn't explain why Gram has had it in for mama all through those years.

The room fills with a cold silence, and if I don't change my thinking, the past is going to suck me under and I will disappear. I can't bear that anymore than I can bear hearing more about Mama.

CHAPTER 54

"Mrs. K," I clear my throat. "About my dress? I was wondering . . . could it be green, and roomy enough to fit over my stomach? White won't do, you know. But don't you think green would be suitable, with my eyes and all?"

"I think green would be lovely, Louise, dear, don't you worry about a thing." She reaches over and pats my tummy. "You know how good I am at adjusting things to fit."

She is back to being her jolly, roly-poly self again, after our talk a few nights ago.

"I'd like to start knitting something for my baby, too," I say. "She'll need a jacket when I take her out in her carriage. Do you think I can make one?"

I know I can, even without Mrs. K saying so. Something inside tells me, these days, I can handle just about anything.

"I'm sure you can, dearie, and I just might have exactly the right pattern for you to use."

She struggles to her feet. "Will you be using blue or pink yarn?" she asks, giving me a knowing smile.

"Pink, of course," I laugh; glad things are near perfect again. "And thank you, Mrs. K." I trail my hand along her arm as she heads toward the door. She smiles and nods, knowingly.

"Why don't you get dressed, Louise," Mrs. K says. "Go for a little walk. You need some exercise. Now that you've stopped working, you don't get out much."

Maybe she thinks I'm gaining too much weight. "Yes, Mrs. K. I'll ask Ellie if she wants to go with me."

"Oh, didn't I tell you, Louise? Ellie isn't home. She went to see her old friend Helen."

Helen again. I suppose Ellie will tell her all about my being in the family way. They'll probably have a good laugh. Well let them. I'm the one who might be marrying Johnny, and I'm the one who's going to have a beautiful baby of my very own.

"I guess I don't feel up to a walk after all," I say. "I'll get dressed and just stay in my room for a while."

"Suit yourself, Louise. I'll be down in the kitchen if you need me."

I'm glad Mrs. K told me those things about my father, but I wish it had been Mama doing the telling. I think it would have been good for her to tell me herself. I'd feel like a real daughter if she would only talk to me as an adult.

I walk to the mailbox, bring in and sort the mail, then go up to my room for a nap.

A post card from Ruthie mailed July 1928.

Dear Weez,

The picture on this post card is someone I don't know but she sort of looks like Gram. I am sending it to you. I am okay so don't worry. Homer is not as nice as I thought. He spent all the egg money and stole some more from a store. He gets jobs and when he doesn't spend it all we mostly get along fine but not always. I'm sorry he took Gram's medicine. It's funny but I miss you. Your sister, Ruthie.

At least she is keeping in touch, but I do worry about her. I close my eyes and finally fall asleep, and I dream.

There is a child. She has fallen into the fast-moving current of a raging river, amidst ice floes and frothy blue-white water. She is being carried downstream toward a giant waterfall. I stand on the shore helpless to do anything. People jump in, but they can't save her. I stand watching, screaming silently, while no one can hear me. Gradually the dream fades and, not knowing who the child is, I wake up in a cold sweat with my heart pounding. Does this happen to all young girls that are expecting an unexpected baby?

CHAPTER 55

No matter how hard I try, I can't reach the buttons on the back of my dress. "Baby face, you've got the cutest little . . ." "Drat these buttons."

"Is that supposed to be singing?" Ellie asks as she stands in my doorway. "Sounds like the cry of a wounded weasel to me. What are you so happy about, anyway?"

My cheeks heat up. "Sorry, I didn't know anyone was listening. Can you help me with these?"

"Sure." She turns me around and buttons me up.

"Thanks," I sigh. "We all can't have voices like yours, Ellie. Besides my voice isn't so bad. Johnny doesn't mind it."

"He'd say you sounded like Bessie Smith herself, if it would make you happy. What's going on, anyway? Why are you changing clothes at this hour?"

"He's coming over so we can work on wedding plans."

"You wearing that old thing again, Louise?"

I stamp my foot. "I can't help it if this *old thing* is the only thing that fits!"

"I'm sorry, Louise. I keep forgetting how touchy you are these days. Must be because you're . . . well, you know. Helen told me her sister gets that way, too, when she's in the family way."

"Oh, It's okay. Just tell me if it looks okay in the back." I'm dying to know what Helen said about me, but I'm not about to ask.

"The middle one won't reach the buttonhole," Ellie giggles.

"Just leave that one unbuttoned. It's in the back; no one will notice."

"It will be our little secret, Weez." She giggles again.

"Ellie, quit trying to be cute, and I've asked you before, don't call me that. Just tell me if I look okay."

"You look like the cat's meow and you're glowing like a new mommy, or should I say, like a soon-to-be new mommy."

If she doesn't stop teasing before Johnny gets here . . . I reach around to the back, but I can't button the middle button, either. I know she's dying to hear what Johnny thinks about the baby and everything. Well, she can just keep wondering. It's none of her business.

"He should be here any minute, Ellie. Please don't embarrass him by talking about the baby. You know how shy he is. Just don't say anything that will hurt his feelings."

"Listen, kiddo, I've known him a lot longer than you have. I know just how much teasing he can take before he gets that pout-y mouth of his going. I used to tease him about Helen all the time."

"Ellie. I don't want to hear it!"

"Okay, okay, Weez, calm down. I'm sorry."

"Look, I'm a little tired. Do you mind?" Every time I'm just about to forget he ever had that Helen for a girlfriend, someone brings her up again, and don't call me Weez!"

"Look, I'll never mention her again, I Promise. And I won't call you 'Weez,' even if it *is* a spiffy nickname. I'm going downstairs. See you later, kiddo."

I ease back onto the bed so as not to wrinkle my dress. Should take it off, but I just need to close my eyes for a minute. It's only two o'clock. He won't be here till later.

"Hey, Louise. When are you going to wake up? It's seven o'clock. We've finished supper already."

"Seven o'clock? Why didn't somebody wake me?" I sit up, and for a second the room spins. I rub my eyes. "Tell him I'll be right down."

"Johnny's not here, Louise. Thought you said he was supposed to come at six."

"He said he'd be here at six. He told me he was getting back from maneuvers this morning. You mean he never showed up?"

"No he didn't. Mom and I finished supper hours ago. She fixed you a plate. It's in the ice box."

"Tell her never mind. I'm not hungry." I can't imagine why Johnny didn't show up, or at least call. We were going to talk wedding plans. Ellie seems so full of concern, but I bet she's gloating inside. I've always wondered if she really wanted Johnny to marry me at all.

"Maybe he had an accident," Ellie gasps. He could be lying somewhere . . ."

Panic grips my stomach before I see she's teasing again. But it could be true. His family would surely let me know. Maybe he just didn't want to come. I feel sick. It's his mother. I know it is. Does she think this baby will just disappear if we don't get married? How can she not want him to marry me, not want a granddaughter? She should know I'd make good wife and mother.

Heading for the door, Ellie stifles a giggle.

"Ellie. Johnny may be hurt somewhere and you're laughing. You think that's funny?"

"You can't believe that, Louise. I think he plum forgot."

"Just go, Ellie. Tell your mother I don't want any supper."

I lay back on the bed. If he's decided he doesn't want me, or the baby, what will I do? I close my eyes, letting the room disappear, the house, the street, the lump in my stomach, everything. That black pit of loneliness creeps in again, spreading up through my legs, my arms. I feel like I'm floating up into a dark, empty sky all by myself. Maybe I'm going crazy. I wonder if there is any of that in our family, besides being in Gram and Ruthie and Mama.

For the next two days I hardly eat anything, and Johnny still doesn't show up. Sleep comes in fitful snatches as strange images in pink sweaters haunt my dreams. I'm back on the farm. Ruthie and me jump into huge piles of leaves. We jump slowing as if time was threatening to stop us altogether.

When I finally feel like getting out of bed, everything goes black. The last thing I remember is the sound of glass breaking.

"Open your eyes, Louise. Drink this." Mrs. K is holding something to my lips. I shutter and push it away. It smells like whiskey.

"It's a good thing she didn't cut herself on that glass." I hear Ellie's voice through a thick fog. "She must have fainted."

A lot she knows. I never faint. If they don't stop making me drink this stuff, they'd better bring me a throw-up pan.

"Take it away," I sputter, my voice scratches like a rusty nail spiking a fence rail. "I don't want it. What happened?"

"You fell, Louise. You've been out like a light for hours." Ellie scowls.

"But don't you worry, dear, you'll be fine in no time." Mrs. K says. "The doctor said you might have a concussion, and we're not to let you sleep just yet. Louise, do you know your name?"

I stare up at her. Know my name? What does she mean, do I know my name. Why don't they leave me alone? I want to sleep, just sleep. Not wake 'til the baby . . . 'til the wedding . . . can't be a wedding without Johnny, but he's gone. Shouldn't be a baby without a father.

"Louise, dear, please, just tell me what your name is."

"My name is Louise, now leave me alone!"

"Oh, good! I guess you're all right, then," Mrs. K says. "The doctor said if you knew your name, we could let you sleep. Did you call her mother, Ellie?"

Mrs. K soothes my forehead and stares down at me. "Yes, I got through to her. She looks so pale, Ellie. Do you think she's all right?"

"You worry too much, Mom. Let her sleep. She'll be fine in the morning. It's just a little bump on the head."

They're talking about me as if I'm not even here. Maybe I'm not here. Maybe I've gone away, too. Disappeared with my baby, but there is no baby yet. No wedding, no Johnny, no nothing.

I wake as the heat of the morning sun floods into my room. Is that Mama's perfume I smell?

"Hi, honey," she says, pushing through the door holding a tray. "So you're finally awake."

It *is* Mama. What is she doing here? She sets the tray down and drapes a cold cloth across my forehead, half covering my eyes.

"Lucy, Mrs. K to you, tells me you haven't been eating enough to keep a bird alive for the last few days, and you cry during the night. What's the matter, Louise, you want to hurt that baby?"

She has circles under her eyes and her penciled-on eyebrows. Her lips are purple, probably from that new lip rouge she uses. Doesn't she know how spooky she looks?

"Just drink this before it gets cold," she says, handing me a cup of steaming tea. She presses a wet washcloth to my forehead. Water drips into my ears as I turn away. She grabs the cloth and drops it into the wastebasket by my bed.

"Don't you know you're going to make yourself sick if you don't eat?" she says wiping her wet hands on my quilt.

"He never showed up, did he?" I ask under my breath.

She wipes water drips from my face with her fingers. Her nails are painted orange-red. What is she doing here, anyway? I didn't think she cared a hoot about what happens to me.

"He's not worth it, honey. If you don't stop brooding about him, look at yourself. You look terrible. You don't want to lose this baby, do you?"

"Would you care if I did," I ask? She pulls back as if I'd hit her.

"Oh, Mama, I'm sorry, I didn't mean that."

I look at her mussed-up hair, her drawn features, and suddenly she looks old.

Gently, she pushes damp hair off my forehead. "We've got to get a comb through this hair of yours. You look like a war victim. Here, let me straighten your bedclothes."

She's trying to be nice, but what is my valise doing on the chair, and my closet is empty.

"Mama?" I manage to sit up. "You can't send me away, you know. I won't go."

"What makes you think I'm sending you away? You're coming home with me."

"But, you said . . ."

"Never mind what I said. I've moved Shirley in with me and Walt, and I've arranged for someone to take Dorothy for a while. Everything will be just fine, I promise."

I roll my eyes at the word, promise. "So it's Walt now, huh? It's hard to keep them straight. You know I'm keeping this baby, Mama."

"Of course you are, honey. We'll talk about that later. Meanwhile, get dressed. I had Lucy order us a taxicab on her telephone. It'll be here in less than an hour."

Saying good-bye to Mrs. K and Ellie isn't what I want to do, but it does feel good to have Mama caring for me. Even if I don't want to go to her house, it seems to be the thing I should do right now.

"I'll come see you after the baby's born, Louise," Ellie says grinning her toothy grin.

"You're going to be all right now, dear," Mrs. K says, bending close. "Didn't I tell you your mother would come around if you really needed her?"

"Thank you, Mrs. K. I'm glad we . . ." I lower my voice to a whisper. "I'm glad we had that talk." I lean toward her. "If you see Johnny, will you tell him . . . oh, I don't know what I want you to tell him."

She squeezes my hand. "Don't you worry, dearie, everything will turn out for the best. But we'll miss you, Louise."

"I'll miss you, too, Mrs. K. I'll come back and visit when I feel better. The baby isn't due for another four months. I'll come soon."

CHAPTER 56

In the back seat of the taxicab, Mama chatters on and on about nothing. It's not until she thinks I'm asleep that she moves closer, puts her arm around me, and lets my head lay on her shoulder. She runs her fingers through my hair and hums softly, stirring memories; memories of a mother who loved me once, a mother I still long for. I move slightly. She quickly moves away and clears her throat. "We're almost there," she says, dabbing at her eyes.

Mama newest child meets us at the door and rushes into Mama's arms. Shirley is already two years old and looks a lot like Ruthie. Behind her is an awkward looking girl about twelve. Mama slips her a handful of coins and the girl leaves.

Shirley hides behind Mama's skirt and points to me. "Who's that?"

"Shirl, baby, say hello to your big sister, Louise. She'll be staying with us for a while."

Shirley peeks out and gives me a slant-eyed look.

"Hey, Shirley," I say, wondering if this new one is going to be ornery like Ruthie, or sweet-natured like little Dottie.

Shirley sucks on her thumb and grins up at me. "Wanna' see my toys?"

Before I can answer, she grabs my hand and we walk through the apartment toward her room. Mama's apartment seems grim, with high ceilings and full-length windows half covered by heavy, maroon drapes. The living room is tightly packed with over-stuffed chairs and a saggy maroon sofa. Off to one side is a small dining room, so perfect it looks unused. A square table is set with four place settings of dishes, silverware, and glasses. Four straight-backed chairs with pink and white gingham cushions are pushed up to the table.

"This is my room," Shirley says as she leads me toward a small bedroom. She rummages in a large toy box, pulling out stuffed animals, blocks and dolls, and tossing them on to the floor until she finally finds the thing she is looking for. It is a black and white, stuffed cat. "Mama don't like this one," she says as she gives it a noisy kiss and tosses it on the floor. Her chubby little fingers pull out a small shoebox. She lifts the lid and tosses out layers of tissue paper.

My throat catches. The box is filled with Ruthie's carved animals. Mama must have taken them when she went to get Gram.

She hands me a small wooden pig. "You can hold him, but Mama says, '*be careful*'.

I ease myself down beside her on the floor as she pulls them out, one by one, making the appropriate animals sounds for each animal. Ruthie's animals, the sheep, the pig, two chickens, and the first one she ever carved, the rough white pine horse with its too-long tail and one ear missing. I can almost hear Gramp's patient words as he guided Ruthie's hands.

She must be fifteen by now. No telling where she is, or what kind of trouble she's gotten herself into. I finger the little white horse. She could have been an artist. I wonder if she ever got her hair to behave? She always said I paid too much attention to mine, back then. She was right, and now my hair is short and dark, and I don't care how it looks. Maybe I shouldn't wish my daughter to have long, blond curls to fuss over. She's got to learn it's what's inside her head that counts.

Mama yells from the kitchen. "Shirley, honey, go wash your hands before supper."

"You're eating for two now," Mama scolds, as she heats up a can of hash."

"Can I help?" I ask, and she shakes her head.

"You need your rest, honey, I'm fixing diner," she says as she opens a can of string beans and a jar of mixed fruit. We don't talk much during supper. I do my best to keep my feelings safe inside while Shirley carries on a conversation with her stuffed cat and peppers me with questions.

"You gonna have a baby?" "Where's the daddy?" "Will you read to me?" "Can you have the baby now so I can see it?" "If it cries too much can we send it back?"

During the next few weeks, while Mama is at work, I spend the afternoons on her dark maroon sofa knitting and re-knitting the pink baby jacket, reading to Shirley, and answering her endless questions. She rattles off her ABC's, and her numbers up to ten, sometimes to twelve. We build Tinker Toys houses and have tea parties, and I pretend she is my little girl.

Every evening Mama fixes dinner. The night she let the canned beans burn and the house filled with smoke, we ended up having peanut butter and banana sandwiches. I can't wait 'til she sees my cookbook with Gram's recipes.

Whenever I mention Gram, Mama rolls her eyes, but I won't let her change the subject. When Shirley is safe in bed in the evenings, Mama brings us coffee in the living room and I pepper her with questions.

"Did Gram mind leaving the farm? What was she like when she was here?" Mama sighs, settles back, and lights up one of her endless cigarettes, even after I tell her I'm not supposed to be around smoke filled rooms.

"Your grandmother turned out to be quite a handful," she says, pausing as she aims smoke toward the ceiling. "I had to watch her every minute. She'd do crazy things like pour her medicine down the toilet, and swear in German at our neighbors. She threw all my plants out the window, said they should be in the ground outside. Once she let the tub run over, nearly ruined my floors . . . nearly got us evicted. She kept sneaking out of the house.

She blows a final stream of smoke toward the ceiling."I couldn't keep her here." She looks around for an ashtray and ends up crushing her cigarette in her saucer. "Anyway, she's better off at the county home. They'll watch her good."

"You mean the poor house," I say hoping she sees how I feel about her dumping Gram. "Isn't that what they call it? If you had me staying here, I could have watched her."

Mama stiffens. "And where would you all sleep? No, it wouldn't have worked, Louise, trust me."

"Trust *you*?" The words come out before I can stop them.

"Listen," Mama snaps back. "You think it was easy sending her away? You tell me, what else could I do? Besides, she's better off there. Can't you understand that?"

I bite my lip, fearing a real argument might wake Shirley.

"I go to see her every week, you know," Mama says, as if that makes the poor house okay. "So," she continues, sinking down next to me on the sofa. "Let's talk." She clears her throat, rubs her hands together, dismissing any more talk of Gram. "Let's talk about you and your plans."

"*My* plans? You want to discuss *my* plans after all these years. Swell." Does she think she can just snap her fingers and we will sit, like good old mother-daughter friends, and she can plan my life, my future? I want to shake her, scream at her.

She smiles weakly, shrugs, and nods, her eyebrows in their perpetual questioning position. "Come on, Louise. Get off your high horse."

My throat tightens but I steady my voice. "Look, Mama, we already know I'm having a baby in a few months and I don't have a husband, and you said there won't be room for me here after the baby's born, which means I can't stay with you. Johnny probably doesn't want me, so there won't be a wedding, and I won't have any money coming in. I don't think there's any more to say about *my plans,* do you?" I boost myself up. "I want to get to bed to bed."

I hurry toward the bathroom but Mama is tight on my heels. Why can't she leave me alone?

"Thought we might . . . talk, Louise, but . . ."

"That's just the way it is, Mama, and I can't do anything about it." I stand at the window. "*You* of all people should understand that."

A blanket of sudden rain turns the air to a sultry gray, giving off a damp, musty smell; the same smell the old stonewalls on the farm had after a hard rain. Memories come flooding in, and with them, more tears. Does she think she can make it all right by talking everything out now? She could have answered my letters.

"Sit down, Louise," she says, smoothing me a place next to her on my bed. I stay standing. "Tell me about this Johnny of yours. He *is* the father of your baby, isn't he?"

"I told you he was, and things haven't changed since then." She can rile me so fast.

Then where is he anyway? Why isn't he here?"

"I don't know." I squirm under her questions, finding comfort in my crossed fingers. She pats the bed again and I sit, like a well-trained puppy.

"It's like this," I say, biting my lip, trying not to give her the satisfaction of tears. "A month ago he went off on maneuvers. Did I tell you he's in the National Guard? He told me he would be gone only a couple of days. He said, when he got back he would come by and we would talk, make wedding plans. I don't know what happened but he never showed up, and I don't know what to think."

"He hasn't gotten in touch with you since he left?"

"No, he hasn't called or anything, and it's been over a month." My voice goes higher as it does when I'm about to cry. "I keep thinking something might have happened to him. He could have gotten hurt."

She hands me her lacy handkerchief. "Or maybe he lied and never wants to see me again. If that's the case," I sniff and turn away, "I never want to see *him* again, either!"

For a moment Mama doesn't say a word. I hope she understands how I'm hoping she knows how I feel about people who lie to me. I thought my tears were all used up, but more come and drip down my cheeks again.

"Stop that blubbering, Louise. Crying isn't going to help."

She hands me a large, white-ironed pocket-handkerchief. H. F. is embroidered in the corner, the initials of one of her husbands, no doubt.

"We've got to think what's best for you, Louise."

I bite my tongue; best for me? Best for *her* is what she means. "I'm tired, Mama, and if you are hinting that I don't want this baby, well you can stop right now. I'll be leaving quietly in a few days, go somewhere far away and have my baby. You can forget all about me, and my little girl. But I want you to know this: I am *not* ever going to give her up. I'll work in a factory, beg, steal, I'll do anything, but I won't give her up."

"How do you know it's going to be a girl?"

Has she even heard what I've been saying? "Mrs. K said it will be a girl," I blurt out starting to cry again.

"Oh, so Lucy Kamens said that, did she? Well, what does she know?" She squints and studies my face. "But, now that I get a good look at you, she might be right. Could be a girl, but if you don't stop bawling like a sick cow, that child won't know how to smile until she's at least a year old. Blow your nose, for God's sake."

"I just don't know what to do. I still love him, Mama, but I never want to see him again as long as I live, and I *don't* want him to see our baby, ever."

"Well, for the moment he's out of the picture. I guess I'll have to put you up here for a while until we can . . . make other arrangements."

I stand up. "Mama, you can't make me give up my baby. I'll never let you, never!"

"Well, it's about time you showed some gumption, Louise."

I look down at her, ready to fight. "How can you talk to me like that? I wouldn't be in this mess if you'd been more of a mother to me. It's your fault that Ruthie ran away, too."

Her eyes flash and her face flushes. "I did the best I could. Can't you understand that?"

"That's what Mrs. K said, but I still find it hard to believe."

"She's been talking to you, has she?"

A full thirty seconds pass as Mama studies me, as if she's seeing me for the first time. A kindness softens her eyes, a kindness I hardly remember. She speaks softly and nods.

"You're right, Louise. I can't make you do anything. You'll have to work some things out for yourself. You can stay here with me as long as you need to. Who knows, maybe your Johnny will come back, after all."

"How come you changed your mind?"

She shakes her head. "You wouldn't understand. You never could understand." Now *her* eyes tear up. Mascara trails down one cheek. I want to reach out to her, but what if she pushes me away again?

"You're tired, Louise. Let's get some sleep. We'll talk in the morning."

I give my nose a final blow. "Good night," I grumble, backing away before either of us has the urge to move close.

CHAPTER 57

In the middle of the night something wakes me. For a second I forget where I am. I grab the quilt and wrap it around me. The living room is half lit from the corner streetlight. The door rattles. I freeze. Mama appears with her hair in curlers. She tiptoes toward me. Her pink nightgown glows in the dim light.

"Mama . . . Someone's out there." I whisper.

"Hush, Louise. Stay close by me."

My heart is in my throat. I can hardly breathe. The door rattles. Someone is testing the lock.

"It's bolted, isn't it?" I whisper.

She nods and puts her finger to her lips.

"Maybe it's Walter, Mama."

"Walt's got a key."

"Mama, I'm scared."

"Wait here," she says as she heads for the kitchen. She comes back toting a broom.

"A lot of good that'll do if it's a burglar," I whisper.

The knob jiggles again. Mama snaps on the light.

"Get away from that door," she hollers, her voice an octave lower than normal. She hands me the broom and grabs a heavy bookend, sending books crashing to the floor.

"We're calling the police," I call out, forgetting Mama doesn't have a telephone.

The knocking stops and a low voice whispers, "Louise? You in there?"

"Johnny? Is that you? What are you doing here?" I start toward the door but Mama stops me.

"I've got to talk to you, Louise. Open the door."

"I've been so worried. I thought you might be dead."

"Just let me in."

"Go away, Johnny. I don't want to see you".

Mama grabs my arm. "Now wait just a minute, Louise. You don't want to send him away until you hear what he has to say. Maybe he has a good reason for being away. Maybe he still wants you."

"He wouldn't be coming in the middle of the night to talk wedding plans. He probably came to say good-bye."

"Now be sensible, young lady. Why would he come in the middle of the night to say good-bye?"

She heads toward the door.

I grab her arm. "Wait, Mama. I haven't decided yet."

Mama rolls her eyes, and Johnny knocks again.

"Come on, Louise, open the door, Listen to me."

I don't say a word.

"Louise?" he pleads, a touch of panic in his voice.

"Don't be a ninny, girl. Answer him," Mama whispers.

"Don't start on me, Mama."

Johnny bangs on the door again.

Mama raises her voice. "Stop that racket out there. You want to wake the whole neighborhood?" She reaches for the knob.

"Wait Mama, let me handle this." I stand in her way but she pushes past me.

"Stop right there," I shout, with a voice that even scares me. "If anyone lets him in, it's going to be *me*."

Mama's head snaps around. She stares as me as if she's seeing me for the first time. She puts the broom down and smiles.

Everything is so quiet I can hear the kitchen clock ticking.

"Well, what's it going to be?" Johnny asks through the door. "I'll leave if you tell me to. I'll walk right out of your life. It's up to you, Louise."

I pull the quilt tight around me. It drags across the floor as I walk towards the door. Slowly I unlock the bolt, and there he is in his crumpled uniform. New stripes decorate his sleeve, and a smile lights up his face. My heart melts at the sight of him.

"Johnny!" I sigh as he pulls me close. His beard is like a cat's tongue against my cheek, and I breath in his smell. He pats my stomach and I blush.

"Ahem," Mama clears her throat.

I take a deep breath. "Mama, I'd like you to meet Johnny. He's the . . . I mean, he's . . . ."

"Never mind, Honey, I know who he is and *what* he's been up to." She looks him up and down, just as Ruthie did the first time she saw him.

He takes off his uniform cap. "It's nice to meet you, Ma'am. I'm Louise's, ah . . . that is, I'm her . . . friend."

"*Friend*?" Mama turns her flat-over eyebrows toward me and shrugs. "So," she says, fluffing up like a hen about to settle a brood of chicks, "and what have you got to say for yourself, young man? I thought you'd be five states away by now."

"Mama, please!"

"Please, what?" she says, starting to take over again.

But not this time, this time I won't let her. "If you don't mind, Mama, I'd like to speak to Johnny alone." My words sting with meaning, and it feels good. "Could you make us a cup of tea or something? *Mother*? In the kitchen . . . *please*?"

Mama stands barefoot, staring up at me. I hadn't realized, but without her high heels, I'm almost about four inches taller than she is.

She pushes a stray lock of hair behind one curler and hums softly as she minces toward the kitchen.

I turn giving him my full attention. "You were gone so long, Johnny. I was so scared, I didn't know whether to worry or curl up and die."

He leads me to the sofa. "It wasn't my fault, Louise. It was the damn Guard. They extended our maneuvers. Didn't even tell us where we were going. Wouldn't let us send word home, no letters, no phone calls. Hell, they treated us like a bunch of snot-nosed kids. Made us march and drill in all kinds of weather for days. We lived on hash and canned beans," I never want to see another stinking can of . . ."

"I don't give a hoot about what you ate, Johnny. What about *us*?"

He moves a few inches away and clears his throat. "Well, Louise, I've had time to think and, well, I've made a decision."

My heart drops. He *did* come to tell me we're not getting married. I pull away. He pats my knee and smiles.

"How can you smile at a time like this?" My eyes full up and my voice hardens. "Just leave if you want to; just go."

"Who said anything about leaving? This kid's got to have a father, doesn't it? Besides, your mother will have my hide if I run off." He puts his arm around my shoulder. "Now, about the wedding . . ."

For a minute I stop listening. He said wedding; we're going to get married, be a family, and my baby will have a father.

" . . . and" he continues, "Ma said we should go over the state line into New York and get it done by a justice of the peace."

"*Get it done?*" I pull away. "Sounds like you're having a tooth pulled or having a mole removed. You're talking about our *wedding*."

"I mean the legal part, you know . . . to get it over with."

"What about my green dress with the jacket?"

"Green dress?" He wrinkles his nose. "What has a dress got to do with anything? At least with a justice of the peace it won't take long."

"Maybe we should just skip the whole thing."

"Geez, Louise. I know you wanted a real wedding, but let's face it, you wouldn't want to walk down the aisle with a . . . you know, a big lump in your stomach, would you?"

"And whose fault is this *lump*, anyway? If we had waited, you wouldn't have to deal with this *lump* at all. You, and your German-hating parents would be off the hook. You'd better go. Just go, and marry that Helen person for all I care."

His brow tightens and his mouth pouts.

Why did I say that? He hasn't mentioned Helen since the first time he told me about her.

"Well, if that's the way you feel about it, maybe I will." He stands and heads toward the door.

"Ohoo!" I gasp, arching my back against the sofa.

"What's the matter? You all right?"

"It's the baby. It's kicking again. Hard this time."

"Does it hurt? What should I do?" He pales under his scruffy beard.

"It doesn't hurt, it just feels . . ." I take his hand and place it where I think her foot might be.

"Now hold your hand right here. Can you feel it?"

He leans down, cocks his head, and listens.

"She's not going to talk to you, silly." I move his hand. "Right there, feel it?"

"I felt it. Wow!"

"She does it all the time."

"Must be a hockey player you've got in there."

"Hockey player? Not if I have anything to say about it. She can be anything she wants to be in this world, but not a hockey player."

Mama comes in with a tray of tea things and sets them on the coffee table. She has put on a fresh robe, combed her hair, and added lip rouge to her mouth. The three of us sit close on Mama's sofa, Johnny on one side of me, Mama on the other.

"Sugar?" Mama asks.

"No thank you," we say in unison.

Milk?" We shake our heads.

"Fig Newton? They're fresh." We ignore her.

"Tell you what, Louise," Johnny leans forward. "How about if we look for an apartment, then go over the state line to New York, get the paper stuff done, and while we're there we can stop for the night at a fancy hotel. Then, when we get back, we can fix the place up and make a room for the baby."

Mama looks from one of us to the other, and smiles. She is probably glad I won't be living with her anymore.

"We'll move in as soon as we get back," he continues. "I'll get Pop to help me paint. That way we'll have it all finished by the time the kid is born."

He sounds almost happy, and he's right about the wedding. I *would* look silly walking down the aisle with my big stomach. I love him so much, and if everything goes as planned, we'll be married before the baby is born.

"Wait, Johnny," I say, as he's getting ready to leave. "I'm not sure I can marry you."

"WHAT?" he shouts. "All this talk about getting married and now you say you're not sure?"

"There's something missing," I say, shaking my head.

His eyes narrow and his mouth pouts. "What the hell's missing, Louise?"

"You haven't *asked* me. You haven't proposed in a proper way. The magazines say . . ."

He sighs and his mouth softens. I can tell he isn't really mad. Then, with a few creeks and grunts, he kneels in front of me and takes my hands in his. They are rough and warm and strong, and I love him.

"Louise?" his voice trembles. "Will you do me the honor of becoming my wife?"

My heart leaps and I feel faint. If only he had asked six months ago.

"Yes, Johnny, I'll marry you, on one condition."

He groans, "Now what?"

"Tell me you love me. Say it. You've only said it once, you know."

He pulls his hands away. "Would I be asking you to marry me if I didn't?"

"Say it, Johnny. Just say it!" He looks down at my stomach and hesitates for a mere second.

"I love you, Louise, I . . ."

"That was perfect, Johnny. Thank you. I love you, too. Won't we make the niftiest parents?"

Johnny stays until after two in the morning. I watch as he walks through the August darkness toward his car. With a little help from me, he's going to make a swell daddy.

If I could push back the clock and do it all over again, I would, and things would be different. There would be no need to head over the state line to a justice of the peace. We would have a wonderful wedding, with a preacher and bridesmaids and a best man, with Johnny in a freshly pressed uniform and me in a real wedding gown, with the lace veil from Gram's trunk. We would fix up an apartment and *then* think about having a baby. I wonder if Mama ever had at least one *real* wedding?

Before I finally go to bed, I write a short note to Mrs. K.

July 1928

Dear Mrs. K,

Just wanted you to know, it's going to happen. Johnny proposed. Please tell Ellie. I doubt it will be a church wedding, but at least it will be legal. I miss you both so much and will come to see you soon. Sincerely, Louise

CHAPTER 58

Mama is heading for the door as I wake up. "Can you make the kid breakfast, Louise? I've got to hurry. I'm late as it is. You'll find stuff in the icebox. I'll be home about six. Good bye."

The springs in the sofa have made impressions in my back, but for the first time in months, I wake feeling happy. Johnny is back and we're going to be married.

I make breakfast for Shirley, oatmeal, and cinnamon toast with the crusts cut off. All the while she chatters, I wonder if Johnny has thought about a honeymoon. I boil an egg for myself.

Mama's kitchen is not what I want at all. I look in her cupboards and drawers. There are no baking pans, no mixing bowls, not even a set of measuring spoons. How does she manage? She never was much for cooking. I remember lunches were often canned sardines sandwiches, sometimes Jell-O for dessert. As I clean up Mama's kitchen I plan what my kitchen will look like in our new apartment.

Shirley and I play go fish and draw pictures in her scrapbook most of the afternoon. We have a pretend tea party with her dolls and her little tin tea set. I wonder if Mama ever takes time to play with her like this. During the second reading of *Goldilocks and the Three Bears*, my eyes begin to close.

Shirley helps me make our lunch of toasted cheese sandwiches cut into triangles, and we sit on the floor for another reading of *The Three Bears*. I put her down for her nap and stretch out on the sofa.

What will it be like staying overnight in a hotel with Johnny? We haven't done anything since that first time in his car. Maybe he won't want to do it while I'm so pregnant . . . maybe we're not supposed to . . . what if he never wants to do it again? It's got to feel better than that first time.

Shirley, where are you? Mama will be home any minute. We've got to get you cleaned up." I hear muffled giggles coming from Mama's bedroom.

"Find me," she sings out from deep in Mama's closet.

"I don't think Mama wants you messing in there, Shirley. What are you doing?"

She comes out of the closet in a pair of high heals and trailing one of Mama's boas. She is holding a cigar box. "I found my crayons."

"Your crayons wouldn't be in here. Let's go look in your room."

"They're in this box," she squeals, holding a shoebox in both hands. She stumbles, the box falls. Several packets of paper tied in ribbons spill out across Mama's rose-colored carpet.

"Where are my crayons? Shirley cries, stamping her foot.

"They are probably in another box in your room. I'll put these things back before Mama . . . Wait a minute," I whisper as she gallops off trailing the boa.

My letters, these are my letters. She kept them. She didn't bother to answer, but she kept them. She must have read them because the envelopes are ripped open. I hold them close remembering the hurt of not getting answers. There is something else in the bottom of the box, held together with Gram's yarn. It is the coil of my blond curls. Tears blur them into circles of gold and I press them to my cheek.

"I found 'em," Shirley yells from her room, as I carefully place the curls and the letters in their box. "I want paper, Louise, so I can draw a picture for my mommy."

I replace the box on the shelf in the closet, just as keys fumble in the lock.

Shirley giggles and hides behind a chair. Don't let her find me," she whispers, as Mama unlocks the door and comes in. Her hair is mussed and her makeup worn off. She looks old and worn.

Too excited to stay hidden, Shirley runs to her. "Mommy!" "Get off me," she snaps. "You want to knock me over?" For the first time I see Shirley stick her thumb in her mouth.

CHAPTER 59

August 1928

Dear Mama,

> *You may now call me Mrs. Johnny Paulsen. We were married on the 15th of this month. I am enclosing our new address. I don't want you to come visit until we have the place looking swell. Then I'll invite you over. Johnny is now an officer with the Police Department in West Hartford. He likes his job. His odd shifts will be hard for me. I'll be serving him breakfast at my suppertime, eating toast and cereal when he comes home wanting a hot dinner. I don't know what I'll do after the baby comes. Johnny will be sleeping during the day and I'll have to keep her quiet. Guess life is never the way we plan is it Mama? Sincerely, Louise*

Being married isn't like I thought it would be. I do all the cooking and cleaning and shopping. On the farm there was Gram and Ruthie to help. Johnny doesn't seem to think it's his job to do any of what he calls, 'women's work'.

It's a lot different than going dancing every Saturday night and having parties. And I don't like going to bed alone. I always thought going to bed with someone you love would be exciting and, well . . . wonderful. But it isn't, and I'm so pregnant, and tired all the time. When we *do* go to bed at the same time Johnny is usually tired and too cross to cuddle. And we can't really make love, not with me being so pregnant. It isn't what I dreamed of. My only hope is that it will get better after the baby comes, but I'm not even sure what I mean by *better*. The magazines say something happens when people are in love, so that everything turns out right.

Sometimes just before falling asleep, I wonder if Johnny really loves me, and would he have married me if he hadn't gotten me pregnant?

He wanted time to be on his own, to be away from his family, a chance to breath. I remember him saying he wanted to wait until he was thirty before he married and start a family. "A chance to live a little before I settle down," he'd said. Well, what happened in the back seat of his car certainly wasn't my fault. But he'll be all right after the baby comes. The baby will make everything all right. I'm sure of it.

I love our apartment. It's in an old, gray, three-story house. It looks like a regular one-family place from the outside, but each floor is a separate apartment. Ours is the one on the second floor, and getting all that furniture up those stairs wasn't easy, especially with his kid brothers doing the helping.

"Johnny, why do we have to take all the stuff your parents want to get rid of?" I ask, as I iron and fold dozens of old dish towels? "Can't we give some of it back?"

He grunts either a yes or a no, I can't tell which. I didn't expect him to answer. He can't very well refuse to take what they offer. "Weld never hear the end of it if we did," he said.

I worry about his mother. His father is okay, but his mother doesn't like me. I don't like her much either, so I guess that makes us even. She blames *me* for getting pregnant. She'll probably hate my baby, too. It's going to be a while before I invite her to our apartment, even after we get settled.

As soon as we got back from New York and moved into our apartment, Johnny and his father started painting. Johnny let me pick the colors for each room. I could see his father wasn't happy with my choices, but I'm the one who has to live with them.

Johnny and his father don't talk while they work. It's as if they don't even know each other, much less are related. Johnny is doing a swell job, but his father complains every chance he gets. I bring them coffee and sandwiches, and try to fill the silences with small talk. The smell of the paint makes me feel sick, but I stay with them anyway, just to make sure they don't blow up at each other.

Then, after days of moving, painting, and cleaning up, they finish.

"Oh, it's just what I wanted. The colors are perfect," I say to Johnny's father, not knowing whether I should call him, Mr. Paulsen or Father Paulsen, or Dad or what. The baby will probably call him, Grampa.

I hug Johnny, and would like to do the same to his father, but he'd probably have a heart attack. It didn't take me long to learn the Paulsen's' aren't much for showing affection. Not a hug or a pat on the shoulder, or a kindly wink of an eye. Instead, when Johnny's father is ready to leave, he shakes my hand, and without even a goodbye to his son, he walks out the door. Maybe Danes are like that.

Johnny cleans the last of the paintbrushes in the kitchen sink, Instead of drying his hands on one of the old castoff dishtowels from his mother, he uses one of my best new ones.

"I'm beat," he says. "Think I'll get a couple of hours sleep before I have to get ready for work."

"I could come lie down with you," I say, straightening the towel.

"Listen, honey. I just want to get some rest. It's been a long day, you know."

I turn away. I can see he knows he's hurt my feelings. He reaches for my hand.

"Never mind," I say, pulling away."

"Gosh, Louise, don't be so damn touchy."

"Why don't you just come right out and say it, Johnny. I look awful and you don't love me. You never did."

"Look, Louise. I told you, I'm just tired."

"*You're* tired? Do you think it's easy carrying this baby around all day? I spend hours cooking for you, scrubbing your dirty clothes, I even iron your underwear, and who do you think keeps the house clean? Did you think your mother comes over and does it?"

"Just leave my mother out of this, will you?" He balls up his fists and stalks off to the bedroom. I wonder if he wanted to hit me.

I sink down into the chair with the doilies. "And next time you go to your mother's house," I yell, "take her damn chair with you. It isn't even comfortable, and you can fix your own breakfast."

"Aw, hell. Have it your own way, Louise. I'll eat at the diner. Right now I need to get some sleep." He slams the door and I'm left alone after our first real fight.

Hot tears trickle down my face. What is the matter with me? I shouldn't act that way. Doesn't he know all I want is for him to show me a little affection? I pick at a worn place on the arm of the chair. Why did I have to mention his mother? I'll make his breakfast. Can't let him eat at the diner. I'll get the house smelling of coffee and bacon and eggs. 'The way to a man's heart,' the magazines say. I heave myself out of the chair and head toward the kitchen. I'll bake him my apple strudel, too.

I measure out flour, eggs, sugar, and spices, just like a good little wife. Maybe he'll forget how I look.

When he comes out of the bedroom he's dressed for work. I have his bacon cooking, his eggs ready and coffee on the stove, perking. I place the hot fresh-from-the-oven strudel next to his plate, and he smiles.

"Johnny," I say, pretending nothing has happened.

"Yah?" he answers, digging into his scrambled eggs that I fixed with tomato and cheese, just the way he likes them.

"Do you think your parents will like the baby?"

He looks up and pouts. "For cripes sakes, Louise. There you go again! Of course they'll like the baby, especially if it's a girl. Pop has always liked girls better than boys. Besides, if it's a boy, I'll have to paint that damn pink room all over again."

He shouldn't talk that way about the baby's room. Maybe he doesn't he want a daughter. I sit down and slice myself a large piece of strudel.

"Maybe next time we can hope for a boy," I say with a smile. We've never mentioned having another baby. I hope he doesn't want to stop at one.

"Yah, I guess," he finally answers. "Hey, can you wrap the rest of the coffee cake? I'll take it with me." He puts his coat on, grabs his cap, and helps me to my feet. He takes my face in both his hands and gently covers my lips with his.

"Let's not fight, Louise."

If my heart weren't beating so loud, I'd be hearing bells ringing. He hurries down the back stairs leaving me with a kitchen full of dirty dishes. I stand in front of one of the mirrors in our apartment. My eyes don't seem as green as they used to. They look tired. Maybe it's because my hair has turned darker, so different from my blond curls. I dampen my fingers and fix a curl on my cheek. I turn sideways, stare at myself as tears start to roll down my cheeks.

So what if I have a mother, who doesn't want me around? And in-laws who don't think much of me, and a husband who probably thinks I look like a balloon? If Gram were still around, but no, she always liked Ruthie best. Well, anyway, pretty soon I'll have my own baby, and I know she will make up for them all.

CHAPTER 60

It's eight o'clock in the morning. I have Johnny's dinner ready and warming in the oven. Meat loaf with apples and cheese, just like Gram's. Baked potato, yellow and green squash, and for dessert a chocolate cake with Grams special adding's.

I sit at the kitchen table, about to have my second cup of tea when I hear Johnny come banging up the back stairs. Usually he's slow and deliberate, and I can count every step. But this morning his step is light and quick, as if he can't wait to see me, or maybe he's just hungry.

There's not much I can do to make myself look presentable, but I push at my hair and pinch my cheeks. Maybe he'll notice. I close me eyes and pretend I'm napping. I hope he realizes I cooked his whole dinner this morning while it was still dark outside. How I'd love to slip back into our cozy warm bed and sleep for another hour, but this is what the eleven-to-seven shift is going to be like. I wonder if I'll ever get used to it.

He bursts in, bringing the crisp smell of autumn in with him.

"Louise? You awake?" I stifle a yawn and smile up at him. A yellow leaf clings to the sleeve of his jacket and I rescue it before it falls. I spin the stem slowly in my fingers, letting the leaf brush my cheek. The maples must have turned and I hadn't even noticed. A memory of Ruthie on the farm jumping into a pile of leaves skips crosses my mind, and my eyes fill with tears.

"You okay, Louise?"

I nod, wishing he'd take me in his arms and kiss me, but there's not even a peck on the cheek for me this morning. He's probably still thinking of last night.

"Your dinner's ready. It's in the oven," I say, turning away from him.

"I'm beat," he says. "Umm . . . Dinner smells damn good. Meat loaf, isn't it?

He hangs up his jacket and cap, unbuckles his belt and holster, and sets them on the high shelf in the closet. I hate having a gun in the house. He slips off his shoes and unbuckles his black leather puttees. He told me if he wears them long enough, they would rub the hair right off his legs.

In a minute he'll ask for a beer. He always wants a beer before dinner, and he'll expect me to bring it to him. Doesn't he realize I might be tired, too?

"A beer would sure hit the spot, Louise," he sighs as he stands his puttees next to each other in the closet, like two patent leather soldiers.

"I'll get it," I sigh, hoping he notices the tone of my voice.

"What did you say?" he asks, sinking deep into his mother's chair.

"Your beer, Johnny. I said I'll get it for you." The thought of drinking anything other than tea at this hour in the morning gives my stomach a turn. I'm going to hate this shift, but at least he doesn't sound mad about last night.

He makes half an effort to get out of his chair to get his own beer, but I can tell he's waiting for me to bring it to him.

"Don't bother, I'll get it for you." I gather myself up and aim toward the kitchen, hoping he'll stop me, but his eyes are already closed.

It's that chair, with the handmade doilies still pinned to the back and arms. I know his mother thinks I should learn to crochet. She never comes right out and says it, but I can tell it's what she's thinking. I can see it in her eyes. She gives me that look when she has a crochet hook in her hand, and a little nod. She always talks to me with her eyes. And when she calls up on our telephone, she never says, hello. It's just, *"Give me Johnny."* Guess I'll never understand her Danish ways.

"Can't think why I'm so tired," I say as I brush by his chair. "I haven't done much all day except sit around knitting on the baby's jacket. Had to rip out three whole inches. I forgot to cast off stitches where the sleeves should go," I say, wiping the bottom of the bottle on my robe before setting it in front of him.

"Thanks," he says gulping it down 'til it's almost gone. "I'm sure she'll love it, even with mistakes."

"I didn't say I make mistakes. I just said I had to . . . oh, never mind."

He gives a loud belch. I'll bet he doesn't do that at his father's house. In about five minutes he'll want his dinner. His face settles into his familiar pout.

"Is something bothering you, Johnny?"

"I'll tell you while I eat. Is my dinner ready?" He hoists himself out of the chair.

"Yes, it's ready." He should know by now I always have it ready when he comes home. I've had a whole month to learn his routine.

"Well," he says, pulling a straight chair up to the kitchen table next to mine. He tucks his napkin into the space between the second and third button of his shirt. Someday I'll ask him to put it in his lap like a grown up, and I'll get him to kiss me when he comes home. We've been married less than a month and already he's acting like an old married man. Next thing I know he'll be eating his dinner in his undershirt.

"Well, what is it, Johnny?" I smile, sitting down with my tea.

"There's been news about Ruthie."

"Ruthie?" I set my cup down so hard tea spills on the tablecloth. "Ruthie? Johnny, where is she? Is she all right?" I squeeze my hands to keep them from shaking. They've found my Ruthie.

"It's not really about her, Louise, it's about that guy, Homer."

"Homer? Don't tell me she's still hanging around with him!"

"We're not sure, but he got arrested up in Massachusetts. Used a forged prescription for some medicine, the kind you get addicted to. A stupid thing to do, they're beginning to check on those prescriptions real good these days. Hand me the butter, will you?" He coats a slice of bread with butter and stuffs it into his mouth.

"Johnny, she wasn't with him, was she?" I cross my fingers, praying he'll say she wasn't.

"They're not sure," he swallows hard. "Seems there *was* a girl in a car, but she drove off before they could get a good look at her. It could have been Ruthie."

He motions for another beer.

"Get it yourself." Can't he see I'm upset? He gets one out of the icebox and brings it to the table. "I knew that Homer would get her into trouble."

"We've told the Massachusetts police, so they're on the lookout for her. I wasn't sure I should tell you. You're not upset, are you?"

"If it was her, at least I know she's still alive."

"We'll know more in a day or so."

My mind trips over the terrible things that could happen to Ruthie. She's so young. And if she's with that Homer . . . . Suddenly I feel weak and dizzy. I should have eaten something with my tea. "Johnny, I don't want to think about what will happen if they catch her. I think I'll lie down, just for a few minutes."

I stretch out on our bed with my eyes closed and my stomach pointing toward the ceiling. Oh, God, If I can just forgive Mama, that might be enough to save Ruthie. If I can forgive Mama, quit blaming Johnny for everything, stop complaining and . . . I finger the chenille bumps in our bedspread. Should have folded it back so it wouldn't get it mussed up. Even with all my bargaining, Ruthie still might get caught. I shouldn't have told her so many times she'd end up in reform school. 'Say something enough times and it turns to truth,' Gram used to say.

I shouldn't let Johnny eat alone, either. I know he likes company, even if he doesn't talk much at the table, but all I can think about is Ruthie.

CHAPTER 61

It's been a whole month and I still can't get used to my new name, 'Mrs. Johnny Paulsen,' and in two more months I'll have a little girl of my very own. If only I didn't feel so ugly. I feel as big and as old as that beat-up chair with the doilies.

He's sitting in it now, reading the paper, a cigarette in one hand and a beer at his elbow. He looks so comfortable. I doubt we'll ever get rid of that chair now.

"Johnny?" He doesn't answer. I know he heard me, but he just grunts. Probably thinks I have some work for him to do. "Johnny, when are you going to give me a driving lesson so I can visit Ellie and Mrs. K? I haven't seen them in so long." He still doesn't answer. "Are you listening? You said after we were married you'd teach me to drive."

"It's too late now, Louise," he says, shaking the paper into shape. "Wouldn't want you driving when you're this far along. Maybe later, when the kid's old enough to walk."

"But, I don't want to wait that long. Come on, you promised you'll teach me. I used to drive a tractor on the farm, you know. If I can drive a tractor I certainly can drive a car."

He lights up another cigarette, blows smoke toward the ceiling, and snaps his paper. "We'll see, Louise."

I can tell by his tone we won't, probably thinks I'll wreck his car. If he thinks I'm going to stay cooped up in this apartment cleaning and cooking for him . . . well, no matter what he says, before this baby gets old enough to walk, I am going to learn to drive.

October 1928

Dear Gertie,

Thank you for the baby book. I love it. I was afraid you'd forgotten me; it's been so long since I've been in your beauty shop. I didn't think Mama would tell anybody. The baby will make her a grandmother, you know. I didn't think she'd ever want to admit to being old enough for that.

I can't wait to begin writing about her in her pink, satin-covered little book. My baby is going to be a girl, you know. I'll bring her in to see you as soon as she is old enough. Maybe you can give her, her first hair cut. Your friend, Louise

CHAPTER 62

Getting from our apartment to Mrs. K's on the streetcar takes over an hour, because it stops at every corner. Another reason I need to learn how to drive. Wait 'til Ellie sees me. Would be just like her to make fun of me, but I don't care. I'll bet she's just jealous.

Should have used the bathroom before I left the apartment. The shape of these seats doesn't allow for much comfort. My back is killing me. Someone walks by, looking just like Ruthie from the back. Could it be her? I tap on the window and she turns, but it isn't Ruthie.

I want so badly to see my little sister again; hear her laugh and make fun of my big belly. Oh, Ruthie, if only you had stayed, you could be with me when my baby comes.

"Mrs. K? Ellie? Are you home? It's me, Louise."

"Louise? Oh my goodness gracious me, you're here. Ellie!" Mrs. K hollers, "Come on down, Ellie, Louise is here!"

She waddles toward me, balancing on her tiny pointed feet. I laugh in spite of myself. How I've missed this little woman and her dear ways.

"Let me look at you. My, oh my, dear child. You look so, well, so . . ."

"I believe *pregnant* is the word you're looking for, Mrs. K," I hug her and laugh.

"Do come in, dear. Do come in, Louise. My, oh my, how you've grown. And you have . . . how many more months? Just two, isn't it? And you managed the streetcar all by yourself?" She leads me toward the sofa. "Come sit, dear, and rest your weary feet." She eases herself down beside me, and I'm wrapped in her warm vanilla smell.

"It wasn't so bad. I just need a minute to catch my breath. I got all steamed up even though there is a touch of fall in the air. The leaves are beginning to turn." I fan myself with my hankie and relax. "Is Ellie here?"

Mrs. K plumps the pillows on the sofa, picks at specks of lint that aren't there, and ignores my question.

"We keep it quite warm in here, Louise. Ellie's thin blooded, you know. Is it too warm for you, Dearie? I'll turn the gas heater down."

"Please don't trouble, Mrs. K, I'm fine." I'd forgotten how wonderfully attentive she can be.

Ellie comes tripping down the staircase dressed, for all the world, like a sailor; blue dress with a square while collar trimmed with red stars, a stiffly cinched belt with a yellow brass buckle, and smelling of beer.

"Well if it isn't Mrs. Johnny Paulsen herself."

Mrs. K scowls. "Be careful now, dear." She reaches toward her daughter, but Ellie pushes her away.

"Looking quite pregnant, I might add," Ellie slurs her words. "'*veddy, veddy*' pregnant indeed."

Without warning, she lurches toward me and sobs, "Oh, Louise, you're so lucky. You've got a husband, and now you're going to have a sweet little baby and live happily ever after. I think I'll just go out and get myself pregnant, too."

"Ellie," Mrs. K scowls." Stop talking nonsense, and leave the poor girl alone. Don't mind her, Louise." She brushes her dress, straightening wrinkles that aren't there, and lowers her voice. "Her latest beau just decided he loves someone else, and she's trying to drown her sorrows. I guess she's had a little too much. Ellie, dear, go into the kitchen and get the presents; wedding presents for Louise, well, not really wedding presents. We thought you'd want to pick out things for your apartment yourself, isn't that so, Ellie?"

"Anything you say . . . Mums-z," Ellie sings out as she staggers toward the kitchen.

Mrs. K. reaches out to steady her.

"I can manage," Ellie shouts, waving off her mother's help.

Mrs. K scowls and she turns toward me. "It's so good to see you, dear."

Ellie staggers back and tosses two packages in my lap.

Mrs. K's face folds into a grin. "They are really for the baby, but you can open them. I do hope you like them, Louise."

I undo the wrappings and hold up a pair of pink knitted booties and a bonnet. "They're adorable, Mrs. K, and so tiny! When I finish the jacket, won't she look sweet in the whole outfit? Thanks you so much. Hardly have time to knit anymore. I fold the paper carefully and tuck it in the box.

"Here's the one from me, Louise," Ellie says handing me the other package. It's shaped like a book. "Just finished yesterday, that's why I'm celebrating." She gives her mother a meaningful look.

"Ellie, you finished it!" I squeal, as I skim the pages of recipes. "They look so professional." I never thought she'd really get it done. "How can I ever thank you, Ellie? As soon as I get them printed up and bound, I'll autograph a copy for you and . . ."

"Oh, please, don't do that, you know I hate to cook. I'll just come to your place for a good meal once in a while." She gives another meaningful look toward her mother, but it passes over Mrs. K unnoticed.

"Louise," Mrs. K clears her throat, "tell us about your wedding. What was it like?"

"Yeah, Louise. Tell us all about the justice of the peace wedding." Ellie sinks into a wicker rocker and her eyes glaze over.

"Do tell us, dear," Mrs. K smiles as Ellie's eyes gently close.

"Well, it wasn't anything like I planned. I guess it was just about what you'd expect from a justice of the peace wedding. We drove to New York State in the morning. Johnny's father didn't think Johnny's car would make it, so he lent us his. I packed some sandwiches and we stopped near a lake along the way for lunch. The mosquitoes just about ate us alive. So we sat in the car and ate.

"For most of the way, Johnny was being his old, quiet self. You know the way he can be sometimes, just grunting answers to my questions and silly chatter. I was afraid he might be having second thoughts."

"Oh, Louise, He was probably just nervous," Mrs. K murmurs. "Don't you think that was what it was, just nerves? You were nervous, too, weren't you?"

"Yes, I guess I was. We both were realizing what a big step we were taking. Anyway, when we finally found the justice's house, we sat in the car for a while. Johnny's hands were shaking so, when he pinned on my corsage, he pricked his finger and got blood on the rose petals and on my jacket, and when he tried to rub it out he made it worse."

Ellie snorts a laugh.

"Ellie?" Her mother threatens. "If you don't act decent, you can just go right back upstairs." Mrs. K rearranges herself next to me. "Go on, dear."

"Well, the bunch of daisies I was to hold was in the back seat without any water. They were supposed to hide the baby, you know. By the time we got to the right address, the daisies were pretty much wilted, but I took them in anyway."

Ellie sputters to life and whispers, "'here comes the bride . . .'" and drops off again.

"Don't pay any attention to her, Louise, she'll have such a hangover tomorrow, it will serve her right."

"Well, the whole thing was pretty laughable, Mrs. K, when I look back on it, but it wasn't at the time. At the time, it was plumb awful.

"The Honorable Otis J. Thornburton, Justice of the Peace, turned out to be about eight feet tall, skinny as a fence rail, and smelling of cigars.

"His wife was a sourpuss of a woman, with sharp beady eyes that darted from our scared faces, to the bunch of wilted daisies that don't quite hide my stomach, to the bloody spot on my jacket, then at Johnny and me again, and back to the flowers.

"And the two witnesses didn't help much, either. We must have interrupted a party or something. They acted like this wedding was the last place on earth they wanted to be. And every time the justice said, *repeat after me*, the baby gave a kick and the daisies jumped, and his wife did her glancing thing all over again."

"Oh, Louise," Mrs. K hides a smile. "That's too funny . . . your first wedding and all."

First wedding? She must be comparing me to Mama.

"The whole thing turned out all right, though," I tell her. "I figured it was something we had to get through, and since I wasn't going to have a nice church wedding the way I wanted, we might as well get it over with as quick as possible.

"Oh, yes, and another thing. They forgot to turn on the phonograph record that played the wedding march until the ceremony was over. By that time, Johnny and I didn't care. We laughed and marched to the music all the way to the car. We didn't even stay for the lemonade and cookies that were included in the price of the wedding."

Mrs. K nods. "It will be something to tell your grandchildren, Louise."

"Grandchildren," I smile. "I've never thought as far ahead as grandchildren."

"I might as well tell you the rest," I say, even though I can see Ellie has fallen asleep. "It rained all the way home. We had a flat tire and Johnny couldn't get the spare on because it was his father's car, and when we got to the apartment it was after two in the morning. We had to break a window to get in because the landlord had forgotten to give Johnny the key. And that's the story of our wedding."

By this time, Mrs. K. is bursting her seams with laughter.

"But you took it all in such good humor, Louise, you and Johnny."

"Well, we're married, and I guess that's all that matters."

But it's not all that matters," she sighs and dabs at her eyes with her lacy hankie she had had tucked up her sleeve.

I know what she's thinking. I'll always be sorry, too, that I didn't have a proper wedding. I wanted Mama to be there, and Ruthie. I wanted a beautiful dress and Gram's wedding veil. I'll probably cry over that from time to time, but I'll mellow and see it as the funny scene it was, and I'll try to make it even funnier than it was if I ever get to tell Ruthie.

I pat my stomach. "Maybe when the baby grows up I'll explain it all to her, so she won't make the same mistakes I did.

CHAPTER 63

"It's three in the morning, Louise, what are you doing up?" Johnny yawns, scratches his ribs and private parts under his pajamas. I wish he wouldn't do that. He looks like Grampa looked, after he started being sick. "What's bothering you? Is it the baby?"

"No, it's nothing, really, it's just that . . . well, lately I've been thinking about Ruthie, wondering if she's okay."

"I told you, we have a file on her at the station. That's about all we can do until we hear any news, Louise."

"But Johnny, I want to do something to help you find her."

"What can you do?" he asks with a yawn.

"Well, I could write a letter."

"How would you know where to send a letter? Come on back to bed. I've got to go to work tomorrow." He rolls over.

I knew he wouldn't think much of my idea. I shouldn't have said anything. Well, I'm going to write a letter, anyway. I know just where to send it, and I'm going to make them think Johnny wrote it. It might not help, but I'll be able to sleep knowing I tried.

Please Post:
October 1928
Company Manager, Amory Mill
Manchester, New Hampshire

*We have received a tip that one of our missing persons may
be working in your factory. I am enclosing a letter to her from
her sister. Please post it on your bulletin board. We don't know*

what last name she is using, but if anyone has information as to her whereabouts, please have them contact the West Hartford Police Department.

Enclosed please find a letter addressed to Ruth Guest. If possible, see that she gets it. Thank you.
Officer John Paulsen

October 1928

Dear Ruthie.

I don't know if you will ever see this letter, but Johnny heard that someone saw you in New Hampshire. They said they thought you were working at a mill in Manchester, so I am sending this letter to the manager, hoping it gets to you.

I think about you every day, Ruthie, wondering if you are all right. I'm married to Johnny now. You remember him. Our baby is due late next month. I am as big as a cow, like Hilda before she had her calf, remember that? Mrs. Kamens says my baby will be a girl for certain.

I worry about you, Ruthie, and pray you are safe and not still hanging around with that Homer anymore. Johnny and I have a nice apartment now. I want you to come and stay with us. We have a room for you. Mama put Gram in the county home. She didn't last long after that. Remember how hard it was for you to handle her after I left? Well, she got worse. We laid her next to Grampa under his apple tree just like she wanted. I'm sorry you missed the funeral. She would have wanted you there. Johnny has a job with the police department. I am so proud of him. Do you remember my recipes? Well, they are all typed now. I plan to go to night school as soon as I can leave the baby with Johnny if his schedule allows. I might even ask Mama. Wouldn't that be funny, Mama taking care of my baby? Maybe night school won't ever happen, but I'm going to try. If you get this letter, please answer. I miss you, Ruthie. Remember, I will be waiting to hear from you.

Love from your sister, Louise.

Maybe I should have told Johnny about the letter. I don't want him to think I am keeping things from him. Mama doesn't know we've heard anything about Ruthie. She has enough on her mind with Shirley and all. The way I figure it, she doesn't seem to know how to love more than one of her children at a time. If I have more babies I hope I have enough love in my heart for all of them.

Wait 'til Mama hears about my cookbook. I'm calling it, *Cooking with Gram and Louise.* That would please Gram if she could see it. Mrs. K is going to help me send it to a publisher. I'm not telling anyone besides Ruthie about it, until it gets published. Then if it doesn't get published no one can laugh at me. Johnny will probably laugh anyway when he finds out.

Mama said she had presents for the baby. Every time the baby kicks I wonder if Mama really does have presents. But as Ruthie used to say, *'Better not hold your breathe on what Mama says.'* Just the same I'm keeping one dresser drawer in her room ready. Just in case.

"Louise, what did you do with that chest of drawers that was next to my chair?"

Now that he's calling it *his* chair, we'll never get rid of it. "I put it in the baby's room, Johnny. She'll need it for her clothes."

"Geez, Louise! You're like a pot bubbling over about that baby."

"I want everything to be perfect for her. You don't know what it's like not having a real family. You've always had one. They cared what happened to you, and that's how it's going to be for our baby."

Whenever Johnny is late coming home and I can't sleep, the old black thoughts cloud over me, setting me to wondering again; did he marry me just because I was pregnant? My heart says no, but I'm still not sure. I've had a lot of practice in not trusting the people I care about, and now he's late again.

"Johnny. Where have you been? I've been worried, worried sick."

"Louise, it's freezing in here. Do you have to keep the heat turned down so low?"

"I'm sorry, Johnny, I get overheated sometimes; it's the baby. I'll be glad when I can wheel her around in that fancy perambulator Mrs. K gave us instead of . . ." but I can tell he's not listening. He digs in his pocket and pulls out a piece of paper.

"Louise, we got a tip on your sister. It came to the station addressed to me. Can't figure how they got my name." I turn away so he can't see my smile. I knew my letter would help.

"Is she's still there?" I ask, knowing in my heart she must be.

"Well, I'm not sure, but as long as there's a chance she might still be in New Hampshire, I'm going to drive up there and check it out."

"But Johnny, what about the baby? She's due sometime this month. If you aren't back in time, what will I do?"

"Don't worry, I'll be back in plenty of time. You want to find your sister, don't you?"

"Of course I do, but . . ."

"You don't have to worry, Louise, I'll be back in time, I promise."

My knees go weak at the word, *promise*. I promised to care for Ruthie and look what happened to her. Our baby is going to learn what that word really means.

"When are you going?"

"Tonight. The sooner I go, the sooner I'll be back. I may bring you good news about your sister, too."

CHAPTER 64

It's been three days and Johnny still isn't back. He could have called. What if he's had an accident?

November 1928

Dear Mama,

My baby is due in two weeks, and Johnny isn't here. He's coming back. Don't worry about that. He's on sort of a business trip, but I can't talk about it. I'm alone and well, I keep thinking, what if something goes wrong? What were you thinking just before I was born? Was my father with you? Was Gram with you? Were you scared? I need someone. If Ruthie could be here or if Gram was still alive, but... Mama, do you think you could come stay with me just until Johnny gets back? Sincerely, Louise

I don't like sleeping in our bed without Johnny. It's lonely. I miss him being next to me. I never got used to sleeping by myself, what with having to share a bed with Ruthie all those years, nestling close, keeping each other warm, filling in the hollow spaces with her bubbly noises. It was different at Mrs. K's house. I had my own bedroom, my own place to be, and besides, who could be lonely with Ellie right down the hall. Who could possibly be lonely with a Mrs. K. in the house?

But now, without Johnny, I feel all that hollow black nothingness crowding in again. I need him. I need him to love me. What good is anything if there is no one to love me, or for me to love? What if he gets killed? A policeman's life can be dangerous. Or, what if he decided he really loved Helen more than me? I pat my stomach. When the baby comes, everything will be different. I won't have these black thinking spells. She'll need me and love me, and I won't have to rely on Johnny or anyone else. I'll have my baby.

"Ow! Baby, you're making my stomach hard as a rock. Relax. It's not time yet. We're going to wait for your daddy. Just settle down." Maybe it's this darn chair that's making her kick so hard. "Darn!" This isn't just kicking; this hurts! "You don't want to be born yet, baby. Wait for your daddy, he'll be here any minute."

I breathe deep, trying to keep calm, but it's not working. My stomach is next to bursting. I'm not even sure I can get out of this chair. The pain is getting worse, too. I'm going to have to use our new telephone and dial for help. Johnny showed me how. I remember he said I should just 'dial '0' for assistance.

It takes me three tries to do it right. When they finally connect me, I hang up. I don't know what to say. It's probably what they call 'false labor,' and I'll feel foolish.

Why did Johnny promise to be back if he wasn't sure? His promises are no better than Mama's."Ooooh!" Always knew I might have to go through this by myself. Somebody ought to be with me. "Oooooh!" Mrs. K. could never make it in time, and I know Ellie wouldn't come.

I relax as the pain lets up. It must have been a false alarm. I dial Mama on the telephone and let it ring. No answer.

The pain comes again. I telephone the taxi company. "Hello? I'm having a baby and I need to get to the hospital. Can you please help me? Yes? Good. Here is the address. I will be waiting downstairs. Thanks you."

I get my valise, which is already packed, climb slowly down, sit on the stairs, and wait for the taxis cab.

Mrs. K talked about ancestors. My great, great, grandmothers must have had their babies by themselves, squatted in a field somewhere, popping them out like Hilda did, or Birdie with her kittens.

"Oh." I grab the stair railing. Maybe I should have called Johnny's mother, but I don't want her with me when the baby comes. What if I faint? Mrs. K said you forget the pain after your baby is born.

"Ooooh." I bite hard on my knuckles. What if the taxicab can't find this address? What if I don't get to the hospital in time? Jesus!" Help me. Please help me! Please, somebody help me! If the taxi doesn't hurry . . . Please, I want my Mama."

The next few minutes are blurred . . . someone banging on the door . . . a uniform? . . . Is it Johnny? No, it's the taxi driver, then a ride to the hospital.

A wheel chair.

I bite my tongue. God damn it, it hurts . . . a brightly lit room.

Everything spins. I hear a scream. Mine? Something over my nose . . . I can't breath . . . I relax . . . no more pain. Am I dying?

"Mrs. Paulsen? Would you like to see your baby?"

"Mmmm?" My eyes won't open.

"You can wake up now, Dearie" Someone shakes my shoulder. "Come on, Honey, open your eyes. Don't you want to hold your new little girl?"

A tiny bundle is placed in my arms. My baby? I'm holding my baby? She's so tiny and sweet. Her perfect little fingers reach out, and my heart aches with love.

"She is so perfect," I gasp, through tears. She has her fathers' dark eyes and a funny, little round nub of a nose. How beautiful she is! She stars up at me, past me, frowning at the world. Oh my!" I laugh. "She's got her daddy's pout-y mouth, too.

"Hi, baby," I whisper. She makes little fists and yawns. I breathe in her sweetness. Something heavy inside me lifts, making a place in my heart for this tiny creature to nestle, forever.

So perfect . . . so trusting. She closes her eyes, content to be cradled in my arms. A nurse hurries into the room, her stiffly starched uniform crackles as she walks.

"I wasn't supposed to leave her in here this long," she whispers, "but you both looked so peaceful, I hadn't the heart to take her back to the nursery."

She must have had children of her own, to be so understanding.

"I'll bring her back in a couple of hours, then you can start trying to nurse her. Get some sleep now, honey. You had a rough time of it back there."

I nod although I don't remember. I'm afraid if I speak, the words will come out as a song, and she'll think I'm crazy and never bring my baby again.

Nobody asked about my husband, or why no one was with me. They probably think someone will come tomorrow. Maybe no one will. Except for showing off my baby, I don't care. I did it alone, without Mama, without Johnny. I know now I can manage on my own. Feelings of relief and pride seep into all the lonely places in my heart. I lie back against the stiff pillow and stare at the ceiling.

What will she be like when she grows up? Not like Mama or Ruthie, not with Johnny and me loving her. My baby will have a lot to live up to when I tell her about her great grandmother.

She'll need a name. I'm not naming her after Johnny's mother, or Mama. She needs to start out with a name all her own.

Nurses in soft-soled shoes scurry up and down the corridor. Their starched uniforms sound as if they are walking through crisp autumn leaves. When I close my eyes I can see the farm, with Hilda, and the apple tree. I smile in case Gram can see me. I think about her and Grampa, and their little girl. Soon they'll bring me *my* little girl. I'll feed her and then I'll sleep.

CHAPTER 65

There is a slight knock on the door of my hospital room and a voice whispers, "Louise?"

"Johnny" Is that you? You're back."

"Yeah, it's me."

He comes rushing into the room, bringing the smell of winter freshness with him.

Tears of fear, anger, and joy erupt, like a dam bursting. "Oh, Johnny. Where were you? You've been gone so long!"

"Don't cry, Honey. Do you feel okay? Can I turn on the light?"

I nod impatiently, wiping my eyes. "The baby's four days old already and her own father hasn't seen her yet," I sob. "You'd better have a good reason . . ."

"Take it easy, Louise. I came as soon as I could. Where is she? It's a girl, isn't it?" He brushes my cheek with the hint of a kiss. I doubt if he's shaved since he left.

"You weren't here when I needed you, Johnny, but . . ."

"I thought for sure I'd be back in time. I'm sorry, Hon."

I want him to say he's proud of me, that he knew I could manage all by myself, but at least he said he was sorry.

"I haven't seen her yet. When do they bring her in?"

"They won't bring her in while you're here, but you can go down the hall and look through the nursery window. Johnny, she is so beautiful. Go down and see her."

"Is she all right? I mean does she have all her fingers and toes, and everything?"

She's the most perfect thing you've ever seen. Oh, I wish we could see her together. They won't let me out of bed for a week. Go on down. Peek at her."

In five minutes he's back.

"She's so tiny, but her eyes were open," he says. "They're blue."

"Baby's eyes usually start out blue, Johnny, and she weighed seven pounds, fourteen and a half ounces. Did you see her little feet? They are so tiny. They'll probably get big like yours, and she's got your mouth, Johnny. Isn't she the most perfect thing you've ever seen?"

"The nurse opened her blanket so we could get a better look. She's even got toe nails."

"Did she smile for you? She smiled at me yesterday. The nurse said it was only gas, but I know it was a real smile. She's just so perfect, Johnny."

"Well, she's no quarterback, but if you squint, she *is* sort of cute."

I know he's teasing, and I love him for it.

"Mama promised . . . well, I mean, she *said* she'd come sometime this week. Ellie will come, too. I hope she can bring her mother, but it's so hard for Mrs. K to get around, with her weight and all. Oh, Johnny, I want everyone to see her. I want to show her off, to the whole world. And how about giving me a real kiss, and the present you said you were going to bring. You didn't forget, did you?"

"No, I didn't forget. I'll have it for you by tomorrow. Think you can stand waiting?"

"Now that I've got the baby, I can stand anything. Johnny, I'm so happy. I just want to hold her every minute."

"At this rate, you're going to spoil her, before we even get her home," he pouts.

"But really, Johnny, isn't she the prettiest baby you've ever seen?"

"Of course she is, she's our daughter."

I lay back against the pillow. "Come on, tell me. Is the present for me or for the baby? And why can't I have it now?"

"After nine months of waiting, you should've learned something about patience.

"Did you notice her eyelashes, Johnny, and her long fingers? They'll be perfect for playing the piano. I think we should start saving now, so we can buy a piano when she gets old enough for lessons. You said your family is musical. I'm sure she'll inherit that."

"Let's let her learn to walk before we have her taking piano lessons."

"I'm serious, Johnny. Are any of your ancestors musicians?"

"Maybe," he shrugs and pulls the chair up close to the bed. "How should I know?"

"You could find out. Maybe you're related to some Danish composer or an artist, a writer maybe. Mrs. K thinks I might be related to that poet, Edgar Guest."

"I suppose I could be related to someone famous. Never thought about it. What makes you so interested?"

"Because of something Mrs. K said. I asked her once if she thought I took after my mother. At the time, I guess I was afraid she'd say yes. She got me thinking about my ancestors, though, way back before Mama. By the way, you can tell your parents, they don't have to worry about me being *totally* German. Tell them my father was an Englishman. That makes me only half German."

"Thought you didn't know anything about your father."

"Well, if you must know, while I was waiting for you to come back, I opened this envelope Mama gave me a long time ago. I figured it was time for me to see it. I found my birth certificate in it. It said my father was born in Nova Scotia, in 1882, and his parents were both English."

Johnny gives me his pout-y look. "So what?"

"Just be sure to tell your mother. I want her to know her granddaughter is at least a quarter English, as well as being part German and part Danish. And tell her I want to know about the Paulsen's history, too. You're probably descended from Vikings. Weren't Vikings pirates or something?"

He shrugs and I can tell he's not following what I'm getting at. "Johnny. Do you think your parents will come to see the baby?"

He yawns and scratches his forehead. "Ma can't come to the hospital. It's too hard for her to get around, and I don't think Pop would come without her. We'll take the baby over to the house sometime."

I close my eyes. "Won't it be fun watching her grow up, Johnny, to see what she'll be like? I think she looks Danish, don't you?" I yawn. "Maybe she will be a pirate."

"Louise, you're talking goofy. What have they been feeding you, anyway?"

"I'll have Mrs. K explain it to you." I yawn again.

The nurse pokes her head in the door, and smiles dryly.

"Visiting hours over in five minutes."

"Already?" I ask, although I'm glad. I'll get some rest before they bring my baby in for her night feeding.

"I'll be back in the morning, Louise," says Johnny, and he leans down and gives me a proper kiss.

December 6, 1928

Dear Mrs. K. and Ellie,

Wait 'til we show you our daughter. You were right, Mrs. K, she is beautiful. She looks a lot like Johnny, even has his pout-y mouth. You will be pleased to know that I finished knitting the little sweater. The few mistakes don't show, really. Johnny will bring the booties and hat you made, and she'll wear the whole outfit when we take her home. We'll bring her for a visit when the weather gets warmer and there is no snow. Won't do, her catching a cold. Johnny has a new camera so we'll bring pictures, too. Love to you both, Louise

CHAPTER 66

"Louise, you awake yet?" Johnny, dressed in his full policeman's uniform, peeks around the door.

"Johnny, you're late. Visiting hours were over hours ago. How did you get past the nurses?"

"It's the uniform," he smiles and takes off his hat. There's a crease all around his head where his hat tightens down.

"I haven't even put on my face." I used to hate it when Mama said that, and now I'm saying it myself. Oh, well . . .

"You look swell, Louise." He gives me a quick kiss and his beard scrapes across my cheek.

"Did you stop to see the baby?"

"Yah, we, ah . . . I looked in as I passed the nursery." He seems edgy.

"I bet you forgot my present."

He walks to the door, turns and raises his eyebrows. I can tell he's thinking I may not like it. Slowly, he opens the door and stands back. And there she is.

"Ruthie?" I whisper, and my breath catches. "Is that really *you*?"

"Can't be two in this world looks like me," she mutters under her breath.

Her speech is slow, as if it is hard for her to form the words. She is thin as a rail. She leans on one foot and then the other, twisting a strand of her stringy hair, then tucks it behind her ear; the same Ruthie hair.

I hold back a giggle and reach toward her. "Oh, Ruthie, it's been over two years." I want to grab her, hug the daylights out of her, but she stands just out of reach.

With one sweep, her dark eyes take in every inch of the room, the tall windows, the bare bulb handing from the high ceiling, the stark white walls.

"How long are they keeping you for?" She smiles her shy, shifty-eyed smile as if she isn't sure she should be here.

"Till I can get around by myself I guess, but come closer, Ruthie. Let me look at you. You've grown, but you're . . . you're so thin. You haven't been eating right, have you?"

She moves tentatively closer. I reach out to take her hand, but she keeps just out of reach. A faded, blue cotton dress hangs like an old wrinkled bag on her thin body. She has a timid, stoop-shouldered look, not at all like the Ruthie I remember. Her eyes are deep set and circled, with a dazed look, like she's been taking . . . no, I mustn't think that . . . mustn't judge her.

"I seen your baby," she says in a slow, shallow voice. "Kind of looks like you." She stretches out her words as if she's not used to talking.

"Wait 'til you see her smile. Oh, Ruthie, I can't believe you're really here. Are you okay? Did you get my letter? I had them post it, you know." For a fleeting second I glance at Johnny. I never told him about the letter. "Why haven't you been in touch with us, Ruthie?"

Johnny comes closer to the bed. "Okay, Louise, ease up with the questions. Aren't you glad to see her?"

"Of course I am. I've never been so glad to see anyone."

Ruthie makes a harsh unfamiliar sound. "Bet that baby out there takes top place in your scale of gladness right now."

"Why didn't you let us know where you were, Ruthie?"

She shrugs as if it isn't important.

"You're coming to stay with us, you know. I won't be out of the hospital for a few days yet, but you can go home with Johnny today. He can make up the couch in the living room until we can get another . . ."

"Hold your horses, Louise," Johnny mutters, "Not so fast. I brought Ruth here this morning, but I have to get her back before dark." He sighs, twisting one hand with the other. "She's been in a detention home, Louise, but because I'm a cop, I got special permission to take her out for the day, so she could come to see you, but I have to get her back. She's got some more time to serve."

"Detention home?" I ask.

"Reform school to you," Ruthie stands straight, jutting out her chin, and for a second I see Homer's face staring back at me. "You always said I'd end up there. Turns out you were right, Weez."

The old nickname pulls me back in time. She's still the same defiant Ruthie.

The three of us stand speechless. The sounds of clinking glasses and cutlery remind me where we are and, in spite of myself, the smell of bacon makes my mouth water. How can I be hungry at a time like this?

"How long will you have to stay there, Ruthie?" I ask, dreading the answer.

"A year if I knuckle under. More if I don't."

She rolls her hair behind one ear again. Her hair is longer now, but it still has a mind of it's own.

"Will we be able to come see you? Bring food and things?"

"You mean like Gram's chocolate cake with a file in it?" She snickers. Her eyes dart around the room, as if she's looking for a way out and I can see she's fighting back tears.

"Oh, Ruthie," I say, giving way to my own tears. "I've got so much to tell you."

I sit up straight and clear my throat. "For one thing, we've got to start listening to our ancestors."

Her eyes slit, a look I clearly remember. "Listening to *who*?" She turns to Johnny. "What the hell is she talking' about?"

Johnny shrugs.

"Oh, you know, our old, oh, never mind, whatever you've done in the past, Ruthie, you can change. When you get out and start living with us, you can get a job, finish school, and . . ."

Ruthie 's eyes flash as she backs toward the door. "She's talking crazy, Johnny. Get me out of here.

"Wait, Ruthie." I reach for her hand.

"Let her be, Louise," Johnny says. "Maybe she'll come around when her year's up."

"Don't hold your breath," Ruthie sneers. Johnny walks toward her and snaps a pair of handcuffs on her wrists.

"Johnny, no!" I gasp, reaching out to stop him. "Do you have to use those?"

"Regulations," he says as they head toward the door.

A nurse pokes her head in. "Visiting hours will be over in three minutes." She doesn't bat an eye at the handcuffs. Johnny must have warned her when they came in.

"Oh," Ruthie says, turning toward the bed. "Almost forgot."

"Come on, Ruthie, we got to go."

She reaches her cuffed hands into her pocket, pulls out a small package wrapped in crumpled yellowed newspaper, and hands it to me. "This here's for you. The kid might like it, too."

Johnny leans down brushes his face against mine. "I'll be back as soon as I can."

They walk out, and I'm left alone with the small package in my lap.

"Oh, Ruthie! I've lost you again," I sob. There doesn't seem to be enough air to breathe. I lay back against my pillow and finger the crinkled paper.

She had all this time to straighten herself out, and she didn't. If I thought it was my fault, this'd be the saddest day of my life. I did everything I knew, back then. I tried to give her love, and she hardly ever gave any back; her and Mama both. If that happens with Johnny, and me, the only thing I'll have left is my baby.

Slowly I unwrap the package, and there, as perfect as it was so long ago, is the baby bird Ruthie carved for Gram. I hold it close to my heart and burst into tears.

That night after visiting hours are long over, Johnny comes in again.

"Well, I got her back in time. But I'm dead tired. Haven't had any sleep since night before last."

"You didn't keep her in handcuffs all the way, did you?"

"Course not. I had to follow the rules before." He flops down in a chair, closes his bloodshot eyes, and yawns. "My present to you didn't work out like I expected. Thought there'd be a happy reunion between you two, but it went sour, didn't it?"

"It wasn't your fault, Johnny. You look so tired; come over here by me."

I make room for him on the bed. He lets out a long sigh, flops down beside me, and yawns again.

"Tears streamed down her face most of the way back." He rubs his rough chin and stretches. "You know, somewhere under all that anger and gruffness, she's not a bad kid. Let's hope she'll straighten out some day."

"She won't if she keeps on with that Homer."

Johnny shakes his head. "He seems to be able to get her to do anything he wants. When he got out on probation, they robbed a dime store, and Ruthie got caught. That's why she's in reform school now. Can you believe it? All he wanted was some some chewing gum, and he made her go in after it, with a gun, for God's sake." He sighs again and stretches. "When she gets out, *if* she gets out, and stays away from him and his steady supply of laudanum, she'll be okay. A year might just do it." He closes his eyes.

"The baby will be walking by then. But I meant it about Ruthie coming to stay with us. She's got to break off with that Homer, and she can't bring any of her old ways with her. I don't want her teaching things to our baby. Drugs. I can't believe it. Johnny, stay awake."

He blows air through his mouth. I brush a strand of his hair back where it belongs. He'll be bald soon, if his forehead gets any higher.

"Johnny, go back to the apartment and get some rest. Tomorrow we'll settle on a name for our daughter. I'd like May for her middle name, then when we have a boy, we'll call him Johnny Junior."

I touch his prickly chin. He'll make a good father, he'd better, but it's up to him. He'd better treat us right. I'm not bargaining for love any more. I can't control anyone else. It's me I've got to worry about, me, and my baby. I'm not responsible for Johnny's actions, or Ruthie's, or Mama's, especially not Mama's.

Johnny smiles in his sleep. I wonder what's going on in his head? I guess I'll never know all the things he's thinking. But then, he doesn't know all that I'm thinking, either.

I stare at him as he sleeps. He looks like a stranger lying next to me. It's moments like this that I still feel that loneliness deep inside. Oh, I'm safely married. I have a proper husband, a beautiful baby, and there's a chance Ruthie might turn out all right. And someday, when my baby is older and I have time, I might want to go back to school. I'm grateful and happy for the blessings in my life. Maybe it's Mama creeping into my thoughts that accounts for me feeling lonely.

But I mustn't dwell on her. It's my baby that I must think about now. My own precious baby, who will have all the love she can handle if I have anything to say about it.

I snuggle down beside Johnny and pull the blanket up over us. I haven't the heart to wake him. We'll wait until the nurse comes. She can wake us both and send him home.

It's a comfortable place between waking and sleeping. That place where dreams are born. I drift off, and there is my little girl dancing in the tall grass on the farm, Gram and Grampa standing under their tree, and Ruthie smiling at me.

It isn't until I hear the steps in the hall that I know someone is coming. Without even opening my eyes, I know by the click of the heels, it's Mama.

"What is God's name are you two doing in that bed?" Mama, whispers through clenched teeth.

I sit up and my cheeks burn. "But Mama . . . we . . . we weren't . . ."

"You ought to be ashamed of yourselves." Johnny stirs without waking. I cross my fingers, and then quickly uncross them. I don't need to do that. We're not doing anything wrong no matter what Mama thinks, but even in the dim light I can see she is smiling. "You're not supposed to be here at this hour." I straighten the coverlet.

"I just breezed in. Nobody took any notice. The nurses must be off drinking coffee."

"You won't get to see the baby until tomorrow, Mama, so why don't you just . . . ."

"Oh, I've seen the baby," she chirps, as she dumps an armful of packages on the chair. "The nursery door was open so I walked in. Poor little thing was fussing, so I picked her up and she stopped right away."

"You held her? Johnny hasn't even held her yet!"

"I told you, no one was around." She points to the packages on the chair. "I brought presents for the baby. Been shopping all day and I'm pooped."

"You brought presents?" I squint in disbelief.

"Well, I *promised*, didn't I?" She aims her straight-across questioning eyebrows at me. "Now, Louise, when have I ever broken a promise to you?"

I can't believe she said that. She moves closer and I think maybe . . . but she steps back. I reach out to her.

"Watch out, honey, you'll muss my hair." She pats at it and brushes a wet finger across her massacred lash. "I can't stay, but I'll come back tomorrow. I promise . . . when you two aren't quite so . . . busy." Like a fluffed-up hen, she minces toward the door.

"But we weren't . . . ."

"Such goings on," she shakes her head as the door closes behind her.

She didn't even say goodbye. She'll never change. Mama will be Mama no matter what. If I haven't learned that by now, I guess I never will. But she's not going to run my life anymore. Not if I can help it. She held our baby. Who does she think she is, anyhow? CHAPTER 68

The next morning Mama comes again, even before visiting hours have started, only this time she doesn't look like my mother at all. She has no make up on, and to my surprise she looks soft and rather pretty.

"What are you doing here so early, Mama? Visiting hours doesn't start until after lunch."

I didn't come to visit. I came to tell you something you should have known a long time ago."

She sits on the end of my bed and there are tears in her eyes.

"Mama?" I ask. "What's wrong?"

"Nothing is wrong, Louise, nothing I can make right, but there is something you should know, and I want you to listen. Don't talk, just listen."

She turns away and sighs, a sigh so deep I can see her shudder. I've never seen her this way, so soft and vulnerable.

It took another few seconds before she started to talk again.

"Louise, honey," she sighs. "I should have told you this a long time ago." She takes another breath and her shoulders straighten. "When I was about six years old, your grandmother had another baby."

"You had a sister? Gram never mentioned she had another daughter."

"Well, she did, but something happened. Something . . . ." Her eyes filled with tears and her voice stumbled. "Her name was Marie."

Suddenly I feel faint. The world is spinning out of my control. She's going to tell me something I'm not sure I want to hear.

"We looked a lot alike," she continues. "We had the same features, same eyes, green like yours and mine, same build, same infectious laugh, and that golden hair.

"Except for the four years difference in our ages, we were like two peas in a pod.

"I adored little Marie. We romped and played together, always laughing and making up games. It gave your grandmother a lot of time to help your grandfather with the farm.

"One day when they went into town to shop, I was to stay home and keep Marie happy by playing her favorite games, Rover, Rover, come on over, kick the can, and her favorite, hide and seek.

"When it was Marie's turn to hide, she ran into the barn to hide in her favorite place. I counted slowly, giving her plenty of time to hide where she hid every time. I counted, and pretended to look in several places where I knew she wasn't hiding, and then something went wrong.

"Nobody ever knew exactly how it happened. It must have been a spark from a passing buggy wheel, or a cigar ash, but whatever it was, a grass fire started. It hadn't rained in a while, and the fire leapt across the dry fields like lightning.

"Marie was safe in the barn, so I began beating at the flames with a shovel. I carried water from the cistern, but suddenly the wind changed, and before I knew it, the fire was heading straight for the barn.

"I ran to Marie's favorite hiding place, but she wasn't there. I called, and called, but she had found a new place to hide, and she wasn't about to answer and give it away. Within minutes, the fire was beyond control. The flames licked at my overalls. I could hardly breathe for all the smoke. I screamed for her. 'Marie! Marie!' I yelled.

"I thought I heard her cry, but instead of my little sister calling, it was the wailing of the damn barn cat huddled in a box with her new litter. In my panic, ran out, and fell to the ground unconscious. When I came to, my hair was singed, parts of my clothes were scorched, and all I had clutched in my arms were the newborn kittens."

"Oh, Mama." Tears stream down my cheeks. I squeeze her hand.

"By the time the neighbors arrived, it was too late. They found her body trapped in a new feed box in the charred remains of the barn. The latch had evidently caught. My burns were minor and the kittens were unharmed.

"In her grief, your grandmother blamed me for saving the kittens and letting her little daughter burn to her death. I knew then she would never forgive me."

"But, Mama, you tried to save her. You went into the barn . . ."

"I know, I know, Louise, but try to tell that to a stubborn woman who has just lost the little daughter she loved."

Mama pats my hand again. "Your grandmother lost one of the most precious things in her life, honey," . . . I don't ever remember her calling me honey . . ."and in her own mind she probably thought, if I hadn't saved those kittens, her little Marie would still be alive. Even though in my heart I know it wasn't my fault, that day has haunted me ever since."

"How awful for all of you. You, Gram and Grampa, and that poor little girl."

"I stayed on the farm as long as I could after the accident, but with all the anger from your grandmother, and my own feelings of guilt, I couldn't handle it, so I left. My life didn't start again until I met your father and you were born. I believe Alma Kamens filled you in with the rest of what you should know of my life."

After a few seconds of silence, Mama straightens, blots her tears, and adjusts her hat. With a dismissive sigh she walks toward the door. "So now, I will leave you and tend to my current life. I don't know why I waited so long to tell you all this, Louise, but somehow it never seemed to be the right time. You have a right to know my past, and how it has inflicted a burden upon your life."

And with that she stood up, adjusted her hat, blew a kiss toward me, and swept out of the room.

When the nurse brings my baby to me, I hold her close and look at her perfect little face and my tears fall on her cheek. "If your daddy doesn't mind, I think we shall name you after your grandmother and her little sister.

December 1928

Dear Mama,

I dreamed of Gram last night. She and Grampa were walking toward me with a little girl walking between them, and they were smiling. Gram kept saying a German word, 'Vergebung.' At first I didn't understand what it meant, but, as if a rock has been lifted from my heart, all my loneliness, all my doubts and blaming slipped away, and I knew Gram was saying, forgive.

Now that I have Johnny and our baby, Mama, I am happy. Things won't always go as I plan, but I think I can handle that now. Johnny will be a good father. He's learning new things, too, and Ruthie will always be welcome to stay with us if she cares to. When I was growing up I didn't understand that giving us to Gram was the only thing you could have done to keep us together.

Soon they will be bringing my baby in to me, Mama. She is the most wonderful thing that has ever happened to me. Johnny will take us home in a few days. I doubt with the baby I will have much time to write. Maybe you can come over once in a while and visit. If Johnny agrees, we will name our baby after you and your little sister. I love you, Mama, I really do.

Sincerely, Louise.

CPSIA information can be obtained at www.ICGtesting.com
Printed in the USA
LVOW062101181211

259987LV00001BA/1/P